Psychology
Of English

Psychology Of English

By

MARGARET M. BRYANT
ASSISTANT PROFESSOR OF ENGLISH
BROOKLYN COLLEGE

ᏬᏬ

JANET RANKIN AIKEN
ENGLISH DEPARTMENT
COLUMBIA UNIVERSITY

NEW YORK: MORNINGSIDE HEIGHTS

COLUMBIA UNIVERSITY PRESS

1940

To Our Students

ACKNOWLEDGMENTS

THE AUTHORS are grateful to the many friends and associates who have helped with the making of this book, particularly Dr. Edward Hodnett, Dean of the College of Arts and Sciences at Newark University; Professors Clinton W. Keyes, of Columbia University, Louise Pound, of the University of Nebraska, and Blanch Colton Williams, formerly Head of the English Department of Hunter College; Mr. Alexander N. Sloan, of the Newark *Sunday Call,* and Dr. Kathryn A. McEuen.

MARGARET M. BRYANT
JANET RANKIN AIKEN

New York
August 19, 1940

CONTENTS

INTRODUCTION

To UNDERSTAND the significance of the present study it will be necessary to sketch briefly certain recent developments in human thinking; for human thought and language, even the English language with which we shall deal, are fundamentally interdependent. We cannot speak or write, to a considerable degree we do not think, apart from language; hence language is peculiarly bound up with our thought processes, and the two must be analyzed together rather than separately.

Now much of the intellectual theorizing, to say nothing of the educational and social practice, of the past century has been directed against the domination of logic. Logic, as first formulated by Aristotle and later developed by Bacon, Mill, Spencer, and a host of others, rests upon the endeavor to define and apply to thought certain fixed rules or principles. Logic is orderly analysis; it rests on the assumption or faith that such orderly analysis is possible and true; it might be called the science of certainty. It involves exact definitions, rigid classifications, and neat patterns, schemes, systems, or colligations of related groups of phenomena.

During more than two thousand years, from the time of Aristotle until the middle of the nineteenth century, logic reigned supreme, forming an indispensable part of the intellectual equipment of any scholar or scientist. Not only that, but to a very great degree logic was determinative in every field of knowledge, contributing to those other sciences the methods and the principles by which alone, it was felt, science could stand. Science was regarded in effect as a body of provable knowledge based upon fixed laws from which all facts and phenomena might be deduced and to which they might be referred.

Scholarly controversy in this earlier period was not wanting; in fact, it was probably more intense than it has been in recent times. But such controversy concerned the precise formulation of these fixed principles, not the question of their existence. Linguists, for example, might debate perennially over the precise theory—bow-wow, ding-dong, pooh-pooh, yo-he-ho, goo-goo—which would explain satisfactorily the problem of the origin of language; but that such an explanation existed and was capable of formulation was not questioned. It was not until the twentieth century that the whole matter was relegated to amateur standing as probably incapable of solution and not worth solving in any case.

The logical theories of this earlier period, moreover, were at one in encouraging their proponents to point back through causative principles to a great First Cause to which all logic in whatever department of study might ultimately be referred. Thus they occupied ground in common with religion, and the marriage of science and faith was largely unassailed by doubt from within or skepticism from without. There was controversy, plenty of it, between rival systems of religion; but this controversy concerned itself with differing formulations of principles, not with the possibility of certainty in itself.

During the nineteenth century there arose two prophets of what looked like a new order of thinking; and their iconoclastic influence has perhaps never been more potent than it is today. Oddly enough, neither attacked logic directly, and both were probably unaware of all the implications of their teachings; but together they have contributed the very strongest impetus toward the downfall of logic. These two prophets, needless to say, are Charles Darwin and Karl Marx.

What Darwin did was to formulate a law, principle, or theory which was so completely at variance with certain beliefs previously held that in assailing these former beliefs it seemed to confute the whole system of religious faith, thus destroying the former certainty and substituting for it a plan of causation, far less "logical," and seeming far less to require the postulation of a First Cause. Somewhat hastily the converts to Darwinism concluded that there was not room enough in their thinking for both God and natural selection. The increase of atheism which followed had its effects upon the systems of logic currently taught, by weakening their hold on the many sciences where evolution now became utilized as an explanation of natural phenomena.

Similar to Darwin's unorthodox view of the origins of human life was Marx's novel approach to history in his theory of economic determinism. His belief was that history must be interpreted, not through the machinations and statecraft of the so-called ruling classes, but through the conditions and methods of commodity production and the economic relations resulting from these conditions. This belief gave a sense of self-importance to the producing and laboring masses and tended equally with the doctrine of evolution to discredit many of the orderly, settled concepts of earlier generations.

Economic determinism substitutes human reactions for scientific certainty; it is personal rather than impersonal. And a by-product of the Marxian doctrine, possibly not contemplated by the Father of Communism, is the denial of fixed principles of human conduct, that opportunism so strikingly exemplified in the statecraft of the Marxists themselves. Certainty in human conduct has gone with belief in the traditional social order.

Perhaps it has not been generally recognized how deeply modern science has been affected by this drift away from certainty. Logic is now a neglected study in our colleges and universities; where psychology classes are crowded, logic is offered perhaps in one section every other year. The very word *science*, with its implication of fixed laws, is today avoided by many contemporary psychologists, economists, and others, who prefer to call their crafts by such names as "the study of human behavior" or "the study of the production and distribution of wealth."

Glance into a textbook of the 1880's, compare it with a manual of today, and the difference will be immediately apparent. Where the older, for instance, psychology began with sets of definitions, distinctions, classifications, and generalizations, the newer book ventures tentative explanations of the subject matter of psychology, perhaps also a distinction between man and his environment, but as soon as possible it is off on the series of statistics, references, and case histories which make up its bulk. General principles are either omitted or proposed with reservations and apologies. By and large, the modern textbook comes more and more to constitute an anarchy of individual instances.

It is not our primary purpose to either defend or attack this very general modern drift away from logic. Quite possibly we moderns are merely tearing down what needs to be torn down, and when the dust settles we may be able to see more clearly the true certainties remaining. Such a readjustment is, at any rate, what we hope to accomplish through this book, which it must be admitted is to a considerable extent a book against logic, a book in the modern tradition of uncertainty. For what we propose to do here is to separate the logic of English from the great mass of linguistic material which is not logical, but psychological, analyzing the latter under appropriate heads.

There is nothing new or revolutionary about such a purpose even as applied to the English language. Many courses on the psychology of language are offered today; however, these usually disregard grammar in favor of vocabulary. In the realm of meanings, or semantics, the attack on logic has been waged already with considerable vigor by such gentlemen as Korzybski, Ogden, Richards, and Stuart Chase, who oppose the very possibility of abstract principles and demand of each usable word that it possess a "referent" or original, which is tangible and concrete. True, the semanticists are quite unable to live up to their own principles, since it is impossible to write or talk concretely; but they are no more out of harmony with practical experience than are the modern determinists, who also find it impossible to live as if no fixed principles governed human conduct. Interesting and daring though it be, the semantics of Korzybski and his associates does not seem a very practical theory, and perhaps determinism also is better to theorize about than to live by.

Grammar is among the last strongholds of the logician, the last of the sciences where certainty is thought to reign. Says a recent authority, "grammatical expression is logic made audible and visible," [1] and except for the author's use of "and" where "or" would have been more logical, we can find no fault with the expression of the sentiment. Says another, "The rules of Logic . . . are found to permeate the entire grammatical structure," [2] while another ventures to defend that limbo of heterogeneity, the English idiom, in the words, "Beneath a surface of apparent whimsicality there is a deeper, finer logic in our English idioms." [3] Some similar statement will probably be found in whatever grammar you may choose to examine.

Now we agree that there is a certain orderliness about English grammar, a certain framework or pattern to which it conforms, which will be described in a future chapter and which might loosely be called logical. But even this pattern seems to be largely fortuitous. It is not found *in toto* in any other language even within the Indo-European family. It has no symmetry or balance of parts such as one could expect from an artificially created system. It seems to be unconsciously or socially rather than logically produced.

So this is our thesis: the English language and grammar are the products of the group thinking of billions of people whose minds have worked psychologically rather than logically; and the fruit of this group thinking is a system which reflects behavioristic patterns rather than formal regularity. It will be our endeavor in this book to trace out the sort of group thinking and acting which has given to English the kind of grammar it has today and which will continue to modify it in the future.

In this endeavor we shall not have to start from zero. One great linguistic principle, psychological in nature, called the principle of analogy, has already been formulated and used to explain items of both "correct" and "incorrect" grammar—for so-called incorrect English has just as much of a grammar as the classicalities of Addison or Dryden. To this principle or explanation which is called analogy we shall attempt to add other factors so as to cover the main aspects of an exceedingly broad subject.

Fortunately, all or most of the material we shall require has been

[1] John B. Opdycke, *Get It Right!* New York, Funk and Wagnalls, 1935, p. xi.
[2] Mason Long, *A College Grammar,* New York, The Ronald Press, 1928, p. 2.
[3] C. A. Lloyd, *We Who Speak English,* New York, T. Y. Crowell, 1938, p. 124.

collected and stored in compendiums any one of which contains all of the facts which would be required to make several volumes as large as this one. Such manuals merely skim the surface of a pond whose depths contain bios which will well repay dredging, sorting, and decomposing. To dismiss, for example, *I only want two* as a solecism is flippancy, and most rhetorics and grammars are flippant after just that fashion. To understand *I only want two* is an education, and that is the sort of education we are trying to secure as well as to impart.

It cannot be gainsaid that ours is an inglorious doctrine by contrast with those which teach that language, the product of the group mind, somehow escaped from the foibles and deficiencies of that mind to make of itself a perfect system, chaste and austere as a table of logarithms, lofty and unassailable as Euclid. Yet however intellectually satisfying the logician's view of English grammar may be, however much of a shock to discover that another prop to our orderly universe has been knocked out, still, if a thing is not true it is not true, and it is not correct to identify English with logic, as the present study will attempt to prove.

For this purpose we shall make no distinction between what is called "good" and what is called "bad" grammar. As already suggested, the word *ungrammatical* is a contradiction in terms, since all expression must be referable to some explanation, and grammar is simply that explanation of the way we talk. Thus *it's them, ain't got no, many a,* and *neither are* are all referable to their proper plan of grammar, conventional or not as the case may be, but still a plan. All are parts of English, all are readily understood, and hence all are to be included here.

While we propose to deal largely with English grammar, as the phase of the subject which has been least explored, still it is impossible to draw a hard-and-fast line between grammar and words themselves; and we shall not try to do so, but shall include semantic material wherever it seems appropriate. A certain amount of repetition is inevitable in a study such as the present one, and we offer no apologies for its presence.

The source material for our study is simple and readily accessible; it consists of the manuals of grammar and rhetoric which are used currently in teaching this subject. Linguists have occupied themselves largely with recording the endless material for linguistic analysis, rather than with the analysis itself. An outstanding example of such recording is *The American Language,* by H. L. Mencken,[4] whose index of words and phrases alone runs to some seventy pages of three columns each, and which, it is safe to say, represents the collection of more linguistic facts than have ever been assembled outside a dictionary. It is no wonder that Mr. Mencken did not do much analyzing of his astounding collectanea.

True, we have found that such books tend to disregard certain expressions which are very common and puzzling in nature; such expressions have been added freely from personal experience. But the merit of our investigation, if it has any, lies not in its discovery of new facts but in its new interpretation of old facts.

[4] Fourth edition, corrected, enlarged, and rewritten, New York, Knopf, 1936.

GRAMMAR AS A STUDY

THE GENERAL BACKGROUND and purpose of this study having been stated, our next task must be to define and explain the most important terms which are to be used. Here definition is less essential than explanation; everyone has a fair working notion of the meaning of such words as *grammar, science, logic,* and so forth, but fewer realize fully the implications and the consequences of these significations.

The simplest definition of grammar is the one found in many of the nineteenth-century textbooks: "Grammar is the science of the sentence." This definition reflects the rigidity of the Era of Certainty, and while the present century has seen few or no attempts to disprove it, it seems to have lost place gradually and naturally, until today it is seldom encountered in grammar textbooks, which indeed infrequently attempt a definition of their subject.

But apart from its present unpopularity, the definition of grammar as the science of the sentence seems obviously wrong. In the first place, it is difficult to justify including grammar among sciences, for the reason that it is not sufficiently universal. One cannot imagine a science altering or becoming invalid at racial or national frontiers, as grammar does. Chemistry, biology, botany could not be formulated so differently by Chinese, Basques, Finns, Turks, and Englishmen.

True, the older linguists and some of the newer ones are prone to assert or to imply the existence of a "universal grammar," a norm or super-system which will comprehend all the various local systems. But it has been demonstrated conclusively, by Jespersen among others, that no such synthesis can validly be made. Science is international; grammar is not. Grammar is a local or national system rather than "a connected body of demonstrated truth" or "observed facts . . . brought under general laws." [1] Nothing in any specific grammatical system has validity for all the world, unless it is the central aim and purpose of all language, that is, communication; and that one common element scarcely serves to justify calling grammar a science.

So it would appear that we must reject the word *science* in the older definition of grammar. And the other key word, *sentence,* is no more acceptable upon close scrutiny. For this word embodies one of the most crucial ambiguities in all the present-day study of grammar, and its use in this definition is impossible to square with its use in other grammatical connections.

Obviously the word *sentence,* as used in the definition under consideration, must mean any communication using words. Thus *Oh!* would constitute a sentence, or *Goodbye,* or the name on an envelope or calling card, since all these unquestionably are complete and communicate. But elsewhere in grammars the term *sentence* is used to designate communications having subject and predicate, and students are even warned away from writing (and presumably from saying) anything but sentences of this second sort. This second "sentence" is of course limited in its application to languages where subject and predicate exist as grammatical concepts, but within these it is ordinarily found with this limited meaning. Thus its use in the general sense of "communication" is fundamentally misleading and renders the "science of the sentence" definition of grammar doubly defective.

One is tempted to look farther back than the "older" grammarians, farther than Kirkham, Brown, and Lindley Murray, to Samuel Johnson and his forebears, even as far as Aristotle and Quintilian, all of whom regarded grammar, not as a science, but as an art, the art of speaking and writing correctly. Certainly a great part of grammar teaching is devoted to the attainment of correctness; but it seems not quite accurate to include all grammar with corrective

[1] Definitions of science in the *New English Dictionary.*

or remedial grammar after this fashion. The defining and recognition of a verb, for example, is not a matter of art, but the result of study of a linguistic plan or system. For the "art" aspect of grammar English has developed a different word, rhetoric, or perhaps several different words, since *composition, elocution,* and *speech* all name studies akin to the "art" of grammar.

As the beginning of a definition, then, we may agree to call English grammar, not a science or an art, but a study or a system, depending upon whether we look at it from the educational or the objective angle. It is, says the *New English Dictionary,* "the system of inflexions and syntactical usages characteristic of a language," or it is, in its other aspect, "that department of the study of a language which deals with its inflexional forms or other means of indicating the relations of words in the sentence, and with the rules for employing them in accordance with established usage; usually including also the department which deals with the phonetic system of the language and the principles of its representation in writing." With the substitution of "in communicating" for " in the sentence," this definition appears adequate.

Such a definition is broad enough to include logical as well as psychological explanations and to cover all the varied material of the present book; but before we leave it and proceed to further explanation it may be helpful to consider another relevant statement: "English grammar is at bottom chiefly a study of the relations of the ideas comprehended in a thought . . . It is not itself a study of pure thought . . . but it may be made a first step toward logic." [2] This statement leads naturally to a consideration of the relation of English grammar to logic and necessitates some definition of the latter word.

The definers of logic cannot seem to make up their minds whether it is a science or an art. The *New English Dictionary* itself defines it as "the science or art of reasoning," while other authorities give definitions such as "the science of reasoning" (Jevons), "the science of the general principles of good or bad reasoning" (Adam Smith), and "the science of proof or evidence" (Mill). Perhaps the best

[2] Blount and Northup, *An English Grammar,* New York, Holt, 1914, pp. 6–7. Quoted by permission.

definition is one of the others given in the *New English Dictionary:* "that branch of philosophy which treats of the forms of thinking in general, and more especially of inference and the scientific method."

Now languages, the English language in particular, are far from being a help to logical reasoning; every student who has tried to use or to formulate logical categories will be found complaining that language is actually a hindrance to his endeavor. The Greek language, the French language, are now and then preferred to English as better media for logical scientific reasoning; but more and more science appears to be turning away from language and adopting mathematical formulae as the least ambiguous and misleading statements of its findings.

In vocabulary a difficulty arises from the facts that words usually have not one but several meanings and that within a single meaning are to be found connotations and implications which are distracting if not actually deceptive to the reader. A very common instance, which Lester F. Ward, the classic sociologist, mentions again and again, is such words as *purpose, aim, end,* and the like, all of which are teleological in their implication of a conscious will, making it impossible for the scientist to indicate result independent of will. It is safe to say that the inadequacies of language constitute one of the greatest obstacles in the way of scientific reasoning.

And it is not alone a matter of vocabulary; English grammar has its definite failings and ambiguities as a medium for logical expression. Our system of personal pronouns, for instance, is seriously defective logically. The word *we* may mean *you and I, he and I, they and I,* and so forth. The word *you* is incapable of distinguishing between singular and plural. *He, she,* and *it* must show the presence or absence of gender, whether or not gender is involved; and it is impossible to refer to, say, a motorist by a singular pronoun which will leave sex out of consideration. On the other hand, *they* cannot show gender even if it is desired to do so. It is only the fact that the pronouns are seldom crucial in scientific reasoning which keeps them from being more often inveighed against by scientists.

It is not only the pronouns which are calculated to make havoc of logic. Everyone knows how easy it is to write a sentence with one intention, only to find that the grammatical structure permits or even makes preferable a different interpretation, possibly even an opposite one. Punctuation may make the difference, for example, in such sentences as *John said Mary was wrong* and *John, said Mary, was wrong*. One of the composition teacher's frequent comments on student papers must be, "You haven't said what you mean here." Shakespeare now and again turns this propensity to ridicule in his plays (for example, *Midsummer Night's Dream,* Act V, scene 1, ll. 108ff.). But the basic fault would appear to lie, not with the writer who falls afoul of grammar, but squarely with the grammatical system which renders such errors easy and almost inevitable.

It is an amusing if somewhat disillusioning game, which may be played with almost any book or article one may chance to read, to take apart minutely a sentence or paragraph, checking on every detail of the words and the grammar. It is rare indeed that such analysis will fail to yield some peculiarity, or even some definite flaw, in order, wording, or punctuation. Such authorities as Ernest Weekley, G. O. Curme, and many others have made collections of the more outstanding flaws and presented them for public perusal, thereby giving the erroneous impression that the authors were defective in their knowledge of English and that wholly perfect English can or should be written. It cannot, even by Curme and Weekley themselves.

Of course, dubious sentences normally give the readers no trouble. The reader must and does depend not only upon the words as they appear on the page but also upon his sense of context, his appreciation of what the writer must have meant. An amusing instance in Shakespeare is given by Dover Wilson, who reconstructs a line in *Julius Caesar* to read "Know, Caesar doth not wrong but with just cause." [3] It is just such a sentence as anyone might write and anyone read without pausing to boggle over logic, and if Ben Jonson had not taken exception to it we might have it still in Shakespearean texts. The average reader uses his intuition or imagination as well as what he sees on the page, and this sort of intuitional reading serves to confirm the English language in its

[3] From Introduction to First Folio Facsimile of *Julius Caesar,* Boston, Houghton Mifflin, 1929.

want of logic. If we really read words and grammar, we might make them more consistently reasonable.

To return to the quoted statements representing grammar as "a study of the relations of the ideas comprehended in a thought" and "a first step toward logic," we must reply that grammar no more than vocabulary is basically or primarily logical. It abounds with anomalies such as *neither is,* which combines a singular verb with a negative-plural subject, and *a good many murders.* If it can be considered in any degree a preparation for logic, it is as much in the shape of a warning as of an epitome. The dissection, not of thoughts, but of expressions or communications, which forms the discipline of grammar, may indeed be made a first step toward the study of logic, but only because the analysis of expressions involves mental processes akin to those involved in logic, not because the system of grammar is in any way identical with that of logic or orderly thought.

Another way of testing the relation between grammar and logic is to consider the two with regard to their susceptibility to change. It is as absurd to think that logic could change as that the multiplication table could become invalid by change of place or lapse of time. Yet grammar alters over the centuries, and not so rarely or so slowly as many grammarians seem to think. English grammar is in many important respects different from what it was in Queen Elizabeth's day. We ask questions differently; our negative statements are differently constructed; even the pronouns have altered in important aspects which have a direct bearing upon our social psychology and which will be more fully treated in Chapter Five.

Occasionally grammatical change seems to occur in the direction of "logic," or rather of consistency and linguistic efficiency. Such a change was the introduction of the possessive pronoun *its,* about three centuries ago. *Its* is far less ambiguous than the former *his,* and its use therefore offers fewer pitfalls for the unwary speaker. On the other hand, grammar has failed to differentiate between *her* as possessive and as objective, and still retains the superfluous possessive forms [4] *mine, yours,* and so forth. And it is easily possible

[4] These predicatives are omitted from minimum vocabularies such as Basic English, which considers that English does not need both *your* and *yours, their* and *theirs,* and so forth.

to instance changes which flout "logic" completely, such as the frequent and predominantly modern constructions where subject and object may actually change places with no change in meaning.

They were assigned places.	Places were assigned them.
She was given a book.	A book was given her.[5]

It is unsafe to assume that English is getting more logical as its grammar develops, just as unsafe as it is to assume any great degree of correlation between grammar and logic.

But if English grammar is not logical, what is it? Our thesis is that it is predominantly psychological and that it can be understood correctly only through a psychological interpretation. It is a product of certain forces working in individuals and in groups to bring about certain equipoises or equilibria which we dignify by the name of rules or laws, equipoises which are as much subject to change as are any other linguistic phenomena, such as word meanings.

It is, furthermore, important to distinguish carefully between the operations of the individual mind and of the group mind in the field of grammar, because it would be so easy and at the same time so inaccurate to analogize from the one to the other. It must be emphasized that language as a group product differs in several essentials from language as used by any one individual, just as in economics individual wealth is a different thing from group or national wealth. The psychology of the individual's grammar is by no means always the psychology of the grammar of the social body.

Nearly always an individual variation or departure from group grammatical practice is regarded as an individual defect and condemned accordingly. Exceptions arise only when the innovator is influential, as President Harding was when he revived the word *normalcy* and the Emperor Charles V, if indeed it was he who introduced the Castilian lisp into Spanish. Normally linguistic change is not sudden, nor does it stem from a single individual.

The individual has constantly to utilize grammar in his speech and writing, and occasionally he is likely to deviate from the system

[5] The verb *begin* permits kindred peculiarities; compare *The war began* and *He began the war.*

followed by members of the group. Such deviations ordinarily have no effect upon the system itself. If, for example, someone uses *man* as an impersonal pronoun meaning *one* or *anyone,* as Scandinavian immigrants frequently do (*Man cannot lift that stone*),[6] this does not mean that the construction will become standard English, even though the same mistake may be made by a considerable number of persons.

But occasionally there arises a linguistic situation in which the same mistake is likely to be made by a great many widely distributed people. To use an instance already mentioned, we may recall the time when the possessive of the pronoun *it* was *his.* At that time it was a mistake to use any other form, and yet because of the ambiguity of *his* and its unlikeness to *it,* a great many speakers were prone to make this particular mistake. The mistake took at least two forms—the uninflected *it* as a possessive and the created-by-analogy *its.* Shakespeare in *King Lear* (Act I, scene 4, l. 238) has the former:

> The hedge-sparrow fed the cuckoo so long,
> That it had it head bit off by it young.

Fewer people, however, used the uninflected *it* than used the analogous *its,* and as this unambiguous, obviously useful form was more and more widely adopted, it gradually became established in the language, so that today it would be a mistake to use anything else.

These examples indicate that individual mistakes are significant in the development of grammar only when the linguistic situation is out of equilibrium, so that such mistakes may, or actually do, point the way to a change in the system itself. Such a tendency in contemporary as well as earlier usage is the widespread substitution of *who* for *whom.* Whether or not this popular "mistake" is ever consummated in the disappearance of *whom* from English, it points to a weak spot in the system of English grammar and illustrates the correlation between individual and group tendencies.

But this is not our whole story, because it leaves out of account the psychological factor, which is the chief subject of the present

[6] The cause is the literal translation of an idiom from the native into the acquired language.

study. Here it is especially necessary to distinguish between the individual and the group if our interpretations are not to be challenged as being out of line with facts. For an instance, we may take the sentence *About my father, I might tell several stories concerning him.* Obviously this is defective from the grammatical standpoint, since we have two synonymous phrases, *about my father* and *concerning him,* only one of which is needed. It is the common error called pleonasm or tautology.

Now in any individual case such a construction might be used by accident, so to speak, without any particular psychological motive. In the inception of such constructions, however, and frequently in their later use, people must have used this sort of tautology out of a desire to be entirely clear—from what might be called conscientiousness. Emphasis, conscientiousness, a tendency opposite to simplicity, what might be called long-cutting [7]—numerous aspects of personality might enter into the choice of such expressions and might make them popular among speakers with a normal unconsciousness of the linguistic means they are employing.

In other words, while psychological factors enter into the beginning and many other individual instances of a particular usage, they will not necessarily enter into every use of that construction. A person may say *Who did you call?* without any reason except that he or she has heard the expression in that or a similar form used by others. Imitation, a very powerful psychological impulse, enters almost immediately to perpetuate a usage which owes its inception to other impulses.

This imitative factor is exceedingly important in bringing about the adoption of any given construction which favors a new grammatical equilibrium, and on the other hand it will operate equally or even more strongly to preserve the *status quo.* That is why it is true that unless a grammatical situation is out of equilibrium, so that the operation of psychological factors will lead individuals independently to make the same "mistake" (or alteration in the established system), imitation will not be a sufficient force to bring

[7] This term *long-cutting* is offered tentatively as an attempt to suggest a neutral name for what might be called opprobriously *procrastination.* So far as we know, there is no good term for the phenomena it names.

about that alteration. The use of *who* for *whom,* mentioned in the preceding paragraph, illustrates a grammatical situation which is out of equilibrium in that the ordinary speaker finds it difficult to use the words traditionally.

The influence of imitation will be more or less taken for granted in the present study, and stress will be laid rather upon the initiating motives of change. If this seems to elevate language too far into the plan of conscious volition, this is a distortion inevitable in such an investigation. Of a million occurrences of *I don't think I'll go,* only one or two percent of the users may have felt consciously or semiconsciously the motives we shall ascribe to the expression, and still that small proportion undoubtedly constituted the genetic power in its development.

To summarize the material of this chapter: grammar is properly to be regarded educationally as a study, objectively as a system, of the machinery of communication. It has to do with logic only in that it embodies some sort of pattern and deals with the same material as does logic, namely, the analysis of idea expression; but it is fully as much a hindrance to actual logic as a help. Grammar changes over longer or shorter periods, usually without opposition from grammarians, and such changes are much more extensive than is usually recognized.

Finally, such changes are the product of widespread imitation of individual variations arising from psychological factors which operate when such changes are favored by some grammatical inharmony or lack of balance. In talking about the psychology of English, therefore, we are analyzing the comparatively few constructions where imitation is not operative and the psychological factor is relatively clear and easy to isolate.

THE LOGIC OF ENGLISH GRAMMAR [1]

BEFORE EXPLORING the behavioristic aspects of English grammar we shall do well to look over what may be called the logic of the English linguistic system, the actual mechanism, pattern, or plan to which most communications conform. There is nothing symmetrical or "groomed" in this pattern. Its every detail shows it to have "just growed," like Topsy, and to have achieved an unpredicted and unpredictable balance after ages of trial-and-error development. Not devoid of beauty, its beauty is nevertheless a natural growth rather than the pure design of a syllogism.

All English grammar is to be referred to four orders or categories of concepts, the first containing five subdivisions; the second, six; the third, an indefinite number; and the fourth, eight or more. First is the category of form, which comprises five units of speech. Second is the category of function, comprising the tasks performed by these units, which are six in number. Third is the category of subordination, for which we may use the term *levels of modification*.[2] And fourth, there are eight main groupings and an indefinite number of minor groupings of a notional character, which we may call aspects.

The category of grammatical units might begin with the sound or the letter, two different units, and might go on with the syllable, word, sentence, paragraph, chapter, volume, or even library. But

---

[1] The material of this chapter is drawn in considerable measure from two books by Janet Rankin Aiken: *A New Plan of English Grammar*, New York, Holt, 1933; and *Commonsense Grammar*, New York, Crowell, 1936.

[2] This use of the word *levels* is not to be confused with the use of the word to express levels of style such as the literary, the colloquial, slang, and so forth.

we shall disregard most of these as not essential in grammar and shall recognize as the physical bits or items of which the pattern of English is composed the word, the phrase, the clause, the sentence, and the nonsentence, or communication in some form other than the sentence.

The next grammatical order or category is the speech function, or the grammatical task performed by a given unit in a given construction. This category has some points in common with the traditional division into "parts of speech." However, a part-of-speech classification is ambiguous in that it confuses unit and function ideas by regarding words as though in themselves they performed one function and only one. While some of the functions of logical grammar are the same as some of the traditional parts of speech, the former terms are used to indicate only work performed, not to indicate rigid groupings. The functions which may logically be recognized and which cover all linguistic usage are six in number: subject, verb, complement, modifier, connective, and absolute. The last-named is the communicating function *per se,* which is discharged by the sentence and the nonsentence.

The units and functions of English grammar operate on an indefinite number of levels of modification, forming our third order or category of classification. These levels are basic in the structure of English and are easily perceived by the analyst. Constructions having five or six levels of modification are not uncommon in English.

These three categories—units, functions, and levels—might be regarded as sufficient to cover all grammatical necessities, just as a machine may be explained by a description of its parts and an enumeration of the work they do and of their arrangement. Indeed, the fourth order of grammatical elements is diminishing in importance and might almost be called a disappearing phase of grammar. However, we must recognize certain scattered notional elements, indefinite in number, which underlie or color grammatical constructions.

As an illustration of such notional elements let us suppose that someone is asked what George is now doing for a living and that he replies, *He is chauffeuring for his aunt.* Here we have a word subject *he,* a phrase verb *is chauffeuring,* and a phrase modifier *for his aunt.* But within these units the word *he* shows number, case, person, and gender and the verb *is chauffeuring* shows number, person, time (a peculiar sort of time, which might be called the habitual or timeless present), progression, mood, and voice. All these are grammatical colorings or refinements of the subject and verb functions, respectively, and English grammar needs a term which will apply to all of them equally and will denote them as a group. In accordance with the definition given in *Webster's New International Dictionary* we shall call them aspects.

While the word *meaning* may be used loosely in connection with these aspects, it is important to distinguish between aspect and meaning, because often this is not done and sometimes it is difficult to do. The aspect of time in the verb *is chauffeuring* is plainly distinct from the meaning of the verb itself; but in a word such as *begin,* time is involved in the meaning, and so it is likely to be called an inchoative or inceptive verb, whereas the time element really belongs with the meaning rather than the aspect.

Eight aspects are most important in English grammar; these are number, case, person, gender, time, comparison, mood, and voice. But in addition to them there are a great many minor aspects which appear now and then in grammatical form—that is, which are expressed in the form of a unit rather than in its meaning according to the dictionary. Among these may be mentioned condition, negation, timelessness, doubt, emphasis, agreement, desire, request. The aspects of the verb will be discussed further in Chapter Twenty-two.

From this brief summary of the "logic" or "system" of English grammar, it is easy to see that one cannot postulate any very logical character for it. The various orders vary widely in their nature and number of divisions. Moreover, they overlap, blend, and combine in endlessly shifting patterns, so that it is almost impossible to give an absolutely complete grammatical analysis of even a very simple sentence, as will be shown later in this chapter. We shall now give a somewhat more detailed statement of the four categories of English grammar.

The five grammatical units may be defined as follows:

1. The word is the smallest indivisible idea unit within the sentence or the nonsentence.

2. The clause is a group of words containing a subject-verb-complement combination or any two of its members, but not constituting a complete communication.

3. The phrase is any other group of words with a unitary idea, within a sentence or a nonsentence.

4. The sentence is a complete communication centering in one or more subject-verb combinations.

5. The nonsentence is any other complete communication in words.

These definitions must not be thought of as logically complete and mutually exclusive. They overlap and combine endlessly. For instance, *yes* is a word and also, used alone, a nonsentence. *In a minute* is a phrase and also a nonsentence. A group of words like *Who called?* may be used independently as a sentence, or it may be used as a clause within a sentence, *I know who called*. All that we can say accurately of the five units is that it is possible in any given instance of their use to distinguish them from one another. And that, considering their psychological genesis and the rudimentary sense of logic of the people who have developed them, is saying a great deal.

To show the actual working of the five units just defined, an illustrative sentence may be analyzed: *Did the boy who spoke say, "Out of bounds"?* Each one of the five units of English grammar is present within that communication. The word is illustrated nine times, in the nine indivisible units making up the whole. It might perhaps be questioned whether *bounds* is actually indivisible, since it will split into *bound* and the plural *s;* but since it is not divided in spelling, it may be called indivisible for our practical purposes.

One clause is present, consisting of the words *who spoke*. It is interesting to notice that these words could make an interrogative sentence without any change. The difference between *Who spoke?* as a sentence and *who spoke* as a clause lies entirely in the presence or absence of that sense of completeness which characterizes the absolute function performed by the sentence and the nonsentence.

The phrase is a less distinct and well-defined unit than the clause, but we may recognize four phrase groupings in the sentence; these are *did say, the boy who spoke, out of,* and *out of bounds.* In each case there is a distinct sense of relationship which brackets the words together as a subgroup within the sentence. The reason for including both *out of* and *out of bounds* [3] is, of course, that these two phrase units perform different functions, the first being a connective and the second a direct object. This is a clear example of overlapping units, or as one might call them, nested units. It would be possible also to call *the boy* a phrase separate from *the boy who spoke,* but this is an unnecessary refinement on analysis.

And finally the words *out of bounds* form not only a phrase but also a quoted nonsentence, being the whole of a complete communication made by the boy. There is no need for supplying words to make this nonsentence into a sentence, especially as no one would know just what words to supply in completing it. It might form a question, an exclamation, a statement, or conceivably a command. It is one of the characteristic forms of expression in English, particularly oral English, which leans to the nonsentence more strongly than does the literary language.

Just as distinguishable, even if just as overlapping, as the five units of English grammar are the six functions, which will now be defined individually.

1. The absolute function communicates; it is the work done by the sentence and nonsentence, both of which can stand alone as communications.

2. The verb function expresses action or assertion with respect to a subject, a complement, or both.

3. The subject function tells who or what performs the action or opens the assertion expressed by the verb.

4. The complement function tells what or who undergoes the action or closes the assertion expressed by the verb.

5. The modifier function describes, designates, or clarifies some other unit in sentence or nonsentence.

6. The connective function joins two or more units.

The absolute function needs little or no explanation beyond

[3] The words *out of bounds* form a nonsentence and also a prepositional phrase of an independent or absolute function. Within this phrase the preposition consists of the words *out of.*

what has been given. It is not the same as what the older grammars called the "independent element," which was ordinarily a modifier. The absolute function is marked by a sense of completeness which makes it stand alone as a separate communication. Occasionally two or more absolutes are joined together, as, for example, *Yes, I think so too,* or *Oh, how pretty it is!* where we have the combination of a nonsentence and a sentence. Or two absolutes may be joined by a connective, as in *Study and you will learn.*

As we turn to the next group of functions, namely, verb, subject, and complement, the remarkable fact appears that these three cannot be defined except in terms of one another. They form what might be described as a family group, a closed corporation. The subject must have a verb to be subject to, and the verb is not a verb without a subject or a complement or both. The complement is the dispensable member of the trio; it is sometimes absent, but when it does appear its appearance is conditioned upon the presence of subject and verb, one or both.

A term used by Jespersen is very useful in understanding this solidarity of subject, verb, and complement. They, or any two of them combined, form a *nexus*. The nexus is the heart of the sentence; it constitutes a drama, while junction, the modifier relation, is like a picture. *The plane speeds* is a story, while *a fast plane* may be static. The former has a nexus; the latter none.

Now the nexus is the heart not only of the sentence but of the clause as well; and this fact makes the definition of the clause much broader than it used to be, because verbids, or verbs which will not carry a sentence, still may and do take subjects and complements. Hence such a unit as the first five words of the sentence *John having called the dog, they went out for a walk,* forms a clause, complete with a three-member nexus. Such a unit is called a verbid clause, because *having called* is not a full verb, that is, cannot be used to carry a sentence; it is a verbid.

The modifier function takes in two of the traditional eight "parts of speech"; it includes the work of adjective and adverb. There is no real functional difference between these two; the traditional distinction, based upon the sort of element which "governs" the modifier, will not hold. Adverbs may modify subjects, as *precisely* in *Precisely what he wanted lay there* and *slowly* in *Walking slowly takes longer.* Often it is impossible to distinguish between the two types of modifier; in *Winding my watch, I dropped it,* the first three words may be either an adjective modifying *I* or an adverb modifying *dropped.* Or, what is probably the best solution, they may modify the whole sentence.

The modifying function may be performed by words, phrases, and clauses, and these may modify words, phrases, or clauses. An extremely common modifier type is the prepositional phrase, which according to one frequency study [4] occurs on an average of once per sentence. Another type, which is commoner than used to be thought, is the sentence modifier. Compare *Positively you must talk* with *You must talk positively,* and you will see that the first *positively* modifies the whole sentence, the second only the verb phrase. These are some of the characteristics of the modifier function.

Connectives are the last and the most difficult functions of the English grammatical units. There are three sorts of connective, called by the cumbrous and misleading names *coördinating conjunctions, prepositions,* and *subordinating conjunctions* (including *relative pronouns*). Under two of these heads are marshaled numerous subtypes, making an imposing array of forms.

The peculiarity of the subordinating conjunctions is that almost always they combine two functions, being subjects, modifiers, or complements as well as connectives. Thus, in the sentence *What happened doesn't matter* the word *what* introduces the clause subject and connects it with the rest of the sentence, but it also acts as the subject of *happened.* In *Where it is doesn't matter* we find the same introductory and connective use of *where,* but this time *where* is an adverb within its clause, modifying the verb *is.*

Like the units of form, the functions of English grammar will often be found to merge, shift, and metamorphose from one to another. No single word can be referred to a single one of them, and not infrequently it is difficult or impossible to tell which of two functions is performed by a given unit.

---

[4] E. L. Thorndike *et al.,* "An Inventory of Grammatical Constructions," *Teachers College Record,* March, 1927.

The levels of English are more stable in character, although here, too, there is some uncertainty. On the main, independent, or primary level stand subject, verb,[5] and complement as the chief elements of the sentence pattern. Below each of these in rank are modifying words, phrases, and clauses, those directly depending on the primary elements being placed on the secondary level, their modifiers in turn on the third, and so forth. Thus the sentence *It was a certainly not very edifying thing to say* shows five levels, with *it was thing* on the first level, *a, edifying,* and *to say* on the second, *very* on the third, *not* on the fourth, and *certainly* on the fifth.

Occasionally it is hard to tell what level to put a unit on. In *Many words meaning nonsense have been coined recently* the verbid clause *meaning nonsense* may be referred to *words,* as its verb and complement (first level), or may be taken as a modifier (second level). Ordinarily, however, it is easy to place sentence units on their proper levels of modification.

The same cannot be said of the grammatical aspects of English, which are shifting and unstable in the highest degree. In general the aspects are characteristic of a primitive period of English and are tending to be lost or rather replaced by other grammatical means, some of which will be discussed in later chapters. It will be sufficient for our purposes to give merely the briefest explanation of each.

1. *Number.*—This aspect is found in most nouns, most verbs of the present tense, and a few modifying words and phrases (*this, those, each,* and *one by one*). One of its oddities is that the ending *s* indicates plural in nouns, singular in verbs. Often number is expressed by context (*deer* in *Two deer were killed*).

2. *Case.*—Every noun in English is in what is called the common case, which simply means that it has no case at all. The aspect of case has to do with the possessive termination, which turns a noun into a modifier, and the objective case, which is distinguished from the nominative in only six words, *I, we, he, she, they,* and *who.* In general in these words the nominative is the subject case, and

---

[5] Jespersen in *The Philosophy of Grammar* places the verb on the secondary level, below subject and complement. It is difficult to understand his reason for this placing, since the verb is in no way to be confused with the modifier.

the objective the complement case, although there are exceptions to this rule. Normally case has no formal indication in English.

3. *Person.*—This aspect is found formally in only a very few words—personal pronouns and some verbs in the present tense. Most nouns show person only by meaning or context.[6]

4. *Gender.*—The words *he* and *she, his* and *her, man* and *woman,* and a few others are the only ones in modern English showing gender. As a grammatical aspect gender survives in meaning and context only.

5. *Time.*—This aspect inheres largely in the verb, especially the auxiliaries and the termination *ed.* These, however, show many things besides time, so that time tends to be driven more and more out of grammatical form and into meanings. The *ed* termination may actually indicate future time, for example, *If I called John at six tomorrow morning, would he get up?* For other instances see Chapter Twenty-two.

6. *Comparison.*—This aspect is confined to a fairly small number of short modifier words, which take the comparative termination *er* and the superlative termination *est.* Ordinarily the words *more* and *most* are the signs of comparison. In the case of *nearer* and *nearest,* comparison is found in a preposition.

7. *Mood.*—This is really, not one aspect, but many aspects, expressing doubt, possibility, condition, negation, condition contrary to fact, desire, and several other aspects under the so-called subjunctive, which in English is expressed formally by only a few verbs, *were* and *be* being the most frequent. Mood is thus a generalized term for a group of grammatical usages. Its full exposition would require much space, but various matters of mood will appear in later chapters.

8. *Voice.*—This also is a verb aspect centering in the auxiliary *be* plus the termination *ed.* The passive voice is altering in modern English usage and is now often found equivalent to the active voice with an unmentioned performer, as was illustrated on page 14.

Mention should be made also of sentence order, which is of considerable significance in English grammar, and has been neg-

---

[6] In such a sentence as *I, James, tell you this,* the appositional subject *James* conforms to the first person subject *I* in verb relation. This shows that *James* is not exclusively a third-person word.

lected by many writers on the subject. Sentence order has its own "logic" and its own rules, and some but not all of them are fairly rigid.[7]

Perhaps the best way to round off this sketch of the English grammatical system will be to take a sentence and show how our various categories apply to it. We shall choose one which is colloquial in character and yet entirely "regular," one which anyone may say and which everyone would understand: *What he said did not strike her as being practical.*

This is a sentence of the declarative, complex type. It contains ten words, three overlapping phrases, and two clauses; one of the clauses is of the type called dependent, or subordinate, while the other is a verbid clause. This verbid clause is the object or complement part of a prepositional phrase. There are sixteen grammatical units to be considered here.

The sentence nexus consists of the clause subject *What he said,* the phrase verb *did strike,* and the word complement *her.* These are the primary elements of the absolute function performed by the entire sentence. But there are two other nexuses in the sentence; the subject clause *What he said* is one, and it is complete with subject *he,* verb *said,* and complement *what. Being practical* is also a nexus, consisting of verb, *being,* and complement, *practical.* Altogether there are three nexuses—two with three members and one with two. One of these is independent, and two are parts of the sentence pattern.

For functions in this example sentence we have: one absolute, consisting of the entire sentence; two subjects, *he* and *what he said;* three verbs, *said, did strike,* and *being;* three complements, *what, her* and *practical;* two modifiers, *not* and *as being practical;* and one connective, *as.* This makes a total of twelve grammatical functions. There are more units than functions (sixteen units, twelve functions) because certain words, like *did,* merge their functions in the function of their phrases.

This is a very interesting sentence pattern. The subject-nexus is nested within the absolute and the modifier-nexus depends like a feather curled below a hat brim. The words *depends* and *below,*

---

[7] For a brief summary see Aiken, *A New Plan of English Grammar,* chap. xviii.

however, are romantic and misleading, as John Dewey once pointed out in a magazine article. The modifying unit does not really "depend below" its "governing" unit, but is superior to it in importance and idea. Thus the key word of this illustrative sentence is *practical,* a word which is here called a complement, but which could equally well be called a modifier.

This brief analysis sketches the units and functions of the sentence *What he said did not strike her as being practical.* It does not begin to analyze the two sentence levels; the sentence order (the shifted complement opening the sentence); or the aspects, discussion of which would lead us into many fresh complications. It would be easy to use this illustrative sentence as the text for an entire volume on grammatical analysis. What has been said is perhaps sufficient to show the intricate and devious organization of sentences which people utter so glibly without the slightest appreciation of their full inwardness.

This chapter has achieved its object if it has shown that English is not lacking in plan or organization, even though that plan is by no means referable to scientific or logical law or system. Why, for example, should English include precisely five units of speech, while functions are six in number and levels and aspects numerically indeterminate? It must be answered that there is no logical basis for having five units, any more than six functions. English has happened to grow in that way. It is unsymmetric, out of balance, fortuitous. In short, its workings are explainable only on a psychological basis.

THE ORIGIN OF GRAMMAR

IN ANY LANGUAGE the structure of grammar tends to grow simpler with the passage of time. It may reasonably be conjectured that we look back at what may be compared to one side of a hill or mountain of complication, and that there must be another side, hidden from our eyes, which includes the stages of grammatical development which occurred while the systems were acquiring complication. Obviously speech cannot have burst complete into being; and it may be profitable to include in our study some conjectures concerning the primary stages of grammar.

Earlier theorists, more naïve than we, were sure there was such a thing as a first word, and they even theorized concerning what part of speech that first word must have been. Was the noun first? Did primitive man learn to point to a tree, a mammoth, a flint, and give to each that particular grunt which was the great-great-grandfather of our word? Now and again one sees references to nouns as "the oldest words," or "the earliest forms of language." How much credence may we place in such phrases?

Similar superlatives are applied to the verb, and it is easy to recognize the usefulness of the verb to primitive man in giving commands, transmitting messages, and generally showing action. Is the verb, then, the oldest word? The term itself, deriving from *verbum,* which means *word,* seems to indicate it.

Few if any linguists have favored the adjective as the earliest sort of word, and yet it may be that it does not lack all claim to that distinction. One can visualize a primitive message bearer gasping out the primitive equivalent of "sick," or "dead." A primitive mother might easily say *Sh-h-h,* or its equivalent, meaning *quiet,* to her baby. And if the tender emotions brought words to man as they brought the mating calls to birds, there must have been very early equivalents for *beautiful* or *dear.*

The interjection was designated by many nineteenth-century linguists as the earliest word. When hurt, even animals emit distinctive cries corresponding semantically to the human *Ow.* Indeed, an entire explanation or theory of language origins has been built on the notion that interjections were the heralds of speech. These independent utterances of no particular grammatical type are still viewed by many as the oldest words.

But today linguists refuse to dwell long on the relative claims to priority of the various parts of speech. The controversy is shelved as not worth fighting over. In the nature of things, it is held, we cannot know what word was first said by man; there is neither television nor telaudition to the past. It is a waste of time to give thought to a matter which must remain in the sphere of what has been called "lunar politics." For is not the genesis of human speech as insoluble a puzzle as that old game of squaring the circle?

It may be possible at least to throw some light upon this question by holding to a psychological view of it and by pointing out as a necessary preliminary to its consideration that language was and is a natural by-product of voice, occurring inevitably and independently as soon as mental development has attained a certain degree or standard.

In the older theories of the origin of language it was a well-nigh universal error to attempt to account for the origin of sound, or of meaningful sound. Since language was thought of as having been created out of nothing, theories were built up to explain what required no explanation. It is entirely true that the old theories of speech origin are vulnerable, but this is because they are all based on a false assumption—the assumption that sounds, even communications, are peculiar to human language.

Everything human has grown out of something earlier, and language is no exception. It grew out of the multiplicity of primitive cries and calls such as are made today by monkeys, birds, cats, dogs, and many other animals. It is entirely probable that this development occurred at the same time or at different times independently in various parts of the earth: it may even be that it has occurred within very recent times. Prehistoric man found himself at the dawn of human language with an animal language already fully developed. From this point on, his speech progress is to be explained by principles of psychology rather than of history or science.

But just what is the difference between animal language and human language? At what point does a significant cry such as the animals make become a human word or sentence? All of us have had experience with the "language" of animals, and we know that it implies a certain degree of reasoning power on the part of the animal using it. What is it then that differentiates such language from human speech?

The key to the solution may be found in the idea of context. Birds, cats, dogs, and monkeys—all the animals capable of emitting significant cries—make these cries in context, that is, in the particular situation which naturally gives rise to them. When a dog growls defiance it is because he means it. His playful growl is a different "sentence," reserved for a different occasion. He cannot talk about growling, cannot tell his master the story of a situation where growling was called for—cannot lift growling out of its context in his mind.

This is not, of course, to imply that dogs lack memory. Given a repetition of the occasion for growls, or even a part repetition of it, the growl may result. But this is still a growl in context. Canine noises out of context, such as the "speaking" which is rewarded by a bit of food, are the result of human training.

In the same way a hen may give a danger signal to her chicks if she sees or fancies approaching danger. It is incredible that such a signal could be given out of context or that on the roost at night the hen should talk over the various perils of the day. In a way it shows a greater honesty on the part of hens, and of the animal world generally, this inability to tell anything but the actual fact about danger. It distinguishes man as the only animal capable of lying; for that is how speaking out of context may at times be regarded.

Human speech alone enables the speaker to talk about his experiences without actually living them, to discuss hunger when well fed and rest when fatigued. And it was at the precise moment when cries came to be used out of context that they became, not cries, but human speech. The word *meow* (as contrasted to the feline cry *meow*) is a word, just because it is not a response to a physical or mental stimulus, but an idea capable of use under any circumstances. The difference between word and cry is not one of genesis, of meaning, or of usefulness; it is a difference of motive, of outlook, of circumstance.

Thus language in the human sense is seen to be conditioned on memory and imagination, the ability to make a topic of conversation out of what one says. The origin of language is subjective rather than objective and denotes a psychological change in the use of meaningful cries. And it is important to remember that at the moment when this subjective change occurred primitive man found himself already supplied with a limited "word-hoard," or stock of cries, which by their new use became language.

Slowly at first, and then perhaps more rapidly, this new use of cries stimulated an increase in the number and complexity of language elements. Speech was found to be a toy as well as a tool, a delightful game as well as a protection and a weapon. This multiplying of speech-cries, of course, served still further to differentiate them from animal cries, which as everyone knows are sharply limited in number, the animal's "vocabulary" seldom or never including more than a dozen items. It is the manner in which speech-cries developed which constitutes the history of primitive grammar.

Consider once again the warning cluck of the hen to her chicks. It may be interpreted variously as a noun, *danger,* as a verb, *beware,* as an adjective, *unsafe,* as an interjection, *scat,* as a preposition, *off.* We cannot read into it a part-of-speech classification; in fact, it is no one part of speech as opposed to any other.

Is it not apparent that this significant cry of the hen has no more to do with English syntax and word-analysis than with Chinese? Completely formulated, perhaps what the hen is saying is, "Danger is approaching, my children, and you had better make yourselves as scarce as you can, as soon as possible." All those twenty words are implicit in the single note. The squawk of the hen is obviously the great-great-grandmother of the sentence, not of the word. In itself it is precisely what we call a nonsentence in modern English.

But here again we encounter the fallacy almost universal among linguists, the fallacy of the sentence. A sentence is, or it is not, a group of words complete with subject and predicate, expressing a thought. If it is, then language is not made up exclusively of sentences, since the nonsentence, a complete thought lacking formal subject and predicate, is extremely common in speech, and to a less degree in writing. It is the nonsentence rather than the sentence which is the primitive unit of grammar, and it is the nonsentence rather than the word which explains the character of the earliest language.

What we may call "pre-language" consisted of meaningful cries used exclusively in context to express emotions, messages, commands, and other necessities of communication. Eventually such cries came to be used apart from the particular situation which might evoke them. People began to "talk over" their experiences, as well as to experience them; and with this "talking over" language and grammar were simultaneously born. The nonsentence is nearer to this primitive type of communication just because it is a conglomerate similar to and less analyzable grammatically than the sentence. Gradually, over long ages of human progress, the word emerged, through the breaking up into parts of this primitive nonsentence. As the word appeared, the parts of nonsentences became free as separate units suitable for recombining, and such recombinations paved the way for the gradual development of the formally complete sentence containing subject and predicate.

These primitive "pre-sentences" came to be broken up, and in the *Ursprache* which ancestored our own English they came regularly or normally to follow the subject-verb pattern. In Chinese, Eskimo, and many other languages, while they broke into parts, they never adopted the sentence pattern. Besides subject and predicate, the Indo-European languages developed more minute subdivisions, which attained great complexity in such languages as Greek and German; in English many such subdivisions have been sloughed off as unnecessary and trammeling.

Thus the progress of language is from significant cries to the pre-sentence or complete communication in unanalyzable form; from this to the word as a separable part of the communication unit; and from this differently in various language families to their distinctive syntactical elements and patterns. It is mirrored in our word *word,* which may apply to a message of any extent and is often used (for example, in the Bible) to mean communication. The first words were words only in this large sense. They were sentence words such as the animals now use, but used by primitive man imaginatively, lyingly, out of their proper occasion and context.

But in pointing out the subjective character of the beginning of grammar and its dependence upon the nonsentence, we are only setting off on the long march from primitiveness to complexity, around the corner, and back toward simplicity. Our next task must be to trace the later development of grammar so that we may understand why it looks as it does today.

We may notice, then, that the primitive cries out of which grammar was to develop were entirely independent of one another, as much so as are today the various items in the cat's "vocabulary." The earliest grammar of all would have consisted merely of an inventory (if primitive man ever bothered to make one) of sound complexes, each as different from the other as a whistle from a sob. No synthesis was possible because there were no elements common to all the nonsentence cries which made up this earliest vocabulary.

Even today it is noticeable that nonsentences are far less analyzable grammatically than are sentences, and this may be one of the reasons why they are almost entirely disregarded in books of grammar. It is the nonsentence which retains most clearly the character of primitive speech, just as the so-called irregular verb is older than the regular verb. And it is certain that long before there existed anything which could be called a verb, man had his little stock or hoard of nonsentences, each one grammatically a law to itself.

Grammar began to develop as more nonsentences began to be added to this initial stock. These new items were, no doubt, often as distinct from all the rest as these had been from one another. But as time progressed, and more items were added to the language stock, it became impracticable to find new sound combinations, even if it was desirable. Synthesis began to come into being.

No doubt primitive ears were not sensitive to such small differentiations in sound as exist, for example, between the words *fern* and *farm,* and the aim in adding new speech-cries was undoubtedly clarity, intelligibility, and differentiation from anything already in the inventory. Perhaps a modern analogy to the progression of primitive utterances may be found in the choice of names for new telephone exchanges. Such names must be very distinctly different from the old, as Susquehanna and Butterfield and Endicott differ from Worth and John and Main. New nonsentences must be easily distinguishable to primitive ears from the old ones, and this necessitated a wide range of speech sounds and clear differentiation of sound combinations.[1]

New speech-cries might be made up out of nothing, but if modern word making is any criterion, it does not seem likely that this occurred often, since it almost never happens in modern speech that a new word is made up out of whole cloth. It seems probable that even at the very start existing speech-cries were modified or combined in the making of new cries. No doubt much innovation took place as well, but it must have been very early that nonsentence combinations were developed. If, for example, there was a grunt accompanied perhaps by a pointing to indicate

[1] In Aiken, *Why English Sounds Change,* it is shown how the range of speech sounds has narrowed even within historic times. It can scarcely be doubted that primitive speech, like animal language, was drawn from a wider vocal area than is civilized speech.

what we call *he,* then this grunt might from early times have been combined with other sounds indicating *danger* or *love* or *discomfort.*

Many speech-cries no doubt were originated which never came to general use; but out of babbling, whining, cooing, growling, grunting, and so forth, there must have emerged the regular combinations which we may call syntactical.

With this combining of speech-cries we have the beginning of grammar; previous additions to the stock of speech-cries were in the nature of vocabulary. Such combining had later to be differentiated into inflexions and syntax, but the latter term better describes this primitive juxtaposing of nonsentence cries. Many speech-cries were no doubt combined in whole or in part to express new ideas or idea-combinations, and it is these new speech patterns which we may call syntactical.

No doubt much grammar was originated by children, and much from play, as well as from the sterner preoccupations of life. The fascination of language juggling must have been early felt, and one new combining led rapidly to another, so that the linguistic stock expanded at a comparatively quick rate because of the pleasures of out-of-context use.

It is important to emphasize that inflexions were in all probability a later development than syntax. As many writers on the subject have pointed out, the pronouns still show themselves clearly embedded in verbal and other affixes in such languages as Latin and Hebrew, and Hebrew also shows prepositional and conjunctional affixes, which may well point to the manner in which case may have originated in the Indo-European group of tongues. Inflexion is a younger process than syntax and one which we may reasonably suppose grew out of it.

If this is the fact, then the earliest inflexion, like the earliest speech-cry itself, was an independent communication. It was not an inflexion in the modern sense, that is, a sound or syllable added to a certain "part of speech" with complete or fair regularity. It was merely a tag or modification in a single word, somewhat of the nature of a compounding, but susceptible of extension to other words after the fashion of an inflexion.

On this basis it is easy to understand how inflexions should have grown up so luxuriantly in the early stages of grammar. Every word was a potential inflexion. It had only to prove itself useful in combination with numerous words, not necessarily all of a single kind, and it was likely to become more and more closely embedded in these words, until finally it lost its separate existence.

Modern English illustrates the process (which of course is recurrent and not confined to primitive languages) in the adverbial termination *ly,* used in *readily, easily, frankly, silently,* and hosts of other English words. Even so recently as the Anglo-Saxon period this *ly* was *līce,* meaning *like.* The compounded adverb is still found, particularly in Irish dialect: *He walked soft-like.* In most uses the word has become a suffix of a semi-inflexional character.

It was inevitable, likewise, that inflexions should be partial rather than complete in their applicability, since several different words might be used for a given idea, such as *many* or *past,* and such words might compound readily with only a few other terms. There is nothing peculiar in the fact that we find primitive languages with a plethora of declensions, conjugations, and other such categories. Even in Modern English, which has dropped most of its inflexional forms, we still have two ways (*more* and *er, most* and *est*) of forming the comparative and the superlative; and plurals are formed in several different ways.

Synthesis is a power relatively lacking in early stages of mental and social development. In many departments of grammar in many languages synthesis has failed to appear, even down to present times. Anyone could construct an English more synthesized than the one we speak. It is entirely consistent with what we know of the mentality of man in the various stages of his development to conclude that he would at first see grammatical relationships one by one rather than in categories. It was only very slowly and gradually that such grammatical categories could have developed, if indeed they ever developed at all.

In the beginning of grammar every word must have formed a category by itself, and it may be that in the Chinese language we have an example of a speech which never abandoned this primitive heterogeneity. Scholars are divided on the question whether Chinese ever went through an inflexional or a syntactical stage; but it is evident that so far as its grammar goes the language is today in a state similar to that which must have obtained in primitive speech.

In Chinese, as is well known, every word consists of a single syllable, and there are no such things as inflexions. Inflexional relationships are indicated, if at all, by separate words. There are no parts of speech; words shift around freely from function to function just as they are increasingly doing in the English language. Intelligibility is attained by sentence order and context. A distinction is made between "full" and "empty" words, the latter being what are known as "structural" words, such as prepositions, conjunctions, articles, and so forth. This absence of inflexions by no means hinders the Chinese from expressing complicated meanings with complete clarity, and it is entirely possible that the inflexionless state of Chinese has existed since the origin of that language.

In the western dialects, as well as in many eastern tongues, categories of person, gender, case, tense, mood, and the rest appeared. In the manner just described these categories multiplied themselves; but no sooner had great diversity appeared than certain categories began to merge and simplify.

To recur to the figure of a mountain used at the beginning of this chapter, we had in the early stages of grammar a steeply ascending curve of grammatical complication. The peak came at the point where the tendency to simplify overtook the tendency to multiply complications, and language began to descend to the state well represented by Modern English, where grammatical complications of form are tending to disappear.

Thus grammar in the shape of inflexions tends to be simple only at the birth and at the complete maturity of a language. In the field of syntax, on the other hand, grammar develops by juxtaposition of elements into a more or less fixed word order, out of which, in the Indo-European and Semitic languages, the sentence as we know it has developed.

The chief syntactical necessity in any language is to achieve a word pattern or group of patterns which will convey meanings with clarity. In Chinese nothing like the English sentence has developed, and the order of sentence elements is extremely fluid. In the Semitic- and Indo-European-language families we have roughly parallel developments into a fixed word order to which the term *sentence* may be applied.[2]

It is worth noting that all these developments into and out of grammatical forms are impelled by a variety of forces, most of them having little or nothing to do with logic. We can understand these forces as they apply to Modern English, and we may conjecture that they were similar at earlier stages of linguistic experience. In this fashion can grammatical origins be analyzed.

[2] This order differs in the Hebrew in that it is ordinarily verb-subject-complement, instead of subject-verb-complement as in English.

ষ্ঠ CHAPTER FIVE ষ্ঠ

CHANGING GRAMMAR

I T HAS BEEN a prevalent assumption that English grammar is something static—a fortress built by former generations, but now established for all time, though menaced occasionally by the assaults of an illiterate rabble who would tear down vital parts of its structure. The descriptive grammarian, who is too often innocent of a knowledge of linguistic history, tends to assume that grammar always was as it is now; and even the scholar, who realizes more fully what changes it has undergone, feels that such changes lie in the past, for the most part in the remote past, and that they are not likely to be repeated in the future. "On the whole, it is probable that the history of English grammar will for a very long time have few changes to record later than the nineteenth century." [1]

This view of grammatical change is of a piece with the current estimate of grammar as in conformity with logical principles, for logic does not change, but merely is uncovered; and it is assumed or inferred by grammarians that English grammar, having attained logical stability, has nowhere further to go. Bradley, who speaks from an unsurpassed knowledge of vocabulary, expresses the current view.

The making of English grammar is now probably a finished process. While it is certain that the vocabulary of English will in future undergo great changes—while many new words will be formed or adopted, and many old words will disappear or change their meaning—there is reason for believing that the grammar will remain for centuries very nearly

[1] Henry Bradley, *The Making of English,* New York, Macmillan, 1904, p. 79.

what it is now. The ground for this belief lies partly in the spread of education. Literary culture perhaps on the whole conduces to tolerance of certain kinds of innovation in vocabulary, but with regard to grammar its tendency is strongly conservative. Another reason is that simplification of accidence has nearly attained its utmost conceivable limit, and that the few further steps in this direction that remain possible would involve practical inconvenience.[2]

Such utterances are basically those of faith—faith in modernity. The scholar looks out upon a world of static (or almost static) grammar and concludes that it will always remain so. The Dark Ages are past. Today is different from yesterday. Grammar does not and will not alter. So he reasons, and such reasoning is the current conclusion on the subject.

However "logical" such views may be, they run counter to psychological observation, which sees constant flux and variation in all things human. If it is true that grammatical change has been or can be stopped or even greatly reduced, then there is no great significance in the psychological analysis of grammatical innovation or change, since such change lies mainly in the past, even the remote past, and all we are doing is to rattle dry bones. If English will be in the year 2950 much what it is today, then it is of merely academic interest to speculate concerning the changes it has undergone in the last thousand years and their causes.

But even while the scholars are assuring us that change in English grammar has ceased, there are many indications that change is still going on. It scarcely seems probable, when one comes to think of it, that today is altogether different from yesterday. For one thing, modern invention assures us that we are living in an era of constant and rapid shift. Wars form a rude stimulant of the perception that after all humanity may not have achieved modernity with stability. And it would seem strange if the alterations which are taking place in all other fields of human activity should not extend to English grammar as well.

It is true that grammatical change is slow and is not usually observable over a year or a decade, but frequently covers a century or more. Moreover, grammatical change is not an even or

[2] *Ibid.*, pp. 78–79. Quoted by permission of the Macmillan Company.

a universal phenomenon, but advances in islands and jagged lines, at first affecting some social groups to the exclusion of others and perhaps never making itself established throughout the social mass. However, this is very different from holding that grammatical change does not occur. Such change may be likened to the god of romance in Kipling's poem, who taught

> His backward-gazing scribes to say,
> The King was with us, yesterday.

It is quite possible that the reason for the failure of linguists to recognize grammatical change is that such change is looked for almost exclusively in the field of inflexions. Inflexional endings in English have decreased rapidly in number, until today there are only some half-dozen left. Whereas in Anglo-Saxon the majority of words showed some formal indication of case, tense, or other grammatical aspect, in Modern English only one word out of half a dozen shows such indication.[3] It might easily seem to be a fact that there can be no very extensive inflexional change in the future, if, as Bradley points out, comparatively little simplification is now possible.

But such a conclusion would be erroneous on several counts. In the first place, it is misleading to assert that inflexions in English are confined to six endings, since this is to ignore the case endings of the pronouns and the many scattered remnants of individual inflexions which clutter the English language and which are frequently discarded in popular speech, as, for example, *whom* is widely replaced by the common-case form *who*. Moreover, this conclusion disregards the possibility that instead of decreasing, inflexional apparatus may actually increase in English. That this is not an impossibility is shown by the fact that recent centuries have witnessed, not one, but several such developments, an outstanding example being the differentiation of *who* and *which*. The first phrase of the Lord's Prayer, "Our Father which art," exemplifies the former genderless or undifferentiated usage, the pronouns having been used interchangeably up to the seventeenth century.

[3] This figure (one in six) is based on an informal study made by a student group.

Today we have developed a complicated set of distinctions between *who* and *which*, but in the main the distinction is between animate and inanimate, *who* representing human and *which* non-human concepts.[4] Such a development actually multiplies rather than decreases the complications of English grammar, and it is interesting to recall that it has occurred entirely unchecked by any opposition from the rhetoricians. The possessive idea in English also has multiplied instead of decreased its complications, which might well be called inflexional, during the past century or two; and other examples of grammatical change looking toward greater complication will be given in later chapters.

When seeking to determine whether or not grammar is currently changing, however, we must not confine ourselves to inflexions, but must include the entire field of grammar. Grammatical change is one thing in syntax, another in inflexion and word formation, and still other things in punctuation, spelling, phonetics, and so forth. It is by no means a single phenomenon, but a group of related phenomena. And while space forbids our setting forth in detail the incidence of change in each of these departments of grammar, a few examples will be useful to prove that change is still active in English.

To consider spelling first, we must admit that so far as formal writing is concerned those who deny change have the facts much their own way. Spelling, which in the Anglo-Saxon was an echo of the voice of the speaker,[5] has become so ironed out and standardized that now the words of the king read like those of the beggar, the poet's like the peasant's. There is little or no room for psychological interpretation in the spelling of formal printed documents in Modern English. It has achieved complete stability, modified only by the existence of a few disputed or alternative spellings such as are set forth in dictionaries. This standardization is probably beneficial linguistically. If everyone spelled as he

[4] It will perhaps be argued that the relation between *who* and *which* is not of an inflexional nature; but, apart from the fact that it is called a gender difference by several grammarians, it is of a nature similar to the distinction between, e. g., *man* and *woman*, which is regularly included under accidence in grammars. Such accidence types seem to be on the increase in English.

[5] That Anglo-Saxon was spelled phonetically is an assumption generally accepted by linguists.

talked, we should have perhaps twenty ways of spelling such common words as *horse* and *hearth,* and this would be confusing.

Yet it cannot be asserted that standardization even in spelling is complete. Frequently minor changes occur, as *airplane* for the former *aeroplane.* Moreover, beneath the surface of the literary spelling of books and periodicals, English shows an almost endless hospitality to misspellings, some of which, like *alright* and *nite,* are making a bid for dictionary recognition.

Misspellings are exceedingly frequent in English, as any teacher of college composition can testify. Sometimes these misspellings represent the individual's attempt at correctness, and sometimes they represent his pronunciation of the word involved. For example, in recent years spellings like *esk* (*ask*) an*d equeduct* have appeared on papers of students in the New York metropolitan district, obviously reflecting the student's idea of the pronunciation of these words.

Thus we see in the field of spelling a formal standardization (which by the way is arbitrary and has nothing to do with logic) and an actual variation and change which represents spoken English as opposed to literary English. Change is not lacking; it is simply driven below the surface. There are also to be mentioned the frontal attacks on our standard spelling from those who advocate simplified systems of one sort or another. Such proposed systems and the degree of logic they manifest would make a separate study in themselves.

The story of change in punctuation is also extremely interesting. So far as the grammars are concerned, the rules for punctuation are rigidly formulated and mandatory; and they have remained practically unchanged for generations. However, these rules are simply not observed in actual literary practice, which has engineered what might almost be called a revolution in punctuation— this revolution centering in the comma and the semicolon.

For purposes of comparison we have studied the editorial columns of two copies of the New York *Times* sixty years apart, the issues of September 25 in 1879 and in 1939. All marks of punctuation found in the first three thousand words on these pages were counted and tabulated, and the results were found to be both interesting and significant.

Sentence length changed only slightly in sixty years; the modern editorial writer used 92 sentences in 3,000 words, while the earlier editor used 105, indicating a slightly shorter sentence. All the older sentences ended with periods; the modern editorials included two questions. It is the impression of many observers that the modern editorial is less formal and more colloquial in its nature than former editorials, but no such conclusion can be drawn clearly from these facts.[6]

If length and type of sentence are inconclusive, however, it is not so with commas. In the approximately 100 sentences of the two periods, the typesetter of 1879 found it necessary to use no fewer than 173 commas, while the 1939 typesetter used almost exactly half as many, that is, 87. Thirteen semicolons were found necessary in the earlier columns, while the latter used but five. Other punctuation marks, such as colons, dashes, hyphens, and quotation marks, were few and showed no very significant variation in the two sets of editorials.

While to be fully conclusive such a study should take account of the structure of individual sentences, still this study is indicative of the decrease in the use of commas over the past sixty years. If the decrease should continue at the same rate, we should have no commas at all in another sixty years; but of course this is not likely to happen. What is happening is that punctuation is growing very much less, in spite of all the rules for its employment to be found in the manuals of correct usage.[7]

In the field of inflexions it is not possible to take so short a view as is represented by sixty years. Here change should rather be charted over centuries; but if we look back three hundred years, to the time of Shakespeare, we find enough inflexional changes to prove that grammar is not so stable as it is represented. To name

[6] It is interesting to see that apostrophes trebled over the sixty year period, numbering five in 1870 and fifteen in 1839; and this may indicate greater informality, but the figures are too small to give a very positive indication.

[7] Newspaper men occasionally complain that the commas in their copy are disregarded by the compositor, who does not like to take the time to set them. The compositor thus may account for part of the decrease in comma punctuation.

but a few such changes we may notice the disappearance of *thou* and its oblique forms, the dropping of the old nominative form *ye,* the use of *my* instead of *mine* before nouns beginning with a vowel.

A cursory study of the first two scenes (roughly one hundred lines) in the folio version of *Twelfth Night* [8] reveals 33 separate grammatical alterations of an inflexional or syntactical sort between Shakespeare's time and the present day. It is to be doubted whether a comparison of a Chaucer manuscript with a Shakespeare facsimile would yield a greater number of changes to the one hundred lines.

Among the features of Shakespeare's English which have been altered are the use of *as* where Modern English would use *like;* instances of tautology like *from hence* (Modern English *hence*) and *though that* (Modern English *though*); the discontinuance of numerous abbreviations such as *o'er, 'tis, e'er, oft;* and the omitted article, as in the line "give me excess of it." [9]

Syntactical change, perhaps, does not need to be discussed in detail, particularly since such change will be analyzed in ensuing chapters; but it is interesting to notice that between Shakespeare's time and ours the rise of the auxiliary *do* has revolutionized our way of asking questions and making negative statements. This is only one of the many syntactical changes which may be noticed in comparatively recent times.

To return to the two reasons given by Bradley for the alleged cessation of change in English grammar, we believe both are less than valid. Scholars have simply missed the abundant room for change in this field, or no one would say that simplification has attained its utmost conceivable limit. As for Bradley's other argument, that education has exerted a stabilizing influence, we think it could be shown that this influence is neither so effective nor so universal as has often been believed. Educational proscription has been effective in controlling the double negative, which has been driven below the level of literary English into popular speech.

[8] William Shakespeare, *Twelfth Night,* a Facsimile of the First Folio Text, with an introduction by J. Dover Wilson, Boston, Houghton Mifflin, 1928, pp. 255–56.
[9] In some modern journalistic styles such as that of the periodical *Time,* the article is very freely omitted.

But can anyone assert that the double negative is not widespread in English? One hears it constantly from people of every sort of cultural background. It would certainly seem that education has not succeeded in stamping out the double or even the multiple negative construction.

What education seems to do is to select certain individual constructions for condemnation, stressing those, but disregarding other constructions, which are thus left susceptible to free change. For instance, it is found that modern grammarians oppose converting *like* into a conjunction and *contact* into a verb, but they entirely overlooked such changes as the conversion of *like, near, nearest,* and *worth* from adjectives into prepositions[10] and *opposite* from a participle into a preposition. Probably nine grammatical changes out of ten take place without permission or opposition from the grammarian, whose function seems to be rather to retard or to drive underground a few specific changes than to obstruct change as a whole.

In this sketch of grammatical change we have not mentioned phonology, but to do this seems hardly necessary. Students of language agree in recognizing more or less widespread and more or less radical change in sounds, even over fairly short periods of time. In British English the fairly recent diphthongization of the vowel in words like *cake* and *note* and the disappearance of the breath consonant in words like *when* and *why* are examples of the strong and continuously operative tendency to phonetic change in English.

What may be in the future an analogy to the development of English is to be seen in Chinese, where we find a literary language which has remained static over thousands of years superimposed upon a popular speech which has changed freely and which very recently has succeeded in unseating and superseding its rival, the literary language. Change cannot be suppressed, even though it may be driven underground for a time. The deliberate, glacial

---

[10] Some of these changes perhaps took place before the grammarian became a very effective power to oppose linguistic change. It should be mentioned also that *worth* is often called an adjective, though its prepositional character seems obvious in such a phrase as *a hat worth a dollar. Worth* is never used without an object, and this fact allies it with the connectives.

forces of grammatical development operate and will continue to operate almost wholly independent of humanly intellectual barriers. We may confidently expect such grammatical development in the future; we can discern it at work today.

In later sections of this book the causes for grammatical change will be analyzed; and it will be noticed that the facts we use derive almost wholly from recent grammatical history. Perhaps enough has been said in this preliminary section of our study to show that English grammar as a system is fortuitous, illogical, and subject to relatively rapid alteration.

CHAPTER SIX

HOW GRAMMAR CHANGES

GRAMMAR is concerned with the use of words rather than with their meanings. Grammar takes account of the way words are altered, added to, or replaced in order to convey an idea of time, number, or other similar notion (accidence), or it treats directly the relation of words to one another in communicating ideas (syntax). Theoretically grammar has nothing to do with what these words mean.

In practice, however, it proves impossible to separate completely the notion of use from that of meaning. Frequently a word becomes significant grammatically just because it happens to mean a certain thing; the auxiliary *do,* soon to be discussed in detail, is an example. Frequently, also, the contrary takes place, and a word loses grammatical significance on account of its meaning; of this an example is *thou,* also to be discussed later in this chapter. And frequently a group of words has a certain grammatical function or standing because its members mean approximately the same thing; thus words of physical or mental perception (*see, believe, think,* and so forth) take the present tense, whereas action verbs (*run, call, read*) are generally put in the present progressive form to show present time. So it is impracticable to keep meaning entirely out of a study of grammar; it is possible, however, to bring it in only as an auxiliary to the facts of its use; and this is the plan we shall follow in this study.

Now in making any communication through speech or writing the maker has of course a semantic aim, which is to transfer to reader or listener the message contained in his words. This aim is not the material for grammatical analysis. It does not concern the grammarian whether what is said is true or false, whether it is cruel or kind, conceited or humble, amorous or hateful. It is *how,* not *what,* which grammar analyzes, the way words are chosen and put together rather than the particular idea they convey. If these words are well adapted and well arranged for their purpose, the demands of grammar have been satisfied, no matter what meaning the words may have.

There is, however, purpose or aim involved in the employment of grammatical means, and this aim is a dual one, corresponding roughly to the eternal duality of the subjective and the objective. The speaker or writer wishes, through the grammar he uses, to satisfy himself in the arrangement and form of what he says or writes, and he wants also to satisfy his hearer or reader, to seem clear and effective to this other individual. These are the twin incentives which lead him to choose any one of various means of self-expression, and they determine the precise form of his communication. Both incentives will be active in inducing him to try to show himself as he is, or as he would like to think that he is. His grammar, like his words, must show him to be modest, impressive, poetic, practical, and a number of other pleasing characteristics. Largely unconscious though it is, this central aim will operate in his grammatical choices.

Always operative will be a tendency toward conservatism and traditionalism. If his father talked a certain way, his strong impulse will be to talk that way also. If he is used to a subject-verb-complement order in statements, he will incline toward it in questions also, and when a *do* or an *est-ce-que* comes his way he will adopt it in defiance of tradition. But he is a bit of a modern also, and sometimes may incline toward change almost because it is change, without any deep impelling reason. Fashion may now and then overcome tradition. Indolence is always operative or ready to operate. Reason, sometimes humanly distorted reason, tends to be an object with the speaker, and impatience in his mind is frequently contrasted with leisureliness, sometimes showing itself through a sense of rhythm which leads him to say more than is necessary, just because it sounds well; and there is an imaginativeness which displays itself in rather astonishing ways.

Thus a variety of motives will lead the speaker away from the grammar which has been used in the past. Sometimes these motives will be easy to detect, simple and clear, as when courtesy leads him to make a request in some form other than the abrupt imperative, choosing, for instance, *Would you close the door?* instead of *Close the door*.[1] Often, however, these motives will be intricate and mixed, sometimes almost impossible to disentangle from one another.

Behind every grammatical innovation, however, lies an indefinite number of individual innovations made by individual speakers. Such motives may or may not lead to actual innovation in the field of English grammar. Because of a feeling for consistency one child or several children may say *sheeps,* and still such an individual innovation never becomes a recognized part of English. On the other hand, when a large number of individual speakers introduce a change in the way of saying a certain thing, it is always possible and even probable that English grammar will actually change in conformity. Thus behind every grammatical innovation lies an indefinite number of innovations made by individual speakers.

While it is true, moreover, that grammatical machinery, such as inflexional endings, tends to decrease, it is scarcely true to say that grammar as a system of communicating devices tends to become less complicated. If we may anticipate at this point one of the many conclusions of this study, we may say that always the grammatical innovations made by an individual speaker will lead him (and through him the English language) toward greater results from less machinery—toward richer and subtler patterns attained by simplified methods.

Few grammatical developments in English are simplifications. In most cases, change is well typified by the word *do,* which is analyzed below. The grammatical uses of *do* have been multiplied, until in Modern English the grammatical usefulness of the word is found to have been vastly increased. And still each development has in some respect acted to simplify our grammar. This richer

[1] See below, p. 152.

use of simplified elements is a natural aim or end sought (largely unconsciously or semiconsciously) by means of grammatical change. It has been the fashion among scholars to emphasize the formal simplification while largely disregarding the pattern enrichment; yet the latter is the more important of the two, as will be seen throughout this study.

It is the purpose of this chapter to give a general view of change in grammar, and for this purpose it seems best to select a very few types of change and to treat their various aspects rather fully. It is seldom that any change is so isolated as to be analyzable by itself, even though in later chapters the illustrations and examples may seem to imply such isolation. Here we shall try to show not only individual change but also its ramifications.

One of the most interesting grammatical developments in Modern English is the emergence and extension of the auxiliary *do*. This verb, while common in Anglo-Saxon, had nothing like its Modern English frequency, which now places it in the second thousand of English words, according to the frequency study by Faucett and Maki.[2] In Anglo-Saxon the verb *dōn* was not an auxiliary; it was a full verb having two sorts of meaning: first, *to make, act, perform, do;* and second, *to cause, arrive at.* Both of these meanings still survive in Modern English, the first in sentences such as *He did his work,* and the second in *He did them harm.* The second meaning is relatively uncommon and constitutes an idiom in Modern English; while in Old English it was perhaps as frequent as the first.

It is this second meaning, *to cause,* which gave rise to the auxiliary use of *do.* In Middle English we have the frequent use of this form with the infinitive, for example, *He dyde him to wit,* meaning *He caused him to know.* But since the causative may form a part of any verb in itself, this causative *do* plus the infinitive came more and more to look like a simple verb with an auxiliary. By the end of the Middle English period (exemplified in the poetry of Chaucer), the causative *do* is very frequent, and many examples may be found in the *Canterbury Tales.*

Later the causative nature of *do* became obscured, and the aux-

2 *A Study of English Word-Values,* Tokyo, Matsumura Sanshodo, 1932.

iliary became colorless and almost meaningless. By the time of Shakespeare we find *do* in fairly frequent use in this colorless fashion, so that *As I do think* meant merely *As I think*. Shakespeare used *do* frequently to fill out a line without giving any particular grammatical significance to the auxiliary. This use also persists today.

Thus *do* became one of a group of unnecessary words which are inserted for emphasis, for rhythm, or for a certain leisurely quality of speech. The auxiliary *go* is used today in much the same fashion; for example, in *I am going to go*. In all such colorless grammatical usages, however, we have a grammatical situation distinctly out of equilibrium, since sooner or later speakers will tend either to discard or to give significance to grammatical elements which lack such significance.

Not one, but three separate grammatical uses were actually given to this colorless auxiliary *do* subsequent to the Elizabethan period. As a general auxiliary *do* became emphatic, and it is emphatic today. This use of *do* for emphasis naturally is largely a matter of oral rather than of written English and is an outgrowth of the frequently operative desire to give one's statements strength and weight.

Another grammatical construction in which *do* became useful is the interrogative. Interrogatives in Elizabethan English were of various sorts, and often when the interrogative began with a characteristic word such as *who* or *what,* the sentence order followed the usual pattern of subject-verb-complement (*Who calls me?*). However, in other constructions the verb was front-shifted; for example, in questions such as *What think you?* which today is *What do you think?* In this situation the use of the auxiliary *do* enables the subject to precede the main verb, even though the complement is still front-shifted. Here *do* came to be used in a fashion similar to the French *est-ce que* or the Latin enclitic *ne*. Its use helped to satisfy a sense of grammatical orderliness in individual speakers.

The third development of the auxiliary *do* is similar to the second. The adverb *not* must have seemed slightly awkward or perhaps lagging, in its use following the verb in Elizabethan English, for instance, in *He went not*. So the auxiliary *do* was again pressed into service, to enable *not* to precede the main verb: *He did not go*. This change was calculated to bring such expressions into line with similar expressions using other auxiliaries, for instance, *He was not told*. The desire to anticipate as well as the tendency toward consistency is involved here. Evidently the speaker desired to make it apparent as early as possible in the sentence that a negative was involved,[3] and this led to the introduction of *do*, which brought the negative before the verb.

The development of *do* has been one of accretion. Today we have every former use of *do* to enrich our grammar. Even the colorless auxiliary *do* is exemplified in much inept poetry. The extension of the grammatical significance of *do* has involved numerous motives, among them the desire for consistency, a feeling for rhythm, a tendency to anticipate, a desire for clarity. And these developments of *do* are typical of English grammatical change, which has multiplied the patterns of this word while striving for simplification. Perhaps it is not easy to see the tendency toward simplification in this process, but it is there, nevertheless, in the unconscious desire to conform sentence order to a standard norm; this desire is at the root of the use of *do* in questions.

The second illustration of the means and motives of grammatical change lies in the history of the second person pronoun, and here we may begin, not with Old English, but with Elizabethan usage. In 1600 the chief forms of the second person pronoun were *thou, thy, thee,* and *ye, your,* and *you*. Of these, only two, *you* and *your*, survive today.

The loss of the singular forms of *thou* may be described as a triumphing of the democratic principle. While the plural *you* was used between strangers and people of equal rank, this form *thou* was used to express intimacy, affection, contempt, snobbery, the relation of master to servant and generally of superior to subordinate.[4] If one will study, for example, the opening scene of

<hr/>

[3] *Cf.* p. 118.

[4] "Thou towards strangers who were not inferior was an insult. 'If thou thouest him some thrice it shall not be amiss,' is the advice given to Sir Andrew Aguecheek when on the point of writing a challenge." E. A. Abbott, *A Shakespearian Grammar*, London, Macmillan, 1871, p. 157.

Othello, where there are some very interesting variations between *thou* and *you,* it will become apparent how undemocratic this alternation was. And it can scarcely be doubted that the discontinuance of *thou* is directly connected with a growing sense of equality and of individual worth, socially, among English-speaking people.

Far less apparent is the reason for the dropping of the old nominative plural *ye* from English. Here we have probably a fairly simple manifestation of the tendency of language toward simplification. One psychological factor which is involved is indolence. Speakers are disinclined to make any greater oral effort than is necessary; and if two words both serve the same purpose reasonably well, it is unlikely that both will survive, unless one is altered to express a different meaning. *Ye* and *you* were a pair, very nearly alike in sound, especially in stressed position; and certainly both are not necessary for intelligible speech. It is normal also that the objective crowds out the nominative, since the objective of this pronoun is more frequently used and hence would come to seem the standard or typical form.

In the King James Bible *you* and *ye* are used according to sixteenth-century views of grammatical correctness.[5] During the centuries which followed, the indolence of speakers caused *ye* to disappear, until today *ye,* like *thou* and its forms, is kept alive only in religious, poetic, and dialectical usage.

Thus far we have been looking at grammar from the angle of the word or words used to discharge a certain function, but it is just as possible to start with the function and see how it is handled in words. We may choose for such analysis the impersonal or indefinite pronoun construction, tracing it from its beginnings in Anglo-Saxon to its present status in Modern English.

We find that in Anglo-Saxon there was one simple mechanism for the impersonal or indefinite, namely, the word *mon* (*man*) as in "sæde him mon" (*one said to him*). This construction English shared with other Germanic dialects, as is seen in the similar use

---

[5] According to Abbott, *op. cit.,* Shakespeare did not keep *you* and *ye* separate, and neither did other Elizabethan writers. The King James Bible then would stand as the last literary monument where the two pronouns are used in the traditional fashion.

of *man* common in Swedish and German today (also see p. 15).

The Anglo-Saxon use of *mon* persisted well into Middle English, with certain variations and additions. Chaucer uses the singular *man* less often than the plural *men*—"Men seyen" (*men say*). Alongside of this use of *men* Chaucer has other ways of expressing the impersonal. Sometimes he uses the word *folk,* the subjectless verb such as *bifel* (*befell*), or the impersonal *it.*

Such Middle English variations are multiplied yet further in Elizabethan English. Shakespeare is not given to the indefinite or impersonal construction, yet it occurs now and then in his plays. For the purpose he may use the plural form, *men,* the singular, *man,* the third person pronoun *he* (*him*), the plural personal pronoun *we,* as well as several other constructions.[6]

Modern English seems to have dropped the noun uses of *man* and *folk* for the impersonal, although *men* is occasionally used in this connection. We have multiplied our use of pronouns for indefinite or impersonal uses so that we may express this construction by *we, you, he, it, they,* or *one.*[7] Another very common mechanism for this purpose is the use of the passive verb. Altogether, Modern English has achieved richness at the expense of consistency in its grammatical method for accomplishing this purpose.

It would require a chapter to discuss fully the psychological bearings of these various devices. The pronoun *you* (*You can't make an omelet without breaking eggs*) has a vigorous idiomatic direct effect, however much it may be frowned upon by rhetoricians. The pronoun *they* removes the thought far away from the speaker and conveys the authority of a vague body of opinion external to the individual. The most "impersonal" of these impersonals are the passive and the pronoun *one,* which convey a slightly arrogant isolation on the speaker's part. Each one of the various devices has its definite place, its reason for being, and its psychology.

It has been suggested (page 44) that grammatical change fre-

---

[6] *I, Henry IV,* Act 3, scene 2, l. 48: "Men would tell their children, This is he." Act 5, scene 1, l. 132: "Who hath it? He that died o' Wednesday." Act 5, scene 4, l. 115: "To counterfeit dying, when a man thereby liveth, is to be no counterfeit." *Merchant of Venice,* Act 4, scene 1, l. 187: "It blesseth him that gives and him that takes." Act 4, scene 1, l. 200: "We do pray for mercy."

[7] *Cf.* p. 204.

quently differs in different localities. This is particularly so in the use of prepositions. British and American usages frequently lean to different prepositions to follow various verbs and adjectives. A good example is the British use of *than* or *to* with the word *different,* while to the American ear these are both incorrect, the preposition *from* being standard. Logically, justification may be found for all three prepositions; the word *than* emphasizes comparison, the word *to* emphasizes contrast, and the word *from* emphasizes dissimilarity. It is a pretty illustration of the variations of human thinking, and each word has become effective in its own locality.

Another type of grammatical change is the differentiation of function between words which have been completely or nearly synonymous. English language seems to oppose synonyms, perhaps because of an instinctive feeling of economy in language; and if two words mean the same thing or fulfill the same function the likelihood is either that one will be lost or that the two will be differentiated. Thus grammars tend to condemn the form *towards* in favor of the slightly shorter *toward.* In the case of *beside(s)* the two forms have survived, but *beside* has been made a preposition meaning *by the side of,* while *besides* has been made an adverb or an adverbial conjunction meaning *in addition to.* This differentiation of function in synonyms is a standard process of grammatical change, and we shall meet it frequently in our study.

It has been said (page 47) that the vast majority of grammatical changes take place without opposition from the grammarians. This is true of many abbreviating changes, which seem to arise from human impatience and desire to get a thing said in the shortest possible way. An example is the idiom *I for one* in sentences such as *I for one hope it will stop.* To explain clearly these three words would require many more words; the language has telescoped thinking so as to satisfy its impatient speakers.

It has been said also that grammatical changes seldom occur in isolated form, but that they ordinarily involve a greater or less number of extra adjustments. In the case of the *who-which* differentiation (page 42) it might be thought that we have an example of isolated change, but it is this shifting which has given to the grammarians occasion to condemn the use of *whose* in referring to nonhuman entities, in such examples as *the book whose cover was torn* and *the cat whose fur had been stroked*. Such uses of *whose* would have been entirely acceptable in earlier stages of the language, but are questioned today solely because *who* is now restricted to human beings.

One final instance of the dynamic development of grammatical machinery is found in the history of the single word *as*. No word *as* existed in Anglo-Saxon; our word has arisen out of two Anglo-Saxon words, *eall* (*all*) and *swā* (*so*), a combination which has given us both *as* and *also* in Modern English. The reason why *also* retains so much more of the original two words is of course its tendency to greater emphasis and stress; human indolence will eliminate sounds in a word which is in an unstressed position. By Middle English the words *as* and *also* were clearly differentiated.

Chaucer uses the word *as* in comparisons, a use similar to its modern function. He also uses it as a subordinating conjunction similar to our *as if*, and he frequently has a pleonastic *as*, particularly with verbs in the imperative or subjunctive; "as sende love and pees betwixte hem two." In Modern English the *as* would be omitted, and perhaps a *may* would be used—*may love and peace be sent between the two*.

The modern uses of *as* are not well understood, or at least it does not seem to be recognized how the grammatical functions of *as* are being altered. To show its present uses some forty examples taken from approximately five thousand words of newspaper English (*The Christian Science Monitor*, issue of December 26, 1939) were analyzed. It was found that the comparison use of *as* is relatively rare, six examples being found. Infrequent also is the semiconnective use of *as* in the phrase *as well as*, of which three examples were found. Other idiomatic phrase uses, *as to, as if*, and *as such*, accounted for five examples; and there was one example of the subordinating conjunction use of *as*, meaning *because*. The bulk of modern examples of this word show it used as a preposition of a pleonastic or appositional nature in constructions such as *Let me say as one who has tried every kind*. Here *as* is obviously a preposition introducing the object *one*, and *one* is as obviously in apposition to the pronoun *me*. This prepositional appositional use of *as* is its typical modern function, and this use goes back to Shake-speare's time, as is shown by the line, "Thou shall present me as an eunuch to him," *Twelfth Night*, Act I, scene 2, l. 54.

Notice that the pleonastic use of *as* has endured, but that now it centers in the noun and adjective rather than in the verb as it did in Middle English. Grammatical uses have multiplied, not de-creased. Each of these uses has its psychological interpretation, most of them arising from the semiconscious desire for clarity on the part of the speaker, a desire which leads to the inclusion of words not strictly necessary, in order to make the meaning plain.

In the following chapters we shall seek to isolate the psychologi-cal factors in grammatical change rather than to trace the change in all its various ramifications. In this chapter our purpose has been to emphasize the fact that change is continuous and expanding rather than fragmentary and occasional. We have also tried to analyze typical developments in grammar in such a way as to show how they operate over a period of time.

CHAPTER SEVEN

CONSISTENCY IN GRAMMAR

IN SPITE of Emerson's dictum that foolish consistency is the hobgoblin of little minds, it is in fact a desire of most human beings, big as well as little, to be consistent. The essence of consistency is harmony—harmony and balance in color, shape, style, pattern, actions, expressions, as well as ideas; and harmony is universally felt to be admirable and desirable.

All these generalizations about the desire for consistency and its frustration are mirrored in man's supreme achievement, language. In fact, a very good place to study the human yearning for consistency, in its finest and, alas, its most deluded state, is within the pages of almost any grammar textbook. Here we may see the eternal strife to make things fit together, even at the cost of not making them fit other relatable things; and as we read on, or as we close the book and hear people speak, we can see how vain have been the grammarian's aspirations.

Consistency in grammar is particularly difficult, if not impossible, to attain; because it is not one harmony, but many different harmonies, which are but too likely to jangle with one another even should they achieve internal concord. Grammatical consistencies may be differentiated under the headings nature, form, function, order, sound, and idea; and each one of these is only too likely to conflict with each other one. A few examples taken from everyday usages will make the facts clear.

CONSISTENCY WITH NATURE

From Socrates to I. A. Richards, grammarians have worried over the relation between language and nature, that is, the external objects which language names. Mark Twain made Eve call the dodo a dodo because it looked like a dodo. Modern linguists talk profoundly of referents; but in the last analysis language bears only a small relationship to the world of things. Language is incorrigibly abstract, whereas things are concrete. Language is emotional, misleading, vague, in a word, psychological, whereas things are factual.

Yet there is one department of English grammar where progress has brought language appreciably closer to the world of nature, and consistency has developed and grown accordingly. The so-called natural gender of English not only sets English apart from and above other Indo-European tongues; it has increased harmony and congruity in English to a remarkable degree.

Laziness had probably as much to do with the disappearance of grammatical gender in English as intelligence had; nevertheless it requires a certain degree of intelligence to harmonize gender and sex, even partially; and this intelligence, this consistency, is mirrored in the contemporary idiom.

No doubt the early scribes, conservative as are most scribes in any age, tried hard to maintain consistency to tradition by retaining grammatical gender in their nouns. When this proved impossible, partly because of general illiteracy and partly through the advent of French, with its different gender system, English fell into a condition of gender anarchy from which it was rescued by the principle of conformity to nature. Gender based on sex was obviously the reasonable thing to establish, and Modern English is largely reasonable from this aspect.

And yet neither is natural gender, by which pronouns apply to objects according to their sex, a complete system, nor was it brought about by any universal perception of the absurdities of grammatical gender. Natural gender inheres only in the third person singular pronoun; there is no way of distinguishing the gender of *me, us, you,* or *them.* Even in the realm of *him, her,* and *it* there are conflicts and discrepancies as well as personifications and poetizings which ascribe sex to sexless beings. And as for the origin and genesis of our natural gender, two forces, neither of them reasonable, appear to have been active. The first was the impact of French upon English, one gender system upon another, with consequent confusion and decay in both; and the second, largely stemming from the first, was the weakening or loss of almost all inflexional endings, perhaps due also to the rise of a stronger first-syllable stress.

A distinction between human and nonhuman, *who* and *which* (page 42), has recently become operative in English. It is useful and necessary because of the rise of natural gender, and it illustrates a further rationalizing tendency of the human mind. There exists in fact a natural division between human beings on the one hand and animals and things on the other; and man through developing a distinction of meaning has ratified grammatically this natural cleavage.

CONSISTENCY OF FORM

Far more usual than conformity to nature in English grammar is conformity to form. Harmony of this sort has a special name in linguistics, and that name is "analogy." Analogy has long been recognized as one of the chief principles of grammatical development, even though its psychological character has not been clearly perceived.

Analogy may be illustrated by such forms as *commoner, perfecter, royaler*, which are formed like *prettier, quieter*, and *lower*, rather than with *more*, as is the standard usage. Analogy, or the tendency to make words fit with one another, is the source of much grammatical simplification. It lies behind the reduction in the number of irregular verbs between Anglo-Saxon and Modern English, since analogy would exercise a strong pull toward the past *ed* ending in place of the older ablaut forms.

Another illustration which seems appropriate to the matter of analogy, or consistency of form, is the so-called illogical comparison of adjectives. Since most adjectives may be compared by the use of *er* or *more, est* or *most*, speakers tend to apply these inflexional devices to all adjectives. However, grammarians discovered that there are words (*round, white, blue, true, perfect*, and so forth) which are themselves in the nature of superlatives and therefore cannot logically be compared. A thing cannot be truer than true, whiter than white, or more unique than unique, as grammar-logicians have pointed out with considerable reason.

Consistency of form here has been contending with logical consistency, and the former has triumphed. So widespread has been the practice of comparing the incomparable that recent authorities have modified their opposition to these illogical comparisons and now generally condone them, even while still recommending *more nearly blue* as preferable to *bluer*. This compromise form is seldom read or heard; to the average speaker all adjectives are comparable, and he compares them all alike. It is a rare issue of your newspaper which will not contain at least one *most unique*.

Another fertile field for the study of consistency in English is spelling. Analogy is not entirely inoperative in our much-abused orthography, and it shows in our tendency to write with *s* or *es*, plurals like *radiuses, indexes, curriculums,* and *hippopotamuses,* instead of the older, foreign forms. Another instance is the hyphen, which has come to be used with fair uniformity for writing compound adjectives, while compound nouns are consistently being written solid if such writing does not look too awkward. The second edition of *Webster's International Dictionary* writes as one, many words which are formerly hyphenated or separated.[1] Such tendencies are progressive and consistent with linguistic progress in the past.

But in other instances not only is spelling consistency lacking, but when it tries to show itself it is stoutly opposed by authority. The spelling *alright* is obviously in line with such spellings as *always, already, altogether,* and so forth; and yet it is branded as an illiteracy by practically every teacher. It would be a fine thing for the English language, as well as for pupils in spelling classes, if the consistent spelling *alright* could find its way into dictionaries and spelling textbooks.

It would unquestionably also be of advantage to English spelling

[1] Between 1928 and 1934 the entire spelling policy of *Webster's International Dictionary* in regard to compound words seems to have changed. A few examples of the older and newer spellings are: *to-day, today; to-morrow, tomorrow; set-up, setup; flash light, flashlight; shame-proof, shameproof.* Among the many words which were not included in the 1928 edition but which appear as one word in 1934 are *beanfield, forksmith, barrelhead,* and even such awkward spellings as *barkcutter* and *bedrail.*

if a wider consistency could be introduced in such spellings as *notable, edible, peaceable; existence, appearance, conscience; to, two, too; principle, principal,* and many other pairs, triplets, quadruplets, and quintuplets of spelling "demons." Such changes would lead to no confusion or ambiguity, since the context would always show which word was meant, just as it does now in both spoken and written English. It is, however, vain to hope for consistency in English spelling.

A very frequent "error" in popular English is the use of the verb *don't* with a third person singular subject. The Leonard Survey[2] includes under disputable forms *Martha don't sew as well as she used to* and *It don't make any difference what you think* (Nos. 175 and 165). Woolley's Handbook[3] goes further and calls it wrong to say *He don't know*. It is easy to see the consistency involved in this grammatical mistake. Since we use *don't* in all the other persons, it seems reasonable to use it in the third person singular as well. English might conceivably be a better or more reasonable language if the form *does* were entirely dropped, and this "incorrect" use of *don't* is just one step in that direction. Here consistency leads toward what is considered a solecism, but one may be pardoned for preferring, theoretically at least, the solecism to the standard usage.

Precisely the same type of mistake is made in relation to the past tense of the verb *to be*. Such a sentence as *You was mistaken about that* is called illiterate (No. 222) in the Leonard Survey; and yet it is simply an extension of the form *was* used in *I was, he was, it was,* and so forth, to the second person pronoun, which like these others is singular in number. Illiterate speakers, with their leaning toward consistency, try to simplify the past of *to be* by using *was* for all persons, or, less frequently, by using *were* for all persons (*He were walking down the street*). The English lan-

[2] Sterling A. Leonard, *Current English Usage,* Chicago, The Inland Press, 1932, hereafter referred to as "The Leonard Survey." A sequel by Albert H. Marckwardt and Fred Walcott, *Facts about Current English Usage,* New York, Appleton-Century, 1938, makes some interesting modifications of the original Leonard conclusions. For the purposes of this study, however, the best authority appears to be the group of linguists reporting in the original Leonard investigation.

[3] Woolley, E. C., and F. W. Scott, *College Handbook of Composition,* 3d ed., Boston, Heath, 1937, p. 373.

guage does not need both *was* and *were* in the past; one form would be sufficient. May it not be that consistency is desirable here, even when it leads away from traditional practices?

While we are on the subject of verbs, certain other constructions may be mentioned. About three centuries ago the third person singular verb ending, in the present tense, was stabilized as *s; eth* had been in frequent (though not universal) use previously. Shakespeare is entirely eclectic in his use of the two endings. A glance at Portia's famous speech concerning mercy will show the two jumbled in hopeless inconsistency.

Here English has taken the obviously reasonable path in standardizing the *s* ending. The only disadvantage of this standardization is to the poet, who no longer has an extra syllable to add or subtract at his convenience. Shakespeare's prosody was no doubt easier because he could choose between the two verb endings.

A final example concerning consistency of form may be given, also from the verb field. The linguists of the Leonard Survey approved as established English (No. 93) the sentence *I wish I was wonderful.* While many grammarians still condemn this use of the indicative for the subjunctive mood, the construction is easy to understand on the basis of consistency, since the verb tends to be in the ordinary form *was,* rather than the form *were,* which after all looks like the plural. What has happened is that the expression of the subjunctive idea, the idea of doubt, possibility, or condition contrary to fact, has been made a matter of context rather than a matter of word form; the idea is no less clear, but the forms used have become consistent with indicative forms. The alteration is distinctly to the benefit of the English language.

CONSISTENCY OF FUNCTION AND ORDER

Analogy, or the tendency to use related forms for what are felt to be similar functions, has been plainly at work in the popular tendency to substitute the objective for the nominative pronoun after the various forms of the verb *to be.* Controversy over *It is me* has raged for many decades, and the expression has finally won a modified approval from the judges of the Leonard Survey already referred to. The linguists of this study regarded *It is me* as established English usage, ranking it 73d in a list of 230 items; and approval is also given to *if it had been us,* which is ranked 102d in the same list. This approval, however, does not extend to *I'll swear that was him* (No. 138) or to *I suppose that's him* (No. 152), both of which were marked disputable. Evidently the first person pronoun has gone farther than the third toward consistency.

The reason for using the objective after the verb *to be* obviously is to bring this usage into line with other complements, which are regularly in the objective case. The unanalytical speaker sees no difference between *I think it was her* and *I think it becomes her,* and since almost all verbs are followed by complements in the objective case, it is difficult for the popular mind to make a distinction between those which should be and those which should not be so followed.

What is happening, clearly, in sentences such as the foregoing, where the pronoun case is changing after the verb *to be,* is that *to be* is being altered from an intransitive to a transitive verb, thus taking a direct object instead of a predicate noun. The matter of sentence order is involved here, since the reason for using the objective case is the pronoun's position following the verb. The change has occurred already in popular English, and it may in the future extend to the literary language.

A like consistency in grammatical function appears in the sentence *All came, he, she, and I,* where the nominative case is used after the verb because the pronouns are in apposition to the subject *all.* In popular speech, however, the sentence order would tend to induce the use of the objective pronouns after the verb, and such constructions as *All came, him, her, and me* are often heard. It is to be expected that the casual speaker will frequently get into trouble in sentences of this kind, where the post-verb position will lead him to choose the objective case.

As suggested, consistency in sentence order is bound up closely with consistency in form and in function. The English speaker has acquired a feeling for the nominative personal pronoun before the verb and the objective personal pronoun after the verb. Forms like *methinks* and *meseems* have become archaic, probably because the objective pronoun is placed before the verb. Such a construction as *Me was given a book,* common in older English, has been changed to the current *I was given a book,* on account of this order consistency which places the subject before the verb even when the idea is that of indirect object.

In the case of the sentence *All but him had fled* there is an awkwardness arising from the fact that the objective pronoun *him* directly precedes the verb. If the sentence read instead *All had fled but him,* the use of *him* would give no difficulty. Our feeling for harmony of sentence order is thus seen to be conditioned on our feeling for the sequence of the main sentence parts.

It is true that in certain other constructions pronoun cases are interchanged in other ways. For instance, a speaker of popular English might say *between you and I* or *Do you want John and I to go?* Such an error, however, is one, not of order, but of the speaker's erroneous choice in the attempt to be grammatically correct. It is a leaning backward beyond correctness. Since *I* is often required (for example, *It is I*), the speaker assumes that *I* is always the better form to use.

CONSISTENCY OF SOUNDS

Analogy is frequently operative in sound change, except that in this field it is called by different names. Assimilation means the accommodating of one sound to another, as when Latin *centum* becomes French *cent,* the *k* fronting to *s* before the front vowel. This is an instance of unconscious sound consistency; another on the semiconscious plane is the repetition of identical or similar sounds which goes by the name of alliteration. Such consistency is illustrated by countless phrases of an alliterative sort—*time and tide, wind and weather, wear out a welcome, here today and gone tomorrow.*

The old English phrase "dæges ond nihtes" (*by day and night*) showed a double genitive which was not in correct grammatical form. As a feminine noun, the possessive of *niht* should have been *nihte,* but the masculine possessive for *dæges* attracted *niht* into conformity with it. It is often hard to separate sound analogy from idea analogy, as in this instance; but there can be little doubt that the alliteration of the endings helped in the establishment of the incorrect form.

A less certain instance of sound analogy is found in the sentence *There was a orange in the dish.* The use of the article *a* instead of the "correct" *an* is due in part at least to the greater frequency of the use of *a* and the desire for sound consistency in the use of the article.[4] This use of *a* before a word beginning with a vowel is, however, infrequent in English, because here analogy is in conflict with a characteristic indolence of enunciation which finds it easier to pronounce the *n* between the two vowels.[5]

CONSISTENCY OF IDEAS

The most frequent sort of consistency in English grammar is undoubtedly consistency in idea. It is such a consideration rather than an analogy of form which is behind the rules given by rhetoricians for the avoidance of unnecessary changes of tense, mood, or voice in sentences. Such sentences as *I set to work, and soon my work was done, Drive south, and then you should turn left* or *He is called, and then his friends greeted him* are called clumsy and defective from the stylistic aspect, and the student is urged to be consistent in his choice of constructions. To be sure, such rules are not universal; a sentence like *Work hard and you will succeed* is acceptable even though there is a change from the imperative to the indicative. However, there obviously exists a striving for harmony of ideas which leads to the condemnation of sentences such as the former examples.

Congruity, which is another name for consistency, has numerous impulsions in connection with literary style. Writers are commonly taught to keep words congruous and to avoid phrases such as *his wet-blanket supper* or the *thirsty rain,* in which the adjective and the noun are incongruous and therefore illogical. Frequently

---

[4] Compare *a historical novel* (American) and *an historical novel* (British), where the difference perhaps arises from a stronger pronunciation of *h* in the United States.

[5] Consonantal glides between vowels are frequently introduced; compare the "intrusive *r*" in the New England dialect, e. g., *the idea-r-of it.*

a sentence is criticized, not for any defect in formal grammar, but simply because its words do not harmonize in their ideas.

Another example of the operation of consistency in ideas can be found in sentences such as *Don't get these kind of gloves,* which is marked illiterate (No. 198) by the Leonard Survey. It is apparent that the plural adjective *these* is chosen in conformity with the plural idea *gloves* rather than with the singular word *kind.* Such sentences have made the phrases *those kind, these sort,* and so forth, extremely frequent in English.[6]

While few or no grammars condone *these kind* or *those kind,* still in the case of words like *number, none, crowd, committee,* which are singular in form but plural in idea, it is permissible according to the rhetoricians to use the plural verb: *A number of students have joined; None of them are here.* These sentences, while definitely out of line with the precepts of twenty years ago, are now established as good allowable English. Liberalism is also apparent in the vexed matter of the plural pronoun *they* referring to such singular words as *each, other, one, everybody,* and so forth. The Leonard Survey linguists viewed as established English (No. 98) the sentence *Everyone was here but they all went home early,* although they listed as disputable (No. 150) the similar sentence *Everybody bought their own ticket.* Obviously this problem is of the same kind as the one previously discussed concerning illogical comparison (page 62), though liberalization has not progressed quite so far.

The opposite view of number is embodied in the recent rule which says that quantities and sums or multiples of numbers, when expressing a singular idea, may take a singular verb. In the sentence *The hundred dollars was very acceptable as a gift* we have obviously a singular idea (*dollars*) in a plural form; and here the consistency of idea has negated the inconsistency of the verb. The same rule operates in sentences such as *Of all the crowd, three-quarters was in favor of the plan,* where the subject is expressed in a plural fraction, but the verb follows the idea in being singular. A related construction is the subject which is compound in form but unitary in meaning: *Her joy and gladness was delightful to see.*

[6] See pp. 95 ff.

The matter of consistency enters into all the minutiae of grammar, and one very fine distinction is made in connection with the possessive case. In the sentence *I bought it at Brown and Morton's store,* we have a possessive consisting of two names taken as a unit, and the *'s* termination is therefore included just once at the end of the compound unit. On the other hand, in the sentence *We combined John's and Bill's cash,* two possessive terminations are used, simply because the two things combined are separate. This is a nice distinction which might easily be missed by hurried or casual writers. It is a matter of idea leading to a distinction in form, but its fineness makes it somewhat difficult for the average person to perceive.

CONCLUSION

Perhaps enough examples have now been given to illustrate the various sorts of consistency which are attempted in the operations of English grammar. If there were but one type, the problem would be comparatively simple; it is because there are conflicting harmonies that so much difficulty arises and English expression becomes so thoroughly illogical and heterogeneous. Consistency in English is now and then desirable in specific instances. On the other hand, it is absolutely unattainable, simply because it will not work the same way in all cases; it is probable that harmony is just as rare in English today as it was five centuries ago, if not actually rarer. Inharmonies and inconsistency are rampant in the English we speak; they are always appearing; and it is unlikely that their number or urgency will grow less in the future.

In all the instances given in this chapter it is important to remember that we are seeing grammar as something very human, something midway between idiocy and logic, something in the vast realm where we conduct our daily lives. In saying "The tumult and the shouting dies," Kipling was utilizing the same instinct which would lead a college student to select a matching tie and handkerchief. In writing *most unique* the student is exercising the same sort of futile attempt at consistency which might lead him to buy roses for one young lady because another preferred roses. Only the myopia of scholarship can lead the grammarian to attempt to put grammar into a pigeonhole separate from living.

INCONSISTENCY IN GRAMMAR

THE EXTENT to which English grammar is inconsistent may be measured by the extent to which those who speak English are inconsistent—and that is very great. It is in fact almost impossible to find any aspect of English grammar unaffected by this normal human quality; and it will be remembered that the examples in Chapter Seven were not unmixed pictures of linguistic harmony and congruity, but were more or less successful approaches to such an ideal. Our task in this chapter is difficult only because we are confronted with such an abundance of material for the proof of our thesis.

We may begin by selecting at random one of the simplest and most ordinary of English sentences, the sentence *It was you,* which anyone knowing anything of English would understand. Long familiarity has so accustomed us to this construction, as to the others we use every day, that we never think of probing below its surface. When we do so we may find, not one, but many inner contradictions. A few of them will be described.

An initial difficulty is that of person. The verb *to be* is a copulative or linking verb, with a function logically much like that of the equals sign in mathematics. Yet here a third-person subject, *it,* is found equated with a second-person complement, *you;* and this is anomalous logically, however frequent such constructions may be in English.

A like contradiction appears in gender. While *you* is common gender, in that it might indicate either masculine or feminine, *it* is distinctively neuter, and in strict logic it should not be equated with either masculine or feminine. Instead of *you, he* or *she* might be used in the sentence. *It was he* would solve the discrepancy of person, but would emphasize this second inconsistency further, since *it* is neuter, *he* masculine.

But worse than either of these inconsistencies is the difficulty in number inhering in *you.* Historically a plural, it is of uncertain number here; it might indicate several persons or one only. If we take *you* as referring to many, it is impossible to justify the presence of *It was* rather than *They were,* which would be defensible numerically, but which is never heard in actual speech. Should we interpret *you* as designating one person, we are still in difficulty, for the verb which custom has selected for *you* as a singular is *were,* not *was,* and yet here we find *you* with a verb which would be called incorrect if used after *you.*

The matter of inconsistency in grammatical number will be considered in detail later in this chapter; here our aim is merely to show how inconsistency lurks in the simplest and most elementary expressions of the English language, just as it does in the most intricate and literary. Contradictions attack standard as well as popular speech, and they may inhere in whole groups of words, such as the one we shall next discuss.

THE INCONSISTENT PREPOSITION

Since relationship is a concept of relatively late development in language, many of the prepositions and conjunctions having no very ancient linguistic history, and the relative pronoun being largely a product of the past thousand years of English, it might be supposed that these small link-words, which make connections between ideas, would reflect a comparatively mature stage in the thinking of our race and would therefore offer poor material for a chapter such as this one. On the contrary, the connectives, and especially the prepositions, offer rich and almost unlimited material for a chapter on inconsistency in grammar, leading the candid investigator to wonder whether human thinking has really logicalized itself greatly in the course of the cycles of human time. And one thinks of Alice's Humpty-Dumpty, who was frank enough to admit that he used words to mean just what he wanted them to mean. "It's a question of who shall be master; that's all."

The uses of prepositions in English are so varied, so heterogeneous, that they cannot be learned by any process of formal education. Books on prepositions have been compiled. Dictionaries do their best to give them meanings and to rationalize their uses; yet all such attempts are failures, since there is no English preposition which has a clear and consistent meaning and use. The correct, which is to say the traditionally inconsistent, use of such a preposition as *of* is to be acquired only through long familiarity with the language, a process which will engender a "feeling" for placing it properly.

There is no English preposition which has one meaning and holds to it, and there are very few which do not shift readily to other grammatical functions. It is necessary to ask for context to determine whether or not a word is a preposition, since so many (*save, toward, through, like*) may perform other functions as well. It is context alone which gives a preposition its meaning. The preposition itself is meaningless until the remainder of the sentence shows its intent.

In the sentence *He presented a book to her* it may reasonably be said that *to* conveys an idea of motion toward, thus having its standard or "dictionary" signification. The book, as the direct object, is the thing which undergoes presentation. The whole sentence looks logical and reasonable until it is set beside another sentence of identical meaning: *He presented her with a book*. Here it is oddly she, rather than the book, that undergoes presentation; and *with* is used in a sense widely different from that of accompaniment, which is the supposedly normal signification of *with*.

Such discrepancies in the use of English prepositions and connectives generally are very common, entering into widely varied fields. Their operation in determining legal action has been analyzed by Margaret M. Bryant in *English in the Law Courts* (Columbia University Press, 1930). Studies in other fields would be valuable.

It may frequently happen, also, that any one of several prepositions, sometimes with opposing meanings, will fit in a given phrase. *With* and *from* would not be considered synonyms, and yet one may speak of a person as suffering *with,* or *from,* a certain disease. We may speak of a man as being careful *with, of,* or *about* his money or his clothes, all three prepositions being synonymous for the purposes of the phrase.

The linguistic significance of the prepositions may best be explained by a somewhat detailed analysis of one, and for this purpose we have chosen, not one of the most difficult such as *to* or *of,* but a relatively simple instance, the word *after.* The first thing one is likely to notice about *after* is its comparative ending, and this ending did in fact carry a comparative meaning in the early stages of the Germanic dialects, when *after* was not a connective but an adverb meaning *more to the rear,* a sense we occasionally find, as in "Jack came tumbling after." *After,* in other words, is a fairly recent member of the preposition family and still bears traces of its earlier state.

The present uses of *after* are by dictionaries neatly separated into types—according to place, time, order, and manner. The first is the literal or primary use of *after,* and it is seen in many sentences, such as *The escort walked after the king. After* in this sense is used mainly with verbs meaning *come* or *go* and is synonymous with *behind.* This is what dictionaries call the basic or key use of the preposition.

From this use grows the idea of *behind with intent to overtake,* so that one may "go after" a thing not merely to follow it but also in a desire to catch up with it. The question *What are you after?* illustrates this use. And from this added idea of overtaking there has grown a thought of *taking charge of.* When one has looked down the street *after* a certain object such as a kitten or a puppy, has taken his hat and gone *after* it, he may then *look after* it in the sense of caring for it when it has come into his charge. Or he may *search after* it, *inquire after* it, *strive after* it, or even *long after* it, in a very different sense from the *long after* used to mean *much later.*

Still, the story of *after* thus far looks fairly reasonable. One meaning has led to another without any great trouble or difficulty.

One can see how English came to widen and shift its uses as it has done, and one's respect for the uses of prepositions is accordingly increased. Perhaps all we need is to arrange meanings reasonably, to find reason and order in this field.

But then we stumble on the first basic inconsistency in the story of *after*. Obviously, meaning *behind* it should have the same meaning when applied to time; and just as obviously this meaning should be *further back from the present,* or *earlier.* Yet *after* means no such thing. On the contrary, it means *later* and can indicate a time which is in advance of now, a time which has not yet arrived, as in *After I finish I shall leave.* Time, the grand confuser of language (see Chapter Twenty-two) has tripped this preposition up.[1]

And so we cannot be surprised to find *after* meaning *in consequence of,* as in *after all,* which is quite incompatible logically with *The escort walked after the king.* Nor can we wonder at the branching out of the word to mean *next in importance, in obedience to, in compliance with, according to,* and *in imitation of* in phrases such as *one after my own heart, named after his father, modeled after Rodin,* and so forth. Logic will take us a certain distance into the history of *after,* will even give us the illusion that there is an orderly pattern running through the whole; but in actuality we can recognize it only as an illusion. *After* is a clear instance of the inconsistency which lies at the heart of English grammar.[2]

INCONSISTENT MODIFICATION

As explained in Chapter Three, one of the outstanding features of the English grammatical system is modification. Sentences and nonsentences are conceived in relation to a series of levels, the primary containing the main verb, subject, and complement, and the others the modifiers of varying degrees. Each of these modifiers has, in grammatical theory, a governing word or word-group on which it depends. In practice there is often confusion among governing

---

[1] If we try to "logicalize" the meanings of *after* by explaining it as *following the present,* we run into the same difficulty, this time with *follow,* which also means *behind in space* and *ahead in time.*

[2] Psychologically it is not hard to see how *after* acquired the contrary meanings *behind* (in place) and *ahead* (in time). The person who is *behind* will arrive *later,* that is, more in the future, than his rival; and this fact probably gave *after* its present time meaning.

elements, so that it is difficult or even impossible to tell precisely what a given unit modifies.

Usually it is not assumed that a sentence as a whole may have a modifier; ordinarily the modifier is referred to the sentence verb. However, if one analyzes the difference in idea between two sentences such as *Happily he did not die* and *He did not die happily,* one sees clearly the difference between the verb modifier and the sentence modifier. The first *happily* qualifies the entire sentence; in the second example the adverb *happily* qualifies only the verb and is itself qualified by *not,* so that the sentence is not a negative sentence in the same way that the first example is negative. According to the first example the man did not die; according to the second example he died, but not happily.

This is an instance of the very subtle and revealing role played by sentence order in English. In sentences of this kind modification is determined by order and follows it. Other examples of the same sort are *Positively you must talk* compared to *You must talk positively,* and *Truly I can't tell* compared to *I can't tell truly.*[3]

Yet sentence order frequently betrays the unwary user of English, particularly when there are two possible governing elements and a modifier is placed in such a position that it might modify either one of them. An example is the sentence *A storm broke just as we arrived with great violence.* Another example is *I want to finish my work very badly.* In both cases the governing element might be either of two things, and the result is a confused and inconsistent impression.

This modifier inconsistency is behind the many so-called dangling expressions in English. According to rhetoricians danglers may consist of participial phrases, gerund phrases, infinitive clauses, elliptical clauses, and other elements like the prepositional phrases instanced in the previous paragraph. So common are dangling gerunds that a large number of these (*concerning, excepting, notwithstanding, granting, considering, assuming*) have gone over into the preposition class, where their dangling character disappears. Such a sentence as *Generally speaking, the decision is a fair one* used to be called defective, since the word *speaking* has no ex-

[3] *Cf.* p. 24.

pressed governing element; but now it is recognized that in this case the words *generally speaking* constitute a sentence modifier. Such a sentence as *Considering his youth, he has progressed rapidly* makes *considering* into a preposition.[4]

It is readily seen that the last few examples are fully as incongruous with logic as examples like *Being poor, help was needed for them.* Yet it is fully as apparent that most danglers leave the meaning clear. The English language therefore assimilates those dangling inconsistencies and offers them wide hospitality.

MISCELLANEOUS INCONSISTENCIES

Contradictions between negative and positive abound in English. The two, which ought to be sharply distinguished, may come so close to the same meaning as to be virtually indistinguishable; for example, *I can but try* and *I cannot but try.* The sentences *He is old, isn't he?* and *He isn't old, is he?* both ask for information on his age, the one on the assumption that he is old, the other that he is not. Yet each contains an equated negative and positive added together for a single purpose. It suggests not only the inconsistency but also almost the perversity of much human nature that if one is expecting an affirmative response he will word a *why*-question negatively, and if his expectation is negative he will be positive. Thus *Why not tell me about it?* contemplates a response such as *I'll be glad to,* while *Why tell me about it?* is calculated to evoke *All right, I won't.* A volume could easily be written on the vagaries of negative and positive which centuries of English-speaking have built into the language.

The numerous double inflexions of English are instances of grammatical inconsistency. The phrase *that house of my brother's* has a double possessive inflexion, the preposition *of* and the *'s* termination, an entirely unnecessary duplication. The predicative pronouns *mine, yours, hers, theirs,* and so forth are further examples of duplicated inflexions, and we have words like *lesser, nearer, innermost, uppermost,* and so forth, which exemplify the same thing.

Grammatical authority frequently proscribes the use of the third person singular *he* with the impersonal pronoun *one.* This proscrip-

[4] *Cf.* Chap. 23.

tion is largely meaningless, since this usage is practiced in popular speech without any anxiety over prohibitions. The linguists of the Leonard Survey marked *One rarely likes to do as he is told* disputable, grading it as No. iii of the list. This common usage shows the ease with which inconsistent constructions may enter English.

The method of forming plurals in English shows little consistency. No one has yet been able to make a rule to determine whether *s* or *es* shall be added to words ending in *o;* no one can tell whether the plural of *fish* is *fish* or *fishes*. We have as a general thing the *s* termination for compound nouns ending with *man, foot,* and so forth; thus *Pullmans, sweet tooths, Germans, Blackfoots*. But on the other side there are *dormice* and *committeemen*. We write *Fairchilds,* but *stepchildren*. Uniformity in English pluralizings would be as desirable as it is nonexistent.

The ordinary speaker is far from consistent in his choice of words. He is given to confusing pairs like *allusion* and *illusion, flaunted* and *flouted, formerly* and *formally, respectively* and *respectfully, militate* and *mitigate*. To say that there is just one "correct" meaning for each member of these pairs is not the whole story, since meanings shift from one decade to another, and these words easily may acquire the very meanings they now tend to have. Their contradictions may in time become a part of the English language.

INCONSISTENCY IN NUMBER

But perhaps the best department of English to study, in relation to the question of inconsistency, is the grammar of number, since for number we have a mathematical norm or standard, severely logical in character, to which to refer grammatical factors.

The first difficulty in the grammatical representation of number is the fact that our language, like most of the Indo-European languages, has only two numbers instead of an infinite number as in mathematics. These two English numbers are named singular and plural, as though they referred to one or to more than one. However, this is not the case. The singular number covers one, zero, and infinity (or the whole), while the plural number is used for any quantity from two up to infinity and is often used also for fractions of one.

Further confusion is caused by the fact that certain words may be thought of as either one or more than one. In English such words are called collective nouns or "words of multitude." Modern rhetoricians permit the use of either a singular or a plural verb with such nouns (*crowd, committee, team, class, number,* and so forth). Even plurals may be treated singularly, as in the sentence *a hundred dollars is ample.* And then we have the so-called invariable plurals, which make it impossible to tell from the word itself whether it is a plural or a singular.

Frequently a plural becomes a singular when it is made into an adjective, as in the phrase *a five-dollar bill* compared to *five dollars.* Other such adjectives are *a two-year-old, a ten-mile walk, a hundred-pound weight.* In rustic or local dialects the adverbial noun is now and then used without the *s* in the plural; *He lived there seven year; He walked five mile;* but this is frowned on in literary language.

Indeed, the taboos of grammatical number are fully as inconsistent as its permissions. The pronoun *you* has developed from a plural into a singular, but the pronoun *they* must not, according to the most respected authorities, be combined with such pronouns as *each other, another, somebody, everybody, nobody, no one,* even when such pronouns are plural in idea. The word *neither* is clearly plural in adding together negative possibilities. But still it is considered a solecism to use *their* with *neither,* or to use the plural verb, as in *Neither of the boys are eating their lunch.*

It is true that English has eliminated certain inconsistencies in the course of the centuries. For example, the ethical dative, which was common in Old English and fairly common in later centuries, has been very largely eliminated in Modern English. In Shakespeare's *Taming of the Shrew* a bit of comedy is extracted from Petruchio's telling his servant to "Knock me here on this gate." This passage reveals a self-conscious attitude with respect to the ethical dative, and it is perhaps no wonder that when its inconsistency was seen it was quietly banished from the language.

Indeed, it might be said that progress in grammar consists of bringing in two inconsistencies while dropping one. Modern English is thus probably even more contradictory than was Old English, even though certain contradictions have been weeded out. Our language, like our people, shows a commendable tendency to strive toward logic; but, alas, it is a tendency which shows no sign of becoming consistently operative.

GRAMMAR IS ARBITRARY

Bᴜᴛ ɪғ ʟᴏɢɪᴄ and consistency do not govern this vast system or pattern or patternlessness which we call English grammar, what does? It would seem that there must exist some principle by which the individual speaker, and through him all speakers of English, make decisions between the two or more ways of saying a given thing. There ought to be some basis for decision, which would stand as a fixed mark in grammatical explorations.

The answer seems to be that not one but numerous fixed marks, principles, or guides exist, so that one can not always tell just which will be operative in any given case. That is the core of our difficulty; grammar is not explicable by any one formula, whether intellectual, emotional, or behavioristic; it is the resultant of the operation of many forces, working now in harmony and now in conflict. Any particular grammatical solution is not a simple reaction to a single impulse, but is the joint product of the working of many complex forces.

We may take as a comparatively simple instance the word *telephone,* devised by Sudre in 1828 and applied by Alexander Graham Bell to his invention in 1876. The coinage followed a common fashion of juxtaposing two Greek roots, both of which have become familiar through this and many other English words, from *phonetics* to *television.* And once coined and applied, *telephone* quickly felt the broadening influence of functional shift, becoming successively a verb (*Have you telephoned?*) and an adjective (*a telephone directory*).[1]

---

[1] There were also formed various derivatives, *telephony, telephonic, telephoner, telephonist,* but these are not very commonly used.

And then as the word grew into increasing popularity it felt the effects of the common human quality of impatience, which seeks short cuts where feasible. *Telephone* was a little too long for the easiest using. Theoretically, either the first or the last part might have been dropped; [2] but *tele* is less of a word than *phone,* and so *phone* came to be the common form of *telephone* in popular speech.

A fourth factor influencing *telephone* next appears, in the shape of conservative disapproval for the abbreviated form. Many, though not all, grammarians proceeded to apply the epithet colloquial to *phone* and to advise the avoidance of this colloquialism. The cause for this disapproval may have included an element of snobbishness and the dislike of hurry. Or it may have been simply an arbitrary decision motivated by prejudice rather than by reason. Other new coinages, other abbreviations, have won acceptance as standard English. If one may say *road* for *railroad, bus* for *omnibus, movies* for *moving pictures,* why not *phone* for *telephone?*

It is uncertain how far this conservative disapproval has been able to affect the popularity of *phone.* No doubt it is still one of the English words most frequently used in conversation; but two competitors, *call* and *ring,* have to a certain degree replaced it, perhaps partly because *phone* is under the cloud of purist condemnation. It is possible that *call* will render *phone* as a verb archaic or even obsolete.

Here in the brief lifespan of *telephone,* covering only a few moments of linguistic time, we see exemplified not one but five or more principles of change and development: the inventive faculty, functional shift, short-cutting, arbitrary conservatism, and linguistic competition. All of these influences have affected great masses of English words, and many others are equally operative. English grammar is a tossing, heaving sea of almost countless tides and currents, occasionally flowing together and occasionally even ceasing to operate, so that we find grammatical effects which appear to have no basis in either reason or psychology, but which are ap-

---

[2] Examples of abbreviation from the end rather than the beginning of words are of course numerous: *taxi* from *taxicab; mike* from *microphone; whoso* from *whosoever.* The last is archaic.

parently as fortuitous as stellar groupings. It is with such arbitrary solutions that we are primarily concerned in this chapter.

Any textbook of correct writing or speaking is a rich source of examples of arbitrary procedure in the fields of grammar and word usage. Here one is certain to find large numbers of dicta which have no particular basis in reason. For example, one may find condemnation of the verb *fix,* used to mean *repair,* and of the combination *to fix up,* meaning *to arrange.* The following sentences are given in one or another authority as examples of poor usage: *That clock must be fixed; With his usual assurance he fixed things up to suit himself.*[3]

Few verbs exist in English which have not altered to some extent in their meanings. The verb *strain* meant to Shakespeare *constrain,* where today its chief meanings are *sift* and *struggle.* This change in meaning has taken place without any opposition or obstruction on the part of the rhetoricians. In the case of *fix* we do have such opposition. Perhaps the reason is the social environment in which *fix* is found in its condemned meanings, but this has not been a sufficient reason to condemn other similar words and phrases. The opposition to *fix* must be put down to an arbitrary and unreasoned dislike for the word on the part of some individual teacher, who then passed on the dislike to authorities generally.

It needs to be remembered that people hear with their habits and prejudices rather than with their ears. The sentence *That clock must be fixed* will sound like good or bad English not according to any inherent quality in the sentence itself, but according to whether or not the speaker or listener has been warned against using *fix* in this construction. The verb itself sounds no different whether it is used to mean *repair* or *fasten.* It just happens that grammarians have selected this particular verb and this particular meaning for condemnation.

And one might make an indefinitely long list of other words and phrases which have undergone similar condemnation in one of or all their meanings, without any sufficient or logical reason for it. A

[3] The Leonard Survey, however, lists as established English in the United States (No. 47) the sentence *Have you fixed the fire for the night?*

few samples will be given in list form, not with a view to justifying
their rehabilitation, but simply in order to point out the arbitrariness of their exclusion from good English.

ain't	I suppose I am wrong, *ain't* I?
allow	I'll *allow* he is a good man.
all-round	She's a good *all-round* girl.
anent	We spoke *anent* the war.
auto	We plan to *auto* through the mountains.
buy	That car is a good *buy*.
calculate	I *calculate* to go soon.
combine	The companies formed a *combine*.
complected	A light *complected* girl passed.
date	He made a *date* for next week.
drunk	The *drunk* came reeling down the street.
eats	The *eats* were swell.
fit	One is not *fit* to vote at the age of eighteen.[4]
heap	I have a *heap* of work to do.
in respect of	*In respect of* his proposal I am neutral.
invite	She got an *invite* for the dance.
liable	It is *liable* to snow tonight.
loan	He *loaned* me his skates.[5]
mad	I was pretty *mad* about it.
nice	There are some *nice* people here.[6]
out of kilter	That machine is *out of kilter*.
party	The *party* who wrote that knew what he was talking about.
piece	Come and walk a *piece* with me.
plenty	That is *plenty* good enough.
price	We stopped to *price* some flowers.
snap	He worked with much *snap*.
steal	That was an absolute *steal*.
suicide	Mr. Clark *suicided* yesterday.
suspicion	He began to *suspicion* something was wrong.
taxi	We *taxied* to the station to catch the train.
tote	Must you *tote* that heavy package?
viewpoint	His *viewpoint* on the matter should be considered.

In other instances of somewhat the same sort one can discern
some shadow of reason or excuse for the opposition to a given word

---

[4] The linguists of the Leonard Survey found this and the next sentence good usage.

[5] The Leonard Survey linguists approved of this and also of *nice, price, snap, taxi,* and *viewpoint*.

[6] Webster and other authorities have come to recognize the use of *nice* to mean *agreeable*.

or phrase. For example, there has always been a tendency for modern grammarians to object to back-formations, even though *beg, peddle, grovel, edit,* and many others are now safely part of the literary language. As eminent and liberal a linguist as Henry Bradley hoped that *swashbuckling* might not meet the general approval it has found, since it is a back-formation from *swashbuckler.*[7] And the widespread objection to *enthuse* (*Don't enthuse before you see results*) is no doubt attributable to the fact that *enthuse* is an irregular wearing down of *enthusiasm.*

The objection by authorities to admitting a new word into close competition with another word which already has the meaning the new word is tending to assume might also be called a reasoned decision. Thus *healthy* is accepted meaning *in a condition of health,* but resisted when meaning *conducive to health,* since for this second meaning the word *healthful* is already available. A like reasoning is behind the objection to *learn* meaning *teach, set* meaning *sit,* and so forth. Again, one questions how far such opposition can be made effective. It has worked fairly well with *learn* and *set,* but seems to have failed to regulate the uses of *healthy.*

Frequently grammarian opposition is based on the derivation or literal meaning of a word. This sort of purism was carried to the point of absurdity in a little book by Ambrose Bierce, where he applied it to words such as *dilapidated* and *candidate.* It is also applied by various authorities to the word *coincidence.* Since this word literally means *falling together,* it is opposed in its meaning of *chance,* and restricted to the meeting of two occurrences. It is difficult to imagine what would happen to the English language if this principle of literal interpretation should be applied to all our vocabulary. It is safe to say that there are few English words which preserve the literal meanings of their derivational elements.

Another instance of the same sort is the word *alternative,* which from its connection with the Latin *alter* (one of two) is frequently restricted to two elements, so that one is not allowed to say *There were five alternatives.* However, the dictionaries now generally support the use of *alternative* to mean *choice* when there are two or more possibilities, and this broader use is also supported by the fact

[7] *Op. cit.,* p. 144.

that in Latin *alter* often had an indefinite meaning and was not restricted to two elements.

Occasionally grammatical taboos are built up simply to establish a distinction between two synonymous words or constructions. While Shakespeare used the word *farther* and *further* indiscriminately, modern authorities tell us to restrict the former to space and the latter to ideas. This seems to be a matter of arbitrary decision rather than any reasoned procedure. It is also difficult to see any logical reason for the frequently stated rule that *so* should be used with negative comparisons (*This hat is not so large as mine*) and *as* with positive comparisons (*She is as tall as he*). Here also we may mention the condemnation of the word *then* in place of *and* or *and then* (*I paddled a while, then fell into a reverie*). There seems to be no reason, except prejudice, why *then* should not have a connective use at times.

In all these cases the condemned expressions and words are stopped in progress from one meaning to another or from one grammatical use to another. The history of the English language is one long series of alterations in use, meaning, and grammatical character; the story of condemnation by rhetoricians is a story of the attempts (frequently futile) to halt such alteration. Condemnation gives rise to a habit of thought which sees in the condemned expression something actually unpleasant in sound. It is a form of linguistic snobbishness which attempts to impose itself upon the entire social mass.

THE PREDICATE ADJECTIVE

For our further study of arbitrariness in grammar it will perhaps be enlightening to select one grammatical construction and trace it historically through its various changes, indicating at just which points arbitrary decisions have affected it. For this purpose we have chosen the construction which is called the predicate adjective. It may be recalled that in Chapter Three complements were distinguished as belonging to any one of four types, namely, direct objects, predicate nouns, predicate adjectives, and prepositional objects. It is the third of these types which we shall now attempt to analyze.

In function the predicate adjective is midway between the complement and the modifier. When it takes modifiers, they are normally adverbial in type, showing its adjective character; but it also fulfills the test for the complement by answering the question *what* after the verb. To analyze the predicate adjective as a complement rather than a modifier is an arbitrary decision. As a matter of fact the predicate adjective fulfills both functions, modifier and complement, at one and the same time.

As it is used in Modern English, the predicate adjective is ordinarily the same in form as the attributive adjective, although there are differences between the two functions. There exists a fairly large group of words, especially words beginning with syllabic *a,* which function always or nearly always as predicatives. Examples are *aghast, astray, afraid, athirst, aware, awry, akin.* Here the initial *a* is sometimes the wearing down of a formerly prefixed *of* or *on,* the predicative form having developed out of a former prepositional phrase. Other distinctively predicative forms are the pronouns *mine, hers, ours, yours,* and *theirs.*

And on the other hand there are certain attributive adjectives which are not used predicatively. An example is the word *very* when meaning precise or exact (*That is the very thing*). Other examples are adjectives such as *only, mere,* and so forth. When such adjectives are used after the verb they are classified as adverbs.

There seems to be no particular reason, except the arbitrary effect of custom, to separate these groups of adjectives. The word *afraid,* for example, is similar in meaning to *fearful;* and yet *fearful* may be used either attributively or predicatively, while *afraid* is confined normally to the latter use. The adjective *only* means much the same as *solitary,* and yet the former is used only attributively, the latter in either function.

The predicate adjective functions in four or five different ways. Its most frequent use is undoubtedly in the position following some form of the verb *to be.* And this use is very old, dating back to very early linguistic times. It is already fully developed in Gothic. In Anglo-Saxon we find "Wǣron æþelingas eft tō lēodum fūse tō farenne" (*The lords were ready to go back to their people*) and "þæt is undyrne" (*That is unconcealed*), to take two examples at random from *Beowulf*. Similar usages will be found in Chaucer, Shakespeare, Milton, and all English writers of late as well as early dates. This use has remained extraordinarily stable, and the chief change which has overtaken the predicate adjective in this basic function when it follows *to be* is that its inflexional terminations have disappeared, as have most other inflexional terminations in English. The modern predicate adjective after *to be* is a good example of linguistic conservatism.

A second type of predicate adjective and one deriving also from an early stage of linguistic history is like the first except for the fact that the verb is not *to be,* but its equivalent. In *He seems bored, He became angry, It sounds melodious* we have an asserting verb followed by a predicate adjective. In each the verb *to be* might be substituted: *He is bored in appearance, It is melodious in sound,* and so forth. Here also are probably to be included many common idiomatic expressions with *get* in the sense of *become* —*He got ready, She got better, It is getting cold.* Slang extends the usage to *He got busy,* which is theoretically no better and no worse than the three preceding examples except that it tends to crowd off the linguistic map expressions of similar meanings such as *commenced, began work, started,* and so forth.

Predicate adjectives are by no means always found with asserting verbs. Modern English uses an increasing number after verbs of action, and one of the uses of such complements is not so much to describe or point out the subject as to indicate the result of the verb's action. *She blushed scarlet* gives in the predicate adjective the result or consequence of the blushing, and a similar interpretation may be made for *The broom sweeps clean, That pencil writes blue, He fell groveling;* though the last is perhaps a bit uncertain and might belong to the fifth type, to be described later.

Concerning our fourth type, it might perhaps be questioned whether it is a predicate adjective at all. It is the appositional, used with acting verbs. An early example of this occurs in the Anglo-Saxon poem *The Fight at Finnsburg,* ll. 35–36: "Hræfen wandrode, sweart and sealobrūn" (*The raven wandered, dusky and graybrown*). Here the predicate adjective has little or nothing to do with the verb, but seems most like an attributive adjective which has happened to come within the predicate. A modern equivalent is *Jane came downstairs, happy as a lark.* Any verb may be followed by such a predicate attributive: *Jack read the book, secure in his thoughts; Have you finished yet, dilatory as you are?* Very often this predicate adjective ends in *ing: She sat on the lawn, smiling and talking.* The adjectives here might be transferred to the beginning of the sentence without changing the meaning of the sentence.

But it is with the fifth and last type of predicate adjective that this chapter is most concerned. This is the modifier which in its meaning, if not in its form, is adverbial: *He played fair, slept sound, stood ready, sat silent, got off easy.* The last is now and then criticised as slang. In the others either idiom or usage favors the adjective, although the meaning is adverbial. This usage is especially common after the passive: *The clothes were packed tight; It was priced low; The theater was built complete with stage.* There may be discerned a stylistic difference, if not a difference in meaning, between *He sat silent* and *He sat silently,* the former being more compact and "literary"; but the meaning is much the same.

Now under this fifth type of predicate adjective fall as well all the "mistakes" in English grammar consisting of the use of the adverb without the termination *ly* or, to use an alternative description, the substitution of an adjective for an adverb following the verb. Examples are: *He did the work good; She spoke proper; They acted noble; Behave modest.*[8]

The tendency to discard *ly* in these and similar constructions may be regarded as a simple sloughing off of an unnecessary suffix or as a tendency to substitute an adjective for an adverb. It is strongly resisted in the examples just given, although, curiously, accepted and even admired in the previous examples and in many other cases which seem related in idea and character.

Sometimes a single sentence may exemplify both possibilities. Recently one of the authors of the present study received a letter

[8] Other expressions occasionally condemned, such as *Drive slow, Speak loud, Walk soft,* are not included, because historically in each case the second word is an adverb as well as an adjective.

from a bank official in Havana asking for a ruling on the sentence, "Expenditures should be reported separate(ly) from receipts." The answer was that neither could be called correct usage to the exclusion of the other; that either *separately* or *separate* could be justified grammatically, according as the word was regarded as adverb or predicate adjective; and that the only criterion by which to choose was style, which seemed slightly in favor of *separate*.[9]

Now when certain constructions of a given kind are allowed and certain others disallowed, it is impossible to escape the conclusion that here again we have arbitrary decisions. English has shown a tendency to get rid of certain adverbial forms. Grammarians have opposed this tendency, but not in all cases; idioms and oddities have slipped through and are now part of the literary dialect. Arbitrary rulings have held up the others.

It is not the language itself so much as those who profess to know and to teach its correct use to which the term *arbitrary* applies. The present chapter covers the conscious, semi-intelligent attempts on the part of students to hold the language in a given mold, and such attempts will rarely if ever be found to reflect an understanding of linguistic harmony and well-being. It is impossible for the close student of English linguistic history to resist the impression that the genius of English is wiser than its professors and may profitably be left to take its own course unobstructed by taboos and prohibitions.

But that is only the linguistic or grammatical conclusion to be derived from material such as we have been considering. The psychological conclusion is no less clear—that arbitrariness is unfortunately a perennial temptation of weak human nature and that the only way to transcend it is by consciously recognizing and resisting it. Arbitrary decisions in grammar are today being increasingly seen for what they are, and it seems probable that their influence is on the wane.

[9] The perennial struggle between *I feel bad* and *I feel badly* belongs under type two of predicate adjectives, and the grammarian's decision in favor of *bad* seems reasonable.

TENDENCY TO CHANGE

No one can contemplate human society or the group mind without perceiving its conservatism on the one hand and on the other its instability, its liability to smaller or greater shifts which are not particularly well reasoned out, but which often seem to be made for the sake of novelty in itself. Just as there is a tendency to conservatism in every department of life, so there is a ubiquitous tendency corresponding to fashion or to what may be termed newfangling, leading to changes veering here and there with no readily apparent reason or aim. And this tendency toward change for its own sake is easily recognizable in the grammar of the English language.

A proper variation in all aspects is one of the elementary lessons in literary style. Readers will condemn alike compositions made up of short, jerky, choppy sentences and those running to ponderous sentence length. Words also must not be uniformly too long or too short, but a mixture of all sorts, with a sesquipedalian now and then appearing to dominate the whole. Rhythm must be likewise varied, and not alone in prose writing; poetry must flash an extra syllable or a hiatus at just the right time if it is to avoid monotony and dullness. Even paragraphs, it is often held, should not be all long or all short, but varied in length, their indentations breaking the page at judiciously differentiated intervals.

It is not that short or long sentences or words are bad in themselves. Occasionally a succession of breathless sentence gasps suits well with a literary atmosphere of tense excitement, and long sentences find ready toleration in much scholarly work. There is nothing wrong with either monosyllables or heptasyllables; it is merely that neither, unrelieved, ministers to that craving for variety which is (along with distrust of variety) one of the basic characteristics of the "inconsistent animal."

Tautology, pleonasm, or repetition is such a fault in English expression as to boast more than one technical name. A sentence like *One rarely enjoys one's luncheon when one is hurried* is unpleasing because of the three uses of *one,* no matter how fully it may follow the dicta of the grammarian; a more common word, like *he* (*his, him*), would not have jarred so perceptibly even when used many times in a sentence; and this fact illustrates the laws of attention as developed by various psychologists. The sentence *They started to go, but a rain started just then, and so a game of bridge was started* is inept in the extreme, whereas *They started to go, but just then rain began to fall and they decided to play a game of bridge* is at least innocuous.

Again there is nothing wrong in repetition *per se,* as is proved by reading the work of any great writer. Walter de la Mare has given a charming little verse picture of moonlight on a brook, in which the effect is gained largely by repeating the word *silver.* The King James translation of the Bible contains much noble and dignified tautology.

And nevertheless the avoidance of repetition is a rule of almost every rhetoric and has become a positive fetish in many newspaper offices. Headline writers will go to the most absurd lengths to keep from repeating a word, preferring even an awkward and clumsy circumlocution. If, for example, the primary headline contains the phrase *rare stamps,* the secondary will have to make shift with *unusual adhesives.* If the first head is *THIRD NATIONAL BANK ROBBED,* the second may say *Cashier of Financial Institution Held Up at Point of Gun.*

Certainly this is carrying rules a little too far. Perhaps the best solution for sensible individuals is to use repetition where any other wording seems clumsy and where repetition is calculated to produce a literary effect. Practice must fit circumstance, and it would be as absurd to eschew all repetition as it would be dull to wallow in it.

Another of the very common manifestations of the tendency to changing fashions in English is the successive advents and exits of slang. A new slang term or phrase is coined, becomes immensely popular, spends its force, and in a longer or shorter time is completely dropped from the vocabulary. Infant mortality is a phenomenon of speech as of society, and it is observable that the words with the best expectations of life are those that have survived their first ten years.

The attitude of the authorities toward slang has been liberalizing. Whereas in former years slang was condemned out of hand, it is now admitted that a slight admixture of this kind of spice does add variety and tang to what is said or written; and the poet's maxim,

> Be not the last by whom the new is tried,
> Nor yet the first to lay the old aside,

is quoted as a good general guide for usage, even though the radical and the careless will disregard it.

There is no particular reason for slang's becoming obsolete; it is just a matter of social whim or fashion in most cases, although occasionally a slang term seems to be pushed off the linguistic map by some more favored newcomer, as *screwball* may have crowded out *nut,* and *cockeyed, haywire.* In all these examples the general notion is *crazy* or *lacking in intelligence,* and this idea, with the related idea of *nonsense,* is the most fertile field in all English for the growth of slang terms. Fashion is rampant here, so that to say *boloney* when *window dressing* is the correct contemporary expression is as bad as wearing last year's hat. *Jitterbug* drives out *finale hopper,* and *mouse* replaces *flapper,* without any reason but fashion.

Slang has a large bibliography, and its genesis and exodus have both been charted with fair completeness. Its extent and importance should not be exaggerated, since it occupies a very minor corner in the realm of English. It is often vivid, occasionally witty, and now and then permanent. It is the playground of fashion in word coinage.

Slang is an aspect of the spoken language which in general tends to be less conservative and more mercurial than the literary idiom. And along the borders of slang lie numerous locutions which like slang are open to change, not indeed so quickly, but over a century or so. If, for example, we should take a series of stage plays (these as representing the oral idiom) at half-century intervals from 1550 to 1900, we could see very clearly the shifts in colloquialities between one period and the next.

Such a study, tempting as it is, would take us too far afield to be made in detail here; but we may suggest a few random comparisons between the English of 1600 and that of today, based on the folio

> If Musicke be the food of Loue, play on,
> Giue me excesse of it: that surfetting,
> The appetite may sicken, and so dye.
> That straine agen, it had a dying fall:
> O, it came ore my eare, like the sweet sound
> That breathes vpon a banke of Violets;
> Stealing, and giuing Odour. Enough, no more,
> 'Tis not so sweet now, as it was before.
> O spirit of Loue, how quicke and fresh art thou
> That notwithstanding thy capacitie,
> Receiueth as the Sea. Nought enters there
> Of what validity, and pitch so ere,
> But falles into abatement, and low price
> Euen in a minute; so full of shapes is fancie
> That it alone, is high fantasticall.
>   Cu. Will you go hunt my Lord?
>   Du. What Curio?
>   Cu. The Hart.
>   Du. Why so I do, the Noblest that I haue:

text of the first few lines of Shakespeare's *Twelfth Night*. We shall give the colloquialism characteristic of 1600, together with the present-day equivalent.[1]

play on	go on playing
so die	thus die
a dying fall	a falling cadence
came o'er my ear	came to my ears
enough	that's enough
no more	let's have no more of it
'tis	it's

---

[1] Notice that this comparison does not involve syntactical change. The first line of *Twelfth Night* begins, "If music be the food of love." The subjunctive form *be* is of course not characteristic of English today, but being a matter of syntax, it is not included here.

art thou	are you
nought enters there	nothing can enter
what . . . so e'er	whatever
even in a minute	in no more than a minute
so full . . . is fancy	fancy is so full
will you go hunt	would you care to go hunting
what	hunting what
so I do	that's what I am doing

That we can see fifteen examples of colloquial changes in only nineteen lines of text is evidence of the abundance of such changes. To be sure, some of these may be explained by reasons other than merely changing fashion; but probably feeling for linguistic variety was a factor in all.

Where the Elizabethans said *some twelve months since* the modern phrase is *a year ago*. Elizabethan expletives—*What a plague, By my troth, Fie, By my halidome, I'faith*—are obsolete practically entirely, replaced by expletives which will no doubt be obsolete in the year 2000. Colloquialisms are seen to be only less ephemeral than slang, only less subject to changing fashion.

FASHIONS IN *KIND*, *SORT*, AND SO FORTH

Another evidence of changing fashions in grammar appears in connection with certain much-used but troublesome words having somewhat the same meaning—*kind, sort, manner, variety,* and *type* being the most common. Several grammatical questions arise in connection with these words, but perhaps the most vexing is whether to use plural or singular for the concrete noun coming after the preposition *of*. Shall it be *all types of community* or *all types of communities; many kinds of books* or *many kinds of book?* And if we choose the first and the third of these alternatives, are we violating any rule of grammar, or are we just showing normal human inconsistency?

Expressions such as these have a very long linguistic history. In early times speakers of the Germanic dialects found frequent use for this type of qualitative genitive, although their fashion of use was different from ours today. Their mental emphasis lay on the concrete things rather than on the abstract class of words, and so they regularly made the expression *books of every sort* or *beast of all kind: alles cynnes dēor.* Examples abound in Anglo-Saxon as well as in later English.

In these early examples the genitive regularly preceded its governing word, so that instead of *wise men of all sort,* we have *of-all-sort wise men: alles cynnes witen.* There is no *of* expressed; the genitive simply preceded the concrete noun, which occupied the emphatic end position. And it was this order which facilitated or possibly even precipitated the grammatical changes which have taken place in this locution.[2]

The preposition *of* entered this genitive construction early, about the thirteenth century, although the older form still lingered, sometimes misunderstood; thus Chaucer has an intrusive initial *s* in a few phrases such as "no skynnes labour":[3] *of-no-kind labor.* By the time of Shakespeare the preposition *of* was standard usage and the traditional order had caused the shift of emphasis from the concrete noun to the abstract or class-noun, as the fashion is today. In the first scene of *Twelfth Night* (line 60) we find "many sorts of Musicke," and in scene 5, "What kinde o' man?" and "What manner of man?"

According to the original form of this qualitative genitive the concrete noun was generally plural, but might be singular or plural according to the idea; and Middle English usage shows plurals freely alternated with singulars: "alle kynne condiciouns," "oþer maner of diadliche sinnes," "fele kyn fisches."

Such alternation between singular and plural has continued throughout the centuries, and it is apparent today, except that in literary pseudo-logical fashion there is a distinct tendency to prefer the singular after the abstract class words. We are encouraged or even directed to say *seven varieties of apple, all types of govern-*

---

[2] This characteristic Anglo-Saxon order may be the progenitor of *these kind* and *those kind,* against which modern school children are forever being warned. Historically *these* and *those* are not plurals but genitives in these expressions, and *these kind of books* may be the modern descendant of *þisses cynnes bēc.* In such a phrase in Modern English it is as though the words *these* and *those* were adjectives modifying *books,* and the words *kind-of, sort-of,* and so forth formed in effect another adjective, also modifying the concrete noun. That this is a distinct linguistic tendency is clearly shown in the modern dialect form *coupla* for *couple of: a coupla bucks.*

[3] The examples in this and the following paragraph are quoted by Leon Kellner in *Historical Outlines of English Syntax,* New York, Macmillan, 1905, pp. 96–120.

ment, every manner of response, and so forth. And still the old plural persists in *all sorts of men, all kinds of children,* and other such common expressions. It would sound absurd to say *all sorts of man* or *all kinds of child.*

The use of the singular form for the concrete noun in such phrases as these has the advantage of compactness and neatness. Probably the fashion of using the singular in some of these constructions will continue, and it is even possible that these will dislodge the plurals which have become a part of the language. For the present, however, a reasonable rule would be as follows: In choosing between singular and plural after *sort, type,* and so forth the singular may be preferred unless it sounds queer or awkward, and then it should be avoided. The choice of the singular is in general not based on any compelling linguistic principle, but rather on the tendency toward change for its own sake.

OTHER FASHIONS IN GENITIVES

It would be interesting but scarcely feasible to go through all the other genitive constructions in English to discover what part fashion plays in them. The genitive is an astonishingly versatile construction. Curme [4] lists eight varieties with subheads, and about as long a list is given by Kellner,[5] who excludes some of these and includes others.

Most of the genitive uses can be traced back to an early stage of linguistic development in English, so that charting their course would take an undue amount of space. Moreover, other factors besides the factor of fashion and the tendency toward change for its own sake enter the history of the various genitives, although fashion influences are frequently discernible. We shall limit ourselves, therefore, to showing the development of the grammatical

[4] George Oliver Curme, *Syntax,* Boston, Heath, 1931, pp. 70 ff. The genitives which Curme recognizes are as follows:
(1) Genitive of origin—the king's son, Dicken's works; (2) Possessive genitive—Bill's car; (3) Subjective genitive—God's love for man, duty's call; (4) Objective genitive—He felt the love of God (of him for God); (5) Genitive of material or composition—a crown of thorns; (6) Descriptive genitive—(a) Genitive of characteristic—a woman's voice, a world's fair, (b) Genitive of measure—a month's rent, a stone's throw; (7) Appositive genitive—city of Rome; (8) Partitive genitive—some of that, a piece of cake.
[5] Leon Kellner, *loc. cit.*

forms used to express the genitive case. These furnish also a good illustration of the tendency toward change.

In its earliest English appearances the genitive had nothing to do with the preposition *of,* which indeed existed in Gothic and Old English, but which is ordinarily translated *from, off* or *by* rather than *of.* The genitive in itself was merely a case marked by various distinctive endings, the most common of which were *es* in the singular and *a* or *ena* in the plural. This case had most of the functions we regard as distinctively genitive today. Certain verbs and adjectives regularly took the genitive; *Beowulf* (ll. 2412–13) has "sē wæs innan full wrǣtta ond wīra"; *it was within full of ornaments and decorations.* The number of verbs and adjectives taking the genitive declined after the close of the Anglo-Saxon period, but we still have numerous idioms with *of: full of water, remind me of the time.*

It was probably a French fashion which led after the Norman Conquest to the use of *of* with the genitive. This fashion spread rapidly, although *of* kept its older meanings for centuries, as is seen by many uses in the King James Bible, such as "He was seen of many." Today these older meanings for *of* have largely been discontinued, and *of* has become simply the sign of the genitive case.

Another fashion which grew up even before the Middle English period was the substitution for the genitive case ending of the personal pronoun in the genitive case: "Enac his cynryn," *Anac his children;* "Africe and Asia hiera landgermircu" *the boundaries of Africa and Asia.*[6]

This usage, which applied mainly to proper nouns and may have been in some degree an attempt to rationalize an explanation of the origin of the genitive case, was continued throughout the Middle English period, increased in early Modern English, and decreased in recent English, although it is still found now and then, particularly in dialects. In the standard literary language it is not common enough even to have the distinction of being ruled out by the authorities. The rise and fall of this construction must therefore be put down to changing fashion rather than to any specific motive.

[6] The examples are from the Alfredian translation of Orosius as quoted by Kellner, *loc. cit.*

During Middle English the *es* case ending was extended by analogy (see Chapter Seven) to the plural and to all singulars; but the apostrophe to indicate the genitive did not become the fashion until much later. Shakespeare was almost wholly innocent of such pointing,[7] and it was not until the eighteenth century that the

> "Dianas lip
> Is not more smooth, and rubious; thy small pipe
> Is as the maidens organ, shrill, and sound,
> And all is semblative a womans part."

modern punctuation of the possessive became standardized. The introduction of the apostrophe cannot be laid entirely to fashion. It shows some ingenuity and perhaps a desire to differentiate singular and plural possessives from each other and from the ordinary plural of nouns.

But the apostrophe had not long been established in the possessive when it was disestablished, particularly in instances in which the possessive word ended with *s*. There is apparent today a growing fashion to omit the apostrophe in such titles as *Pikes Peak* and *Teachers College*. Other such phrases, for example, *Jesus' sake, Dickens' works,* take only the apostrophe and omit the following *s*. Writers like George Bernard Shaw and Robert Bridges are doing even queerer things with apostrophes. It seems apparent that there is a swing of the pendulum back to the genitive lacking the apostrophe.

Today there are in common use at least four different forms for expressing the genitive relation. Undoubtedly the most common, as well as the most awkward and circumlocutionary, is the *of*-genitive which French fashion introduced and popularized in the Middle English period: *a book of two hundred pages, the first chapter of the book.* In an analysis of the six opening paragraphs of a recent publication,[8] there were 45 such genitives, or about two-thirds of the total number.

Next numerically come genitives in pronoun form—*his, their, your,* and so forth. Sixteen of these occurred in the paragraphs an-

---

[7] *Twelfth Night,* Act I, scene 4, ll. 31–34, has three examples.

[8] Hazleton Spencer, *The Life and Art of William Shakespeare,* New York, Harcourt Brace & Company, 1940.

alyzed. All were attributives; the predicatives *mine, yours, theirs,* and so forth are comparatively rare in English usage and might almost be said to be disappearing from the language.[9]

The genitive in *'s* or *s'* comes fourth on the list (seven examples), third place (ten examples) being taken by a construction of very distinctively modern fashion. Increasingly often English-speakers are tending to turn an *of* phrase into a positional genitive in uninflected noun form. Instead of *the top of the table,* for instance, one will say *the table top.* This genitive by functional shift is compact, easy and convenient. It may confidently be expected to increase in the future in phrases like *battle field, tortoise shell, profit sharer,* and so forth.

It may seem a far cry from the latest creation in feminine headgear to functional shift and its effect on the genitive construction in English grammar; but that there is a connection seems undeniable. People see a new way of expressing old ideas; the new way spreads and popularizes itself. It may become a permanent part of the language, or it may decline and disappear. It is simply a matter of linguistic fashion. Perhaps men's styles in clothes, with their somewhat more deliberate rate of change, are better analogies to linguistic fashion than the kaleidoscopic alterations of women's fashions, and yet now and then new styles of speech seem almost to burst forth overnight.

Such change may be pleasing or annoying according to the temperament of the hearer or user. Two examples from recent practice are the introductory *too* and the misplaced *not only: Too, he wanted fame not only, but love as well.* Conservative speakers will view such locutions with disfavor, while those modern Greeks who are always ready to hear and to see some new thing will adopt them for that impact of novelty which they may bring to the reader.

Languages themselves may differ in their hospitality to change for its own sake. Icelandic, which has remained largely unaltered over the past thousand years, presumably had little to do with fashions in grammar and wording. English, on the contrary, is a language which is very open to new forms. A story goes that on

[9] Basic English, an "international" vocabulary of 850 items, omits the predicatives altogether.

one New Year's Eve a colored celebrant stood on a street corner and shouted "Halleluyear" and that before morning the word was all over the city. Such a word of course is not likely to become a part of the language, but there are plenty of examples of phrases and even of grammatical constructions which have begun as fashions in English and have gone on as parts of the English language.

Of course, too, one may say of language, that the more it changes the more it is the same thing. Fashions are not much more than skin deep and do not by and large affect the stronger currents of linguistic change.

CHAPTER ELEVEN

EXPEDITION, IMPATIENCE, ANTICIPATION

A COMMON HUMAN CONVICTION, very strong among the English-speaking peoples, is that if a thing is to be done, it is well that it be done quickly. Expedition is generally accepted as an admirable human quality, even sometimes where it topples over into impatience. Action has been and continues to be the key to social progress; and the energetic and active man, rather than the dilatory or apathetic, has been and continues to be the model for human endeavor.

Both expedition and impatience often manifest themselves in a tendency to anticipate accomplishment. What is the setting up of a scientific hypothesis but anticipation of results not yet achieved in fact? And such hypotheses are not only helpful but also necessary in scientific work, where Browning's words about a man's reach exceeding his grasp are particularly applicable.

But we do not have to look to scientific research for evidences of the human tendency to anticipate. They are all about us, in the English language, which we may see leaping at its own conclusions, making short cuts, and anticipating future expressions, in a great variety of grammatical patterns. Perhaps the verb and the adverb form the clearest instances—the former in its relation to time, and the latter to sentence order.

VERBS MEANING *HOPE* OR *EXPECT*

With *expect* the future tense is commonly used: *I expect he will be here shortly; She expected that he would arrive shortly*. Such sentences as *I expect he comes tomorrow* would be rated as "foreign" English. And yet there is a curious anticipatory use of *expect* in which this verb is equivalent to *think or suppose: I expect he knows his lessons*. This usage, which was marked disputable (No. 144) in the Leonard Survey, shows clearly the human tendency to anticipate the future. The future word *expect* becomes present time for the speaker's purpose of anticipation.

The verb *trust* may show somewhat the same impatience. *I trust you agree* asks for agreement expeditiously and well-nigh peremptorily. In its ordinary uses *trust* is followed by the future: *I trust I shall hear from you soon*. There is no particular anticipatory flavor here.

The verb *hope* has recently broken away from its related verbs and abandoned the future for the present tense. It is rare today to hear such a sentence as *I hope he will win;* it is more likely to be *I hope he wins*. Sentences like *He is hoping he gets home early* and *I hope the letter comes tomorrow* are very common usage. The present *hope,* in such sentences, anticipates the future and brings it down to the moment, leaping at the result before it is attained. It is an interesting detail in the grammar of Modern English.[1]

WILL AND SHALL

The perennial choosing between *will* and *shall* has in it various elements of anticipation or short-cutting and is worth while going into in some detail. While the verbs *shall* and *will* both go back to earlier-than-Anglo-Saxon times, it is generally agreed that the primitive Germanic dialects did not contain any future tense. Two tenses only, past and present, were marked by inflexional terminations. However, in Anglo-Saxon there did exist certain verbs which might be used to express future time.

Of these verbs the most common was *willan,* which meant *to will, to be willing, to wish,* or *to desire,* as well as *to be used to* or *to be about to*.[2] This verb *willan* covered most of the modern uses

---

[1] If rhetoricians have objected to the use of the present tense with *hope,* such objections have not been advertised widely. The change seems to have taken place normally and naturally, without any opposition from the grammarian. It is perhaps a little less complete in literary than in oral English.

[2] John R. Clark Hall, *A Concise Anglo-Saxon Dictionary,* 3d ed., Cambridge (England), Cambridge University Press, 1931.

of our verb *will,* including even the use to designate habit, as in the sentence *He will get up mornings at about six.*

Particularly in narrative use the verb *sculan* (*shall*) might be used to designate the future; its various meanings, as given by Clark Hall, are *to be obliged, shall, have to, must, must needs, am bound to, ought to,* and *owe.* These meanings in modern English have largely transferred themselves from the "present" form *shall* to the "past" form *should,* which very regularly conveys a sense of duty or obligation.

From the very earliest times *willan* has been used in all persons, for simple futurity. The objection to *will* as a simple future in the first and second persons did not become articulate until about the nineteenth century, when various authorities opposed it in favor of *shall.* Rules were worked out for *shall* and *will,* varying in declarative and interrogative sentences, so complicated that probably no one, not even the rule-makers themselves, was able to follow them consistently in practice. Today the authorities seem to be inclined to liberalize their dicta. So persistent and obstinate is the popular preference for *will* that in the most recent edition of the classic Woolley's *Handbook of Composition* the permission is given, "In informal speech and writing disregard many of these rules [for *shall* and *will*]." [3]

There can be little question but that the verb *will* is better to use for the future than *shall.* This verb *will,* with its greater sense of determination, seems to leap at the future condition just as the present tense after *hope* does.[4] If we compare the usual *I would like* with the recommended *I should like,* it is clear how much better the former anticipates achievement and gives an effect of expedition. And the same is true of *I would prefer, I would be glad,* and many other such expressions where *would* is used and *should* is recommended.

The English language has played one little trick on the authorities by permitting the abbreviation *'d* to be used indiscriminately for *would, should,* and *had;* so that *I'd rather* can be expanded into

[3] Earlier editions of Woolley gave mandatory instructions for upholding the usual *shall* and *will* rules.

[4] *Will* is regular Scottish usage in all persons, and American usage except in New England, follows Scottish rather than British English in this respect.

any one of the three auxiliaries. The very use of the clipped form shows the linguistic tendency to expedition and impatience.

ANTICIPATION IN THE HEADLINES

Every teacher of composition knows how hard it is to get the student to observe a neatly consistent series of verb tenses in his writing, particularly if the composition is of a narrative sort. The present tense is always breaking in, and often the transitions between present and past are clumsy. Thus a student giving the story of Hamlet might write "The ghost of Hamlet's father appeared to him and tells him that he must avenge his death." What is this present tense but an impatient projection of the story from the past into the present?

Such schoolboy impatience has, however, been elevated to a system in a field of modern English which has been completely neglected by the grammarian; we refer to newspaper headlines. During the past century expedition, impatience, and anticipation have all become operative in and determinative of the headlines we read. The story is an amusing one.

Looking back to the first issue of the New York *Tribune,* founded October 18, 1843, under the editorship of Horace Greeley, we find few headlines, and when used they partook of the nature of labels, rather than epitomes. They give subject matter rather than summarize action. Here are all the headlines used in the issue quoted; only the fourth and the seventeenth could conceivably be used today.

Letters from Italy
The Ladies of Italy and the Ladies of New York
Unitarian Convention
Murderer Arrested
"The Present"
Trial of Cissius M. Clay
Speech of Henry Clay
Visit to the White Mountains
Life and Speeches of Henry Clay
Somers Mutiny
Useful Works for the People
Ellsworth's Report

The Improvements in Agriculture, the Arts, etc. in the United States
Dr. Lardner's Lectures
Griffith's Chemistry & Dalton's Philosophy
Glimpses of Europe
Another Revolutionary Soldier Gone
Amerigo Vespucci
The First Bank of the United States
Canal Lots
Kidnapping
Association
Proceedings of the Western Fourier Convention
"Morals are no better, and the fish no worse"
Literary notices

If from this naïve list we turn to the sports section of the New York *Herald-Tribune* for Sunday, February 18, 1940, we shall find on the first page alone a total of 47 headlines, all but 8 of which contain verb forms. Of these just one ("The Time Was 1:52.8") has a verb in the past tense to indicate past time.

Of the 47 headlines, 29, or almost exactly three-fifths, use verbs in the present tense to indicate past time: "Crosetti Enters Yankee Fold"; "Scalzo Beats Vaughan"; "Yale Five Crushes Penn." Next most frequent is the use of a past participle (really the present passive construction) to indicate past time: "Shortstop Set for Ninth Year with Champions"; "Game Delayed 40 Minutes." There is one instance of a present participle used for past; "John Woodruff Nipping John Borican." And in three cases future time is indicated, once by a future tense ("Brown Mentor Will Guide Graduates") and twice by the present infinitive ("Tuss McLaughry to Coach College Football All Stars" and "Staff to Assist Coach").

From these examples it is clear that anticipation is the normal plan in news headlines. Since now is the news moment, the headline writer regards past events as though they were still in process of happening and so places them within the present tense. Except for an occasional participial use, the present is the tense to use in headlining events occurring in the recent past.

But when we analyze headline presentation of the future, we find the same situation. "NBC Symphony Visits Newark on Wednesday" means that it will do so next Wednesday. And if the present tense is not used, it is likely to be the present passive infinitive: "Contest to Be Held in Geneva Next June."

In short, headline time is just one thing—the present. Past and future are drawn into present time in order to make the desired effect of immediacy. As a result, it is frequently impossible from a headline such as "Piscator Starts Rehearsals" to tell whether the rehearsals have started, will start in the future, or perhaps are starting at the very moment you sit down to read the paper.[5] By and large, newspaper headlines are a single-tense matter, and it is the reader's task to unravel past, present, and future by reading the article that follows.

This present-tense anticipatory practice, which has grown up within the past half century, has not extended itself to colloquial speech to any very great extent. Newspaper articles, except for headlines, use verb tenses in the conventional fashion for the most part, and convention is also followed in literary and colloquial English. Occasionally such questions are asked as "When do you start?" and the answer may be given, "We start next Thursday"; but such use of the present for the future is not very widespread.

With the verb *say* this anticipatory present use has become fairly widespread in popular speech, although the authorities condemn locutions such as *He looked at me and says, "How are you?"* Such use of *he says, she says, I says* is probably somewhat less frequent today than yesterday. Certainly the formerly popular *says I* is archaic, although a few years ago there was a recrudescence of the present-tense *says* with the pronoun *you*, to indicate incredulity and skepticism.

Little more need be said about these common constructions for expressing future time in English.

1. I shall call.	4. I will call.
2. I call.	5. I am calling.
3. I am to call.	6. I am going to call.

Of these the last is not to our present purpose, but belongs to the material for Chapter Twelve. The third, *I am to call,* is ordinarily

[5] All headline examples are taken from the Sports and Drama Sections of the New York *Herald-Tribune* for Sunday, February 18, 1940.

used to express obligation or a mild degree of compulsion. Of the other four constructions it is uncertain which are the more frequent. Two are in the present tense used with future signification, and it is these two which best exemplify the anticipatory tendency in the language which we are now studying.

ANTICIPATION IN ADVERBS

Aside from the matter of time, the stronghold of expedition, anticipation, or short-cutting in English is in sentence order. Frequently a sentence element is pushed forward from its logical position so as to anticipate a thought which logically might belong later on.

One of the commonest usages in the English language is a sentence such as *I don't think I'll go;* and yet certainly this sentence does not say what it means. What it says is that the speaker *does not think;* what it means is of course that he *does think,* and what he thinks is that he *will not go.* Logically it would read *I think I'll not go,* but this is seldom heard.

The negative adverb *not* has in this type of sentence been shifted to modify the main instead of the subordinate verb, simply because of the unconscious desire of the speaker to make it plain early in the course of his words that the sentence is to be a negative one. If he began with the positive words *I think,* the listener might jump to the conclusion that he would go; with the negative applied prematurely to *think,* his drift is made clear from the very start.

The average speaker of English cares little or nothing about fitness or logic, and it comes as a shock to him to find that *I don't think I'll go* is less than logical. In speaking he simply realizes that a negative is coming, and he tries to introduce that negative just as soon as possible, so as not to run any risk of misleading the hearer. So common is this *I don't think* construction that few grammarians or other authorities bother to condemn it. Anticipation has triumphed over logic and established itself in the everyday English language.

Some opposition is expressed, however, to a parallel case of adverb anticipation. In connection with sentences such as *He only had a dime,* the speaker is warned to place *only* near the word with which it belongs, in this case the noun *dime*. It is recommended that the sentence should read *He had only a dime*, or even *He had a dime only*.

This misplacement of *only* is one of the exceedingly common constructions in popular speech. People say *I only wanted to say hello, He only lost his handkerchief*, and so forth indefinitely.

In mentally composing such a sentence the speaker realizes that the qualifying word *only* is coming, and in order not to mislead the hearer he puts this qualifying word just as early in the sentence as possible. If one said *He had only a dime* one would imply, at least by the first two words, that he did have something substantial; whereas the sentence reveals that he had practically nothing. Putting *only* before *had* gives the hearer warning that what he had was little or nothing; it anticipates the facts in such a way as to give the hearer an immediately correct impression of the situation.

There is a large group of other adverbs which are subject to the same logical "error" as *not* and *only*. Among them are *merely, just, almost, every, hardly, scarcely, quite*, and *nearly*. In every case the psychological aspect is the same. When one says *We nearly got home before the rain started* he is anticipating an essential restriction on the word *home* and thus trying to give a more accurate picture of what happened. Attempts to establish a logical usage in these words would probably be futile in view of this psychological bias.

ANTICIPATION IN SOUNDS

The principle of short-cutting, or anticipation, extends even to the sounds of the English language. An outstanding example is to be found in one of the phonetic principles of Anglo-Saxon, the principle called umlaut. There were various sorts of umlaut in the Primitive Germanic out of which Anglo-Saxon developed, but in every case a vowel in a later (usually a final) syllable influenced a vowel in an earlier syllable, the speaker anticipating the sounds he would next have to make and conforming his tongue to them even to the extent of altering the earlier sound. Theoretically one would expect it to be the other way round.

To give a concrete example of umlaut, the plural of *fōt* (*foot*) is in early Germanic reconstructed as **fōtiz*. The *i* of the plural termination caused the first-syllable vowel to change, and (the termination later dropping) we get *fēt* (*feet*) as the Anglo-Saxon plural.

Umlaut is not an isolated phenomenon. In fact, it is an accepted rule in phonetics that sounds influence the sounds which precede rather than those that follow them. Here again we find anticipation at work, and almost any phonetic change occurring in combinations will exemplify it.

Many other matters of word order might be referred to anticipation or previewing. The consciously distorted orders which we sometimes find in speech and writing are often determined by the desire to anticipate some element which in its normal or logical order would come later in the sentence. Adverbial clauses in general can come after the main clause and do not require any preceding punctuation (*He came when he was ready*). However, such adverbial clauses are frequently pushed to the beginning of the sentence and followed by a comma: *When he was ready, he came*. This order shows an anticipation of the subordinate element, takes it out of its normal position, and gives it artificial prominence in the sentence.

The present chapter has by no means exhausted the list of manifestations of short-cutting in English grammar. Letter-writing practice has cut down on its complimentary openings and closings, obviously in the interests of greater expedition. What in the eighteenth century was "I am, Sir, your most obedient and humble servant" has become "Yours truly" or "Yours sincerely." Addresses have been shortened by modern Post Office practice. Epistolary art has grown briefer and more efficient.

And then there is the vast list of verbal abbreviations in English—*York* out of *Eoforwīc*, and *taxi* out of *taximeter-cabriolet*. All those attest the leaning of English-speaking people toward making speech short, sharp, and to the point. All are short-cutting in the field of English.

Of course there are counter-impulses which oppose the operation of short-cutting in English grammar, as in the lives of the people who speak English. Impatience is not generally regarded as an admirable trait, and so it is combatted actively through various linguistic conventions which demand the use of what may be termed "long-cutting," or circumlocution. Laziness also passively opposes the energetic and anticipatory use of language.

It is only here and there that expedition can make its effects felt in the grammar of the English language, and it is natural that it should appear just where we find it. Anticipation is natural in connection with hope, with the headlines, and with sentence qualifiers; and it is readily seen in precisely these fields.

LONG-CUTTING IN ENGLISH GRAMMAR

HOWEVER ADMIRABLE expedition may be considered, there is something also to be said for the elegant leisure which never permits itself to hurry or to take short-cuts; and this leisure, like all other aspects of human character, is reflected in the English language and its grammar. English is lazy, just as those who speak it are lazy; and English cultivates leisure much as its speakers may do.

This long-cutting, or procrastination, is clearly observable in present-day practice in business letter writing. Within the past decade usage in letter headings has changed so that today good stenographers avoid end punctuation and abbreviations in the lines of the return address and superscription. A letter heading formerly might read

> 421 W. 117th St.,
> New York, N. Y.
> Oct. 12th, 1920.

Messrs. Henry Crawford & Co.,
4620 Chestnut St.,
Phila., Pa.

Today, however, the same heading would be more likely to read in this way.

> 421 West 117 Street
> New York
> October 12, 1940

Henry Crawford and Company
4620 Chestnut Street
Philadelphia, Pennsylvania

The modern practice uses a little more space and typing, but it compensates for this fact by its general air of neatness and attractiveness. Compared with the fashion of twenty years ago, it is long-cutting; but this long-cutting seems to be amply justified by its effect.

LONG-CUTTING IN VARIOUS PHRASES

It would take undue space even to make a list of the phrases which show the tendency toward procrastination, or circumlocution, in the English language; suffice it to say that their number is legion. We all know people who find it impossible to say *Every item was defective,* but who must say *Each and every item was defective.* Certain people never do things *for a reason;* it must be *for the simple reason that,* and so forth. People of this sort say *in any way, shape, or manner,* rather than simply *in any way.* They *continue on, return back, finish up, ascend up, descend down* in an endless variety of tautological expressions.

If we study carefully such long-cutting phrases, we may see in them a certain aspect of emphasis and prose rhythm, which further their use. To *finish up a job* seems perhaps just a little more emphatic than merely *finishing it;* and the word *simple* adds impressiveness to the noun *reason,* so that doing a thing *for the simple reason* sounds perhaps more reasonable than just doing it *for the reason.* The verbal circumlocutor does achieve some degree of rhythmic and emphatic prose.

Long-cutting is seen in numerous rhetorical precepts, warning against the use of short or syncopated words. Thus Webster lists the word *movies* as United States slang, evidently preferring the more elegant length of the phrase *moving pictures.* Woolley warns against the words *Jap* and *ad* as colloquial abbreviations, recommending the use of the full words for *Japanese* and *advertisement.*

Even sounds are not permitted to drop from words. The Leonard Survey lists as illiterate English (No. 192) the form *busted* for *burst,* and periodically teacher's examinations in the United States dwell on the iniquity of saying *goverment* for *government, resevoir* for *reservoir,* and *reconize* for *recognize* in spite of the fact that these shortened pronunciations are extremely widespread and seem relatively harmless.

A NEW AUXILIARY

Long-cutting has given to English a new set of verbal auxiliaries, the forms with *going to*.

I am going to call.	We are going to call.
You are going to call.	You are going to call.
He, she, it is going to call.	They are going to call.

These auxiliaries are rather distinctively American and probably not more than a century old; but they have established themselves very firmly in the English language, so that they must be reckoned with as much as any others of the verbal auxiliaries of English grammar. The form *I am going to go* is of course pure tautology; nevertheless it enjoys immense popularity among speakers of English. It is probable that more people say *I am going to go* than *I am going,* to express the intention of future action.

Here again the matter of prose rhythm enters. There is a different rhythmic feeling about *He is going to call* than about *He will call;* the latter sounds somewhat abrupt and crude, whereas *He is going to call* has a pretty lilt about it. It is uncertain what part this prose rhythm has played in the establishment of *He is going to call* in English grammar, but the rhythm itself is unmistakable and attractive.

Many authorities in grammar have objected to the use of *if* in place of the longer form *whether,* although the linguists of the Leonard Survey listed *I don't know if I can* as established usage (No. 60). Here also rhythm enters and works, it seems to us, somewhat in favor of the word *whether,* which has on the whole a more attractive rhythmic pattern. It is probably the pull of expedition, or short-cutting, which makes *if* a frequent substitute for the longer word.

Rhythm also enters into the question of the omitted relative in sentences such as *There is a man (whom* or *that* [1]*) I used to*

---

[1] Authorities frequently direct that *that* be avoided where the antecedent is a person rather than a thing; but the use of *that* as a personal relative seems to be rather definitely established.

know. Quite apart from the difficulty of deciding whether to use *who* or *whom* in this construction, the rhythmic pattern is different with the relative omitted. Several authorities favor the use of the relative, at least in literary prose; and its use may be regarded as another instance of procrastination or long-cutting.

LONG-CUTTING AND SYLLEPSIS

A minor example of short-cutting in English grammar is the figure of speech known as syllepsis, examples of which are: *She went off in a rage and a Buick car* and *He took a knife and his life.* In such expressions it is easy to see how short-cutting, or the using of a single word in two discrepant senses, has led to a ludicrous effect. Long-cutting in such sentences is obviously the correct solution, making them: *Enraged, she stepped into her car and drove off* and *He took a knife and ended his life.*

The tendency to syllepsis has been discouraged in the rhetorical rule: "Do not make a single word serve as principal and auxiliary," which rule applies to one particular aspect of the tendency toward syllepsis. Examples of sentences illustrating the disapproved word are: *At first it was interesting and liked by the men; I have a book and gone home;* and *He got a book and through.* Such sentences are obviously defective, and here again long-cutting or procrastination is necessary.

Another illustration of long-cutting has to do with the frequently stated rule for pronoun antecedents: Never use a pronoun without a specific noun antecedent. To be sure, this is a rule which is violated widely in practice, and almost necessarily so, since one could scarcely expect a noun antecedent for a pronoun such as *nobody* in the sentence *Nobody was there* or for *whoever* in *Whoever came was welcome.* However, this rule does have some aspects which are interesting in the present connection.

Take, for example, the sentence *She ignored him, which did not bother him at all.* Here obviously *which* refers, not to any single word, but to the entire clause *she ignored him.* Careful rhetoricians would direct the insertion of some such word as action to make the construction complete: *She ignored him, which action did not bother him at all.* This added word *action* is a good example of long-cutting, even though it would be used only in the most meticulous sort of literary prose and would scarcely be found in colloquial speech, which with no hesitation whatever uses a relative pronoun to refer to an entire clause.

Occasionally grammarians invoke the bogy of ambiguity in order to induce long-cutting. For example, sentences such as *I like Mary better than Jane* are used every day and are perfectly clear and sensible, yet they are said to be ambiguous and therefore we are advised to change to either *I like Mary better than I like Jane* or *I like Mary better than Jane likes Mary*. Obviously the first of these interpretations is to be preferred here. A slightly different example is *He likes golf better than his wife,* where the preferred meaning seems to be *He likes golf better than his wife likes golf*. In any case, the enlarged statements of comparisons are seldom heard. The English language seems definitely given to expedition in such constructions, and it avoids many of the procrastinating constructions which grammarians recommend.

Occasionally grammatical short-cutting goes wrong, and the following rule is framed to prevent such errors: When words are understood as repeated, they must fit in both places. An example of illogical practice is *The fire was built and the potatoes baked;* it is apparent that if something is supplied after *potatoes* it must be *were,* not *was;* and this shift in the word to be supplied is regarded as a grammatical flaw.

It does not seem to be very much of a grammatical flaw. Indeed, a variant of it occurs in a famous line of Keats' "Ode on a Grecian Urn": "Forever wilt thou love and she be fair." A good practical rule seems to be that unless such a construction is really awkward (for example, *He did what others have and are doing*) there is no particular need to follow a meticulous long-cutting.

Another example of this sort of thing, slightly different, is *A dispute arose as to whom the honor belonged*. Here the word *to* is taken in two connections, so that the sentence in complete form would have to repeat *to*. This construction is perhaps somewhat awkward and in need of change.

A related error, which also inheres in comparisons, is reflected in the rule: When *than* and *as* are both used, the second part of the comparison should come after the comparison word. The type example is *She is as tall if not taller than he.* Here long-cutting would require an *as* after the first *tall,* but on the other hand, the sentence with such an *as* would seem intolerably clumsy and awkward. The way out, as suggested by the rule, is to put the second comparison by itself at the end of the sentence, saying *She is as tall as he, if not taller.* In this construction the ellipsis is not noticeable; the only trouble is that this wording is far less prevalent than the logically defective wording first instanced. Another example of the same sort, marked disputable (No. 118) in the Leonard Survey, is *He can write as well or better than I.* This is a difficult sentence to put into logical form, and it seems to call for some degree of long-cutting.

The same thing occurs with other sentences implying comparison; *He is one of the greatest if not the greatest author of our time.* The word *author(s)* makes the trouble here, and the solution is again obviously to say *He is one of the greatest authors of our time, if not the greatest.* In literary language such a construction might be used; in colloquial spoken English it would be difficult to avoid the more usual order.

LONG-CUTTING IN PHONETICS

Certain words in English show the effects of a process of long-cutting in sounds which occurred in former centuries. An example is the word *near,* with its comparative *nearer.* This word *near* is the descendant of an inflected form of the Anglo-Saxon *nēah,* which has given us the somewhat archaic *nigh* in Modern English.

It was the comparative of the word *nēah* which gave us our modern word *near,* and the comparative character of *near* is seen in the final *r.* However, this comparative character of *near* was lost sight of, so that *near* seemed to be a word of positive degree and finally acquired an intrusive comparative, in the form *nearer,* which thus is historically a double comparative.

The form *nearest,* which was latest originated, is doubly illogical, since it is a superlative grafted onto a comparative; both forms are examples of long-cutting in inflexions. A similar development, to which exception is sometimes taken in modern rhetorics, is *lesser,* which is a tautological form built on the comparative *less.* This *lesser* is listed as standard English in the second edition of *Webster's Dictionary.*

In the same way that an intrusive *r* has attached itself to *near,* an intrusive *d* has attached itself to *sound* (*noise*), which historically should be *soun.* Our form *sounded* is thus tautological, but it is standard English nevertheless, unlike *drownded,* which tried to go the same path, but was prevented by grammarian disapproval.

Besides tautological *r* and *d,* the sibilant *s* endings, used in the plural and the possessive, are matters of much uncertainty in pronunciation. In sentences such as *All the Dickens' relations came* many speakers will be uncertain whether to pronounce the possessive *Dickens* or *Dickenses,* and in phrases such as *the three Misses Fish* and *the three Miss Fishes* uncertainty becomes intensified. Certain phrases involving sibilants, such as *for Jesus' sake,* are fairly well standardized, but in others there is no easy choice between short-cutting and long-cutting.

An odd example of phonetic long-cutting is the intrusive consonant which appears in phrases such as *the-y-east, to-w-aid,* and *the idea-r-of it.* Such consonants are actually easier to pronounce than not, coming as they do between vowels of various sorts. This unconscious phonetic long-cutting is frequent in English, particularly in certain local dialects such as that of New England, where the intrusive *r* abounds.

Among other interesting examples of phonetic excess in English grammar are the various doubled plurals—*brethren, children, kine.* If these words had all developed normally from Anglo-Saxon to Modern English, we should have as their plurals *brether, childer,* and *ky.* The word *brother* had an umlauted plural much like the plural *men* for *man,* and this plural *brether* was made into a double plural by adding the termination *en* to it. At the same time a "regular" plural, *brothers,* was introduced, and this became the standard form of the plural for *brother, brethren* being confined to religious and poetical uses.

The plural for *child,* according to standard Old English grammar, was *cildru,* and in Irish dialect we have still the form *childer,* which reflects this older form. In the standard English, however, the plural termination *en* was added, thus forming a doubled plural. No regularized plural *childs* was introduced, so that *children* is today the standard plural form for this word.

Ky, or *cy,* was the umlauted plural of the Anglo-Saxon *cū,* from which we get the Modern English word *cow.* Again we have a duplication of plurals through the adding of *n,* with a regularized plural in *s* also introduced. Today *cows* is the standard plural for *cow,* and *kine* a poetical word not generally felt to be associated with the word *cow.*

OTHER MISCELLANEOUS EXAMPLES

We have already mentioned the word *up* as having played a great part in long-cutting in English grammar. Its use is redundant, that is, superfluous, in such phrases as *dress up, wake up, get up, look up, speak up,* and *call up.* Perhaps, with its explosive consonant, it provides a sort of period for the verbs it follows. Certainly its use is increasing rather than decreasing, so that every once in a while one gets a new combination of *up* and a verb (*let up, point up,* and so forth) with which it forms a new idiomatic meaning.

Another word which has much to answer for in connection with long-cutting is the pronoun *all.* Frequently *all* is used in connection with an *of* phrase, *all of you, all of us.* In such phrases it does not seem very redundant. In certain dialects, however, *we all* (occasionally *we-uns,* meaning *we-ones*) and *you all* have become almost substitutes for *we* and *you.* The perennial controversy between Southerners and Northerners on the question whether *you all* is ever used as a singular pronoun in the South has not been officially decided. It is clear, however, that the South is very hospitable to the use of the phrase *you all,* which is so commonly heard that it often merges into a single syllable *y'all.*

Prepositions are frequent sources of redundance, in sentences such as *He came (at) about three o'clock* and *He took the book from off (of) the table.* In general, the preposition has become an increasing factor in English idioms, and it might be expected that many of its uses would be unnecessary and matters of long-cutting.

Frequently long-cutting in English grammar is a matter of mere wordiness—of clauses used when a word would suffice, of a sentence which is worth no more than a phrase. Such wordiness is all about us and is to be encountered at any time in newspapers, books, magazines, sermons, and lectures. It is the luxuriant over-growth of the English language made possible by the use of the printing press and typewriter, and the extension of literacy; and it is likely to increase rather than to decrease in the future.

Such wordiness is sometimes a symptom of self-importance on the part of the speaker or writer, but probably oftener it is symptomatic of "padding," or the necessity of filling a certain amount of space with words. Modern life presses hard upon its articulate members to produce voluminously in the form of speech sounds and of printed pages, and it would be indeed remarkable if a goodly number of the words this pressure produces were not mere verbiage.

The part played by rhythm in long-cutting has been suggested; and indeed to the truly aesthetic ear, unspoiled by subservience to grammatical dicta, there is a fine cadence about certain of its manifestations. The *for* in the sentence *I want for him to get to work* adds something which is not present if this preposition is omitted. And the redundant *why* in *Tell me the reason why* [2] seems to make the sentence better rounded off and filled out than it would be without this word. Even circumlocutionary expressions like *Mr. Evans of Seattle his gloves* and *It is his book my teacher Mr. James* have about them a fine flavor showing that humanity is grasping at meanings.

So it is impossible generally to condemn the frequent manifestations in English grammar of laziness, procrastination, repetition, and long-cutting, in spite of the recognized social tendency to-

---

[2] The Leonard Survey linguists list as established usage (No. 80) the sentence *The real reason he failed was because he tried to do too much.* Such a sentence is obviously redundant and yet is just as obviously general and normal popular usage.

ward disapproval of these qualities. At their best they contribute something to the English language. At their worst they are to be set down as just human, just further instances of the psychology of English speakers, reflected in their speech.

IMAGINATION AND STRIVING
FOR BEAUTY

IN CHAPTER FOUR we suggested a possible explanation for the origin of language, or in other words the shift from animal cries, which are not language, into the complicated and extensive system which we call human speech. In this explanation one aspect of the evolution was neglected: the motive or motives which may have led to the extension of meaningful animal cries into language.

If we survey the field of animal cries we shall find that many of them are motivated by utility, or the instinct for self-preservation. Cries of warning, of hunger, of rage are evidently framed for use, not for beauty; and it is even probable that the utilitarian motive dominated primitive language, whether animal or human, so widespread and potent does this motive seem to be.

But in fact there is a great part of the pre-language of animals which is not utilitarian but aesthetic in its nature, and this fact points to the possibility of an aesthetic motive in the extension of animal cries into human speech. The cat probably purrs as often as she mews. The birds sing for joy as often as for hunger or warning. Every creature with a voice has its imaginative as well as its practical expressions, and it may be questioned whether the imaginative or the practical predominates in quantity and importance.

So the earliest extensions of the animal cries out of which human nonsentences were developed may not have been, and in all probability were not, of an exclusively practical sort. They may have included laughter and joking, love-talk and a primitive kind of crooning, the enjoyment of comfort after toil, and many other such forms of imaginative expression. It is certain that such expression has during historical times formed a very large element in language and that it bulks enormously in the language of today. Possibly more writers at the present moment are turning out "literature" (including news, entertainment, uplift, narrative, and so forth) than will be found grinding out words of a strictly utilitarian sort.

English grammar is thus affected by both practical and aesthetic impulses, and it will be our task in this chapter to describe a few of the latter. How does the striving toward beauty, the aesthetic impulse, affect English grammar?

SHAKESPEARE'S AESTHETICS

Probably no literary craftsman dealing in English words has attained a greater degree of linguistic beauty than has Shakespeare, and it is worth while to consider some of the means by which Shakespeare's word-magic was achieved. These means are interesting alike to the student of grammar and the student of literary style.

One of these means (one might almost call it a trick) which Shakespeare used for verbal effect was functional shift, or the employment of words out of their normal functions as verbs, adjectives, or what not. In the line "The dark backward and abysm of time," we find the adverb *backward* used as a noun; and "The be-all and the end-all" shows verbs in the same use. Tamora is told to "Patient yourself," and Cleopatra fears lest "Some squeaking Cleopatra boy my greatness." Functional shift is not overworked in Shakespeare; it is a touch used sparingly to achieve particular effects of beauty, and it never fails to accomplish its end.

Keats, whose work contains so many reminders of Shakespeare, uses functional shift in much the same way. In the first stanza of his "Ode to a Nightingale" he has "And Lethe-wards had sunk," and "full-throated ease." Other examples of functional shift for literary effect might be multiplied from writers both before and after Keats.[1]

A second grammatical or linguistic means by which Shake-speare achieves aesthetic effects has been studied exhaustively in one of the most original and penetrating works of recent Shake-speare scholarship, *Shakespeare's Imagery,* by Caroline Spur-geon.[2] It is by the image or figure of speech, the comparison expressed or implied, that Shakespeare attains much of his word-magic.

Let us analyze one well-known example, from Act II, scene 2, of *Antony and Cleopatra.*[3]

> The Barge she sat in, like a burnisht Throne
> Burnt on the water: the Poope was beaten Gold,
> Purple the Sailes: and so perfumed that
> The Windes were Loue-sicke with them.
> The Owers were Siluer,
> Which to the tune of Flutes kept stroke, and made
> The water which they beate, to follow faster;
> As amorous of their strokes. For her owne person,
> It beggerd all discription, she did lye
> In her Pauuillion, cloth of Gold, of Tissue,
> O're-picturing that Venus, where we see
> The fancie out-worke Nature. On each side her,
> Stood pretty Dimpled Boyes, like smiling Cupids,
> With diuers coulour'd Fannes whose winde did seeme,
> To gloue the delicate cheekes which they did coole,
> And what they vndid did.

No fewer than seven images appear in these sixteen lines, some fully stated, some implied by a single word. The first of these, comparing Cleopatra's barge to a throne, is complete, while the second consists of the single word *burned,* which forms a picture of the barge compared to a fire. The third image, contained in the word *love-sick,* is of the sort which Ruskin designated pathetic fallacy.

---

[1] This tendency of Keats was ridiculed in a famous review of *Endymion* by John Wilson Croker, who mentioned particularly "turtles *passion* their voices" (l. 248); an 'arbor was *nested*" (l. 431); a lady's locks "*gordianed* up" (l. 903); and "wives prepare *needments*" (l. 208).

[2] New York, Macmillan, 1935.

[3] Except for the transference of two words which are plainly mislined, the spelling and wording here are those of the First Folio.

Pathetic fallacy inheres also in the next image, which centers in the word *amorous;* the fifth is a direct comparison between Cleopatra and Venus. This comparison is repeated in the likening of the boys to Cupids, and then the whole is rounded off with the fanciful comparison of the fanning to the action of wind.

In a well-known analysis of these lines [4] the sounds themselves are shown to have made no little contribution to the poetic effect. The repetition of *b,* especially the combination *bur* in the first few lines, varied with the sound *p* and the combination *pur* (in *purple* and *perfumed*) contribute directly to the pictorial effect; and the alliteration, which is frequent in the lines following, likewise reinforces the poetic images. Thus to his word-magic Shakespeare added sound-magic, which we shall not analyze in detail.

RESTRAINT AND AESTHETIC EFFECT

One of the perennial struggles in the field of aesthetics is between restraint and rant, or understatement and violence. In general the untutored mind prefers the latter and the discriminating intelligence the former in each pair. Shakespeare's early work shows fairly frequent lapses into rant and violence, which mar even the exquisite lyricism of *Romeo and Juliet.* When Shakespeare comes, however, to his mid-career, in *Hamlet,* he puts into words his own judgment against rant.[5]

Excellent examples of his great mature style are the two death scenes in *Antony and Cleopatra,* where the emotional exclamations are held within the strictest limits of understatement and the height of tragic effect is achieved by Cleopatra's poignant speech

> Peace, peace:
> Dost thou not see my Baby at my breast,
> That suckes the Nurse asleepe?

---

[4] R. L. Stevenson, "Technical Elements of Style in Literature," *Letters and Miscellanies,* New York, Scribner's, 1898, p. 261.

[5] Opening of Act III, scene 2. "Nor do not saw the air too much with your hand, thus; but use all gently: for in the very torrent, tempest, and—as I may say—whirlwind of passion, you must acquire and beget a temperance, that may give it smoothness. O! it offends me to the soul to hear a robustious periwig-pated fellow tear a passion to tatters, to very rags, to split the ears of the groundlings, who for the most part are capable of nothing but inexplicable dumb-shows and noise: I

In modern writing, particularly dramatic writing, there is plenty of rant and violence; it is the stock in trade of such writers as Eugene O'Neill, Clifford Odets, and other well-known moderns. However, in the related field of advertising, understatement seems to have come into its own. Here, in place of the superlative, common a generation ago, we have the multiple comparative, as, for example, in this bit of an automobile advertisement: "It gives you greater room in which to take road-life easy. . . . It puts a sturdier, higher-crowned Turret Top overhead and more rigid, shockproof reenforcements all around—to add to your security." [6] This use of the comparative is characteristic of present-day publicity and seems symptomatic of an appeal to mature rather than to juvenile intelligence.

There has grown up in English a whole group of intensives, mainly adverbs, which are frequently used as heighteners of aesthetic effect. The impression produced by these is, however, the opposite of restraint or understatement, and their use is questionable. Among the intensives in English are such words as *so, very, quite, just, unique,* and *such.* The inexperienced writer is likely to use them as in the following example: *Ann dropped into a chair; she had had such a hard day and she was so tired. She had had a hard day and she was tired* gives the effect far more completely and wholly than the construction with the intensives.

In general the intensives give a distinct impression of amateurishness. Such a sentence as *The swamps were just beautiful, so many birds were flying, and the sky was a unique blue* sounds immature and overdone. The use of intensives weakens the effect. A very useful rule for the writer is to avoid such words in their intensive use.[7]

BEAUTY IN PUNCTUATION

The example of letter-heading punctuation given at the beginning of Chapter Twelve illustrates the aesthetic effect of punctua-

---

would have such a fellow whipped for o'er-doing Termagant; it out-herods Herod: pray you, avoid it . . . Be not too tame neither."

[6] *The New Yorker,* issue of February 25, 1940.

[7] Another example which has been suggested is *very* in the phrase *a very good woman* as compared to *a good woman.* It is easy to see how the intensive is a weakener here.

tion used sparingly. The decline of the use of commas, mentioned and illustrated on page 44, is also a contribution to aesthetic effect, since little marks of punctuation tend to make a page of type look unattractive and cluttered.

Certain experimenters with punctuation have gone even further than the general public in minimizing this sprinkling of marks. George Bernard Shaw and Robert Bridges have already been instanced as radical in their use of punctuation. Modern usage also tends strongly toward leaving out end punctuation in titles, inscriptions, headings, and other single-line locutions. The age of a public building can almost be calculated by the presence or absence of punctuation following the inscriptions on its walls. Certainly the style without punctuation seems aesthetically the better.

Among the punctuation marks which are becoming less frequently used than formerly are parentheses. Such marks indicate a break in the thought, and beauty of diction demands smoothness and a flowing style unmarred by jerkiness. The exclamation mark also is becoming a rarity in modern literature.

One university instructor of our acquaintance gave in his composition classes a rule that a sentence is defective if it calls for any internal punctuation whatever. This is no doubt a counsel of perfection, and yet it is true that it may stand as the ideal toward which English is tending. Unquestionably internal punctuation is decreasing; and just as unquestionably this fact makes for the advantage of the English language.

BEAUTY IN SOUNDS AND WORDS

As for separate sounds, it is not always easy to distinguish the aesthetically appealing from the aesthetically unattractive or repellent. Generally consonants are considered less beautiful than vowels, and yet the tendency in English has been strongly toward increasing the proportion of consonants to vowels; Modern English is a very consonantal language in comparison to Italian or Modern Greek. Jespersen [8] speaks of this preponderance of consonantal sounds as making English a "masculine" rather than a

[8] In *Growth and Structure of the English Language,* 4th ed., New York, Appleton-Century, 1923, chap. i.

"feminine" language, but he evidently does not consider English less attractive on that account.

Among the vowels, phonetic aestheticians often disparage those which are said to be nasalized, or formed with the nasal passages open rather than closed. Americans are adversely criticized in England because of their alleged tendency to vowel nasalization. As one wit put it, "Americans and Englishmen speak the same language, but through different organs."

It seems plain that these critics tend to hear with their prejudices rather than their ears; for across the Channel in France is a language which frankly nasalizes many of its vowels, yet it is considered a beautiful speech. Probably American English is condemned as much for being different as for nasalization, since this is not considered a defect when found in other languages.

Another vowel sound often avoided in both British and American English (though probably more in the latter) because of its unpleasant sound, particularly in certain consonant combinations, is the sound *æ,* the vowel of the word *as.* Probably the objection to this sound is partly the unpleasant facial expression it involves,[9] with the lips flattened and the nose drawn up as if apprehending some unpleasantness. Words such as *path, laugh, calf,* and *bath* seem especially objectionable with the *æ* sound; and students are often taught to pronounce them either with the broad *a* (*ah*), or with a sound midway between *ah* and *æ.*

In a recent popular song a syllable used to express derision and scorn is *nyah* (pronounced [*njæ*]). The combination of the nasal consonant with this disliked vowel *æ* appeared to express particularly well the juvenile emotions represented.

Occasionally words may be coined by a speaker; a young man of our acquaintance created the word *twot* to designate any person he did not like, and we seem to recollect that P. G. Wodehouse has invented *twerp* for the same purpose. Another person, a student, created the surprising word *euphemious,* and in a recent broadcast Walter Damrosch referred to flames as flickering and *flimmering.*[10] Such coinages may have considerable aesthetic

[9] As pointed out in Aiken, *English Present and Past,* p. 155.
[10] Perhaps a "portmanteau" of *flickering* and *shimmering* (or *glimmering*).

value, and at their best may even pass into the language. At their worst, of course, they are facetious and ephemeral.

With respect to words rather than sounds, it is often assumed that certain words in themselves are aesthetically desirable, while others are aesthetically undesirable. Thus *garbage* would be called a distinctively unpoetic word, while *moonlight* would be called poetic. The relation of sound and meaning in such pronouncements perhaps needs some clarification.

It appears to be unquestionable that we hear with our minds rather than with our so-called auditory organs, and that meaning is far more potent than sound in determining the aesthetic value of a word. For example, if a person is asked to evaluate sound in the word *vermin,* the judgment will probably be that *vermin* is an intrinsically unaesthetic word, one which "sounds bad." Yet if the same question be asked regarding the word *ermine,* which is practically identical in sound pattern with *vermin,* the answer is just as likely to be that *ermine* has a wealthy and luxurious sound and is aesthetically attractive. Other similar pairs are *garbage* and *marriage, traitor* and *greater, dope* and *hope.*

How readily words may be used and enjoyed so long as their meanings are not taken into account is proved by the true story of a group of children who in writing and producing a play named one character Diarrhoea just because they thought it a pretty name. It is intrinsically a pretty name, comparable to Isabella or Dorothea; but to most people the meaning would obscure any beauty of sound it might possess.

In various contests and inquiries concerning words the word most disliked has been invariably one of unpleasant meaning, and on the contrary the word selected as most lovely is determined by the meaning rather than the sound. Such a word as *nightingale* is by no means intrinsically attractive from the phonetic aspect; yet to most people it would stand as a beautiful word.

It would be unsafe to assert that there is any single word in English which is positively and completely unaesthetic. Probably every English word is capable of successful use for poetic effect. In Shakespeare's plays and poems homely and even commercial words, like *brag, lease,* and *chimney-sweeper,* are freely used with an effect of perfect fitness. Such words are so beautifully incorporated into the thought that they give precisely the right poetic effect.

AESTHETIC FEELING AND FIGURES OF SPEECH

It should not be assumed that the feeling for aesthetics in English speech is confined to discriminating or scholarly minds. Even the most commonplace middle-class individual has some feeling for aesthetics in speech, and it is a matter of frequent observation that the ignorant orders of society possess speech which is vivid, racy, and occasionally poetical.[11]

Such vulgar speech is likely to include a good deal of personification. The owner of a rattle-trap automobile will give it a name such as *Susie* or *Estelle*, and will use the pronoun *she* in referring to it. The same personification is almost universal with boats. It is only a step from this crude sort of personification to the figure of speech employed by the poet who speaks of "Time in his course" or "Stern duty, daughter of the voice of God."

Figures of speech other than personifications also abound in homely and untutored language. A recent rhetorical authority gives seven rules for figures of speech, saying that they must be (1) fresh and original, (2) spontaneous, (3) in good taste, (4) essentially true, (5) used sparingly, (6) not too detailed, and (7) congruous. All these requirements, especially the first, are observed in the speech of many farmers, laborers, salesmen, and others with a spontaneous feeling for beautiful and vivid language.

The use of many figures of speech which have knocked at the door of the English language has been extended from just such popular levels. The word *partial,* for example, is ordinarily used with persons or animals, so that one may be *partial to a particular cousin,* but scarcely *partial to sugar.* Yet the use of *partial* in referring to inanimate things like sugar, as a figure of speech, is vivid and scarcely merits the condemnation which some authorities have expressed for it. A homely expression of a like variety is *I don't take any stock in his reforming.* While speakers are warned

[11] Dramas frequently catch this poetry of the masses. An example is *Liliom,* by Ferenc Molnar.

against this expression in some books of writing, *Webster's Dictionary* gives it as good standard English.

It is plain, from the examples given in this chapter, that in languages, as in life, beauty is subjective rather than objective. Beauty must exist first in the mind and spirit of the writer or speaker, who must then be able to express that beauty so as to make it seem a discovery for all mankind.

There is no objective standard for linguistic aesthetics; the authorities may define tendencies and principles, but the fact remains that in the last analysis their precepts may be set aside at any time by a genius capable of redefining beauty in his own terms and convincing the world of the truth of his perceptions. Shakespeare did this more than once, and his methods are worth study.

There was a story, years ago, of a little boy in a New York City public school who wanted to bring his teacher an especially desirable gift. Having observed what his father brought his mother one night, and her joy, he purloined the present and took it to his teacher, who found it to be a rent receipt for their poor flat for the current month. She told the child he had brought her a beautiful gift and gave him the kiss he shyly angled for. The story is not without its linguistic parallels.

CHAPTER FOURTEEN

HUMDRUM AND ESCAPE

IT CAN SCARCELY BE DOUBTED that to almost everyone his own life looks uninteresting. Seen from near at hand experience is too likely to flatten out into the humdrum and the repetitious. Disregarding the obvious fact that any life pattern will seem romantic and adventurous to someone, somewhere on earth, people hasten to disclaim any accusation of living an exciting life, obviously convinced within their own minds that their particular round of occupation holds no excitement whatever. One successful celebrity said that her attainment had been "the achievement of dullness"; and Hamlet, who managed to stir up plenty of adventure, nevertheless complained

> How weary, stale, flat, and unprofitable
> Seem to me all the uses of this world!

Now people who take the humdrum view of life are conscious of a recurring need for an escape from their beaten path; and this escape may come in either of two typical ways. They may lose themselves in the rose-tinted realms of glamour through fiction, radio, and dramatic presentations which will lift them into a never-never land of bliss and love. Or, in contrast, they may escape by plunging into the world of pain and crime in the tabloids, in stage tragedy, and in personal gossip and rumor-mongering. The latter world is just as much a never-never land as the former, but to many persons it gives more of the illusion of reality and hence is more often labeled "realistic." As a matter of fact, neither world is realistic, since both partake of the extraordinary, which is not likely to occur often in individual experience.

HUMDRUM IN ENGLISH SENTENCE ORDER

As with everything else involved in human experience, both the humdrum and the two escapes from it are mirrored in sharp outline in the English language, its vocabulary, its grammar, even its spelling and punctuation. What is our established sentence order of subject-verb-complement but a beaten path, gray and dusty, along which we route our words over and over, always the same, sentence upon sentence, and chapter upon chapter? Small wonder that the early cinema, striving perhaps unconsciously to escape from this regular round, made "Came the Dawn" (verb-subject) universally known as characteristic movie patter.

Sentence order in English is standardized in a more rigid and thoroughgoing way than most of us realize. Some score of typical patterns exist, varying for interrogative, imperative, and exclamatory sentences, for different kinds of clause, for modifiers and their governing elements, and so forth. It is rare, indeed, that a sentence fails to conform to some one of these types, even in the most complicated construction. Here are a few of the characteristic English sentence orders.

1. Article—adjective word—noun—adjective phrase—adjective clause: *the young farmer of Centerville, who was now thirty years old.*

2. Relative pronoun as subject of clause—verb of clause: *the boy who entered.* This follows the basic subject-verb-complement order.

3. Relative pronoun as object of clause—subject of clause –verb of clause: *the book that I asked for.* Here the connective function of *that* has front-shifted it.

4. In interrogative sentences with no interrogative word, auxiliary verb—subject—main verb—complement: *Has George bought the steak?* Compare the French *George has he bought the steak?* and the German *Has George the steak bought?* In each case a small change in order is introduced to show the interrogative nature of the sentence.

5. In interrogative sentences with an interrogative adverb, first the interrogative adverb—auxiliary verb—subject—main verb —complement: *When did he buy the steak?*

6. In interrogative sentences with an interrogative pronoun as subject, the ordinary sentence order is followed: *Who bought the steak?*

7. In interrogative sentences with an interrogative pronoun as complement, complement—auxiliary verb—subject—main verb: *What did he read?*

8. In exclamatory sentences with *what, what*—article—adjective—complement—subject—verb: *What a good cook she is!*

9. In exclamatory sentences with *how, how*—predicate adjective—subject—verb: *How cold it is!*

10. If there is no predicate adjective the exclamatory order may be *how*—adverb—subject—verb—complement: *How well he knows his lesson!*

11. In prepositional phrases, preposition—article—adjective word—object of preposition—adjective phrase—adjective clause: *in an old manuscript of my grandfather's, which was discovered recently.*

12. Verb—indirect object without preposition—direct object: *gave Bill the book; asked me a question.*

13. Verb—direct object—indirect object with preposition: *gave the book to Bill; asked a question of me.*

All these orders, and many more which might be added, are standard and fixed in English. They represent the beaten path of humdrum expression. They are to be encountered in 99 percent of all sentences spoken or written. And it is from them that escape, in sentence order, is occasionally attempted. Such escape sometimes consists of employing free words, words whose place in the sentence is not fixed. There are very few words in English which are even partly free, and the vocative is typical of them. In the imperative sentence *Go down to the store for a pound of butter,* the vocative *Ellen* may be placed either at the beginning or at the end of the sentence, or, less plausibly, after *go* or *store.* In *Well now, tell us the whole story,* the vocative cannot go at the beginning, but will fit after *now, story,* or, less neatly, *us.* The vocative is thus not so much a free word as one having alternative positions within the sentence.

Some adverbs share this modicum of freedom. While the adverb *not* is fixed, between parts of the verb phrase or after the verb *to be, never* may precede the verb (*He never did that*), poetically follow the object (*He did that never*), or, with an inversion, begin the sentence (*Never did he do that*). And *homeward* in *They turned their steps homeward,* while fixed for practical purposes as a last word, may with a slightly poetical flavor be placed initially or after *they* or *turned*.

A few word adjectives may or must be placed after the noun, but this does not make them free words, only exceptions to Rule 1, above: *bread enough, life everlasting, choir invisible, nothing whatever, anyone else.* It is interesting to see that the last of these combinations has become so firmly welded together that it takes the possessive inflexion in the adjective rather than in the pronoun: *anyone else's book.*

Now and then an exclamatory sentence contravenes Rule 8 by placing the verb before the subject: *What a good dinner is this!* This order, however, is felt to be poetical. And in connection with certain words Rule 8 establishes an order according to which an adjective may precede rather than follow the article *a: what a pity, such a crime, many a man.* These, however, are not free orders so much as fixed exceptions.

Occasionally, for variety or for emphasis (see Chapter Seventeen), the subject-verb-complement order is altered. Ordinarily this is done by means of an adverb (often *here* or *there*), a prepositional phrase, or a simple inversion. *There went Harry; Here comes Jane; In the drawer lay the purse;* and *This farmer the government forgot.*

Even the interrogative order may be altered if the verb is *to be,* which still clings to the verb-shifted order of four centuries ago rather than the auxiliary-shifted order of today: *Is this your book? Was the boy Jim? Has* and *had* sometimes have the same order as *is: Has he any money? Had he the car when you saw him?*

Altogether we find variety coupled with rigidity in English sentence-order patterns. The rules are not so simple or so uniform as to be uninteresting. Most people to whom English is a mother-tongue absorb them unconsciously and follow them without ever thinking them out.

On the other hand, escape from this beaten path of sentence order is very difficult. Even a slight divergence will attract attention. Such divergence is now and then practiced in the periodical *Time,* in phrasings such as "Shelved was a scenario," "Spread Eagle she did over," and "Hush-hushed was the effect." [1] This divergence from standard sentence order as practiced by *Time* has not been widely imitated. Speakers and writers of English are, like it or not, held in a mold of sentence order from which they can escape only under penalty of incurring that most undesirable of epithets—queer.

ESCAPE IN GRAMMAR

So-called bad or incorrect grammar may constitute an escape from the dead level of standard English. One small boy of our acquaintance insists that he prefers *like* (for *as*) and *ain't got no* because they sound nicer and are "different" from the ordinary speech of his Olympians. In the same way, Hyman Kaplan and Florian Slappey achieve a humor beyond and above the humor of situation, through the astonishing way in which they treat English vowels, consonants, and syntax.

For the reader or speaker such escape is in the nature of comedy-romance. Bad English may, however, hold within it elements of tragedy when it is indulged at the wrong places. Either sort of indulgence may be escape, but the type of escape will depend on the individual outlook.

And on the other hand, to the illiterate or semiliterate speaker good English stands as a heaven to which he aspires and toward which he labors. It gives him a goal for which to work; these aspirations enrich his life and lift it out of the realm of the commonplace and the trivial. Probably most simple minds view good English as a realm of culture inhabited by superior beings.

---

[1] *Time,* issue of February 12, 1940. This is only one of the linguistic innovations made by *Time,* which also omits articles, coins words such as *cinemactor* (*movie actor*), and short-cuts generally. It is a question whether *Time's* linguistic experimentation has increased its circulation, although it has certainly brought publicity. Ordinarily the linguistic tastes of readers are likely to be conservative.

Grammar, like sentence order, is full of rigidities. There is ordinarily one way, and only one, which must be followed in uttering a given construction. Free choice, such as the choice between omitting or retaining *whom* in *the girl (whom) I met,* is rare. English grammar in general is very much a beaten path out of which one must not stray.

The English language compensates for this fact, however, in part at least, by offering many choices of wording for saying one thing. Not only does English offer a wide variety of synonyms or semisynonyms for particular words; it offers many alternative choices of construction.

Take, for example, the simple sentence, *John got to work.* One can readily construct at least ten other ways of saying the same thing.

1. John began working.
2. John started his task.
3. John commenced toiling.
4. The job was now undertaken by John.
5. A beginning of work was now made by John.
6. The task began to melt away in the heat of John's endeavor.
7. Well begun characterized John's start on his job.
8. Industry now became John's watchword.
9. John's hands now began to move.
10. The long struggle between John and job was joined.

It would be a fascinating task to analyze minutely the differences between the literary and other linguistic values which distinguish these and other possible ways of saying the same thing. The sentence *John got to work* is at once simplest and most direct, while the eighth is the most generalized and vague. The sixth attempts some sort of image, the ninth visualizes the working process, while the tenth approaches the facetious. The fourth and fifth, which are passive constructions, sound clumsy and dull.

These sentences illustrate the possibilities for escape from the commonplace way of saying a thing, according to the predilections of the speaker. Which type of expression he chooses will determine the quality of his result. In a famous chapter called "Jargon," in his book *On the Art of Writing,* Sir Arthur Quiller-Couch states the case against expression involving verbiage and pleads for direct, vivid, concrete English. It must be admitted that such English is very rare. Written and spoken expression is full of more or less meaningless clichés, for example, *under these circumstances, along these lines, in this connection, in this field,* and so on endlessly. We do not altogether share Quiller-Couch's dislike of such expressions. They may come upon reader or listener with a comfortable sense of normality, tiding over his attention between one idea and the next, whereas speech which is always vivid and concrete might offer too concentrated a diet for human consumption. Perhaps the English language, like the human stomach, can use what is called roughage.[2]

ADVERTISING AND ESCAPE

The language of advertising, to which reference has already been made in other connections, is essentially a language of escape—almost always escape of the comedy-romance sort, although the tragedy note is not entirely absent, for example, in persuasions in favor of dentifrices, mouthwashes, and deodorants. Even tragedy, however, must be followed by a happy ending, according to the artists who call our attention to these products.

Rhetoricians have too often adopted a distinctly supercilious attitude toward advertising English. One authority lists specific advertising terms, such as *beautician* and *shoe-conscious,* as expressions which are to be avoided by careful speakers. Even idioms like *to put a deal over* and *to contact the key man* are frowned upon by educators. The pretentiousness which calls a floorwalker *a section manager* and a nightgown *sleepwear* is to such experts unjustified and crude.

A psychological approach leads to no such lofty and critical position. The masses of the people want and perhaps need escape. They get tired of saying things literally, tired of calling a spade a spade and a real estate agent an agent. They want to be dazzled, and dazzling is what they get in the advertiser's world, where all misses are smart, all men distinguished, and all life exciting. In advertisements magic is still possible, and one may give a confident "yes" to questions like "Do you want your complexion to

[2] See also Chapter Nineteen.

look divinely fair?" and "Would you enjoy this mellow moment?" The advertiser is selling more than goods; his words form one of the great media of escape for the average person caught in the squirrel cage of modern civilization; and it would seem ill done if the advertiser's raptures should be quenched by the self-appointed guardians of the English language.

When the advertising method and aims are taken over by the government, however, a more difficult problem arises. Modern politics has by no means eschewed the advertiser's weakness for making his product look romantic and salubrious, whether it is or not; and there is a whole list of recent titles and phrases, from *preparedness* to *home relief,* which if analyzed closely will be found to be of an advertising rather than of a humdrum nature. It remains to be seen whether glamour and politics form a good combination; to the conservative mind it may seem that the proper view of government should be as commonplace as possible [3] and that spellbinding is a dictator's weapon.

Politicians are given to coining phrases such as *Square Deal, New Deal, Good Society, Coöperative Commonwealth* to describe their utopias. There are also many political synonyms for the under dog—*The Forgotten Man, The Underprivileged, The Client* (in relief bureaus). Introducing *the Forgotten Man* to *the Good Society* is the politician's province, and if he favors his job he will never admit that he does not know precisely how this may be done or hesitate to do it.

Recently many studies of propaganda have been made, but none of a purely linguistic nature. Yet propaganda works almost exclusively by words and employs typically the two escapes already defined in this chapter. On the one hand is the tragedy of things as they are; on the other the joy of things as they might be. Apparently the safe way for the individual is to distrust both linguistic methods and cling to his commonplaces. If he can learn to see how much better conditions are than they might have been,

[3] News note: "William F. Gailing, Chicago Republican candidate, appeared on the street (February, 1940) in a full suit of armor, promising to 'rescue the First Ward from politics.' Perhaps Mr. Gailing has at last succeeded in making advertising subservient to the humdrum."

how much worse they might become than they are, he has done his bit in neutralizing propaganda.

In this chapter we have tried to suggest a few of the opportunities for the study of humdrum and escape in the English language, but no one could be more conscious than we of the inadequacy of so brief a treatment of so vast a theme. We can but hope that these few hints may stimulate broader research and investigation.

It would be a useful public service and a desirable benefaction from some public-spirited man of wealth, if a foundation could be established to investigate escape coinages and usages in the English language. Such a body would watch for new phrases, words, and constructions and would then analyze them psychologically to show their associations, their implications, and the facts actually basing them. Such phrases as *share-the-wealth, home-owners-loan, and favorable balance of trade* would be profitable items for analysis. It is to be hoped that a Word Analysis Foundation may one day be a reality.

The ultimate in public education would be to change the average man's picture of life from the one described at the beginning of this chapter to a view which embraces the commonplace and delights in its infinite possibilities and opportunities for interest. Such a world is not yet reflected in the English language.

ARROGANCE AND THE DESIRE
TO IMPRESS

THE CONSULTING PSYCHOLOGISTS of the present day are given to advising their clients to cultivate self-confidence and the attitude which will command success. While they may occasionally warn against arrogance or an unpleasant aggressiveness, such warnings are very likely to be drowned out by the chorus of warnings against timidity, self-consciousness, and knuckling under.

Impressiveness is a frequently desired end in the English language as in life, and impressiveness may be achieved in any of various ways. Dullness itself is occasionally impressive; emphasis is impressive; length is impressive. And on the other hand, brevity, casualness, and wit have their share of the ability to attract attention and admiration.

THE IMPRESSIVE PRONOUNS

Ever since Omar Khayyam, as translated by Edward Fitzgerald, said "myself when young did eagerly frequent," rhetoricians have been striving to undermine the beauty of the line by pointing out that it is not good English to use the form *myself* as the subject of a sentence. Still one must admit that there is impressiveness about *myself*. To say, as many under-cultivated speakers do, *Bob and myself* went to the play is underlining the first person pronoun and giving it more of an impact. Bad English or not, this use of *myself* has its effect in swelling personal pride.[1]

[1] The sentence *Yourself and your guests are invited* was labeled "disputable" (No. 146) by the Leonard Survey linguists, while *They invited my friends and myself* was marked "established English" (No. 91).

The first person pronoun itself has undergone some weakening since the Anglo-Saxon period of English, when it was a two letter word *ic,* perhaps similar in pronunciation to the Modern German pronoun *ich.* This Old English pronoun survived in dialect to Shakespeare's time; in *King Lear* is to be found the form "Cham" for *I am (ich am).* It may even possibly survive today in rustic English dialect. Standard English, however, has weakened the pronoun to a single vowel, which often becomes very light in pronunciation and frequently is entirely omitted in conversational or epistolary use: *Went downtown today and had lunch with Evans.*

This weakening of the first person pronoun results in the opposite of impressiveness, although the very frequent use of *I* in letters and other documents indicates the widespread possession of a sense of self-importance. According to an investigation of words used in telephone conversations [2] the pronoun *I* was much the most frequent word, occurring 3,990 times, or 450 more than its nearest competitor, the pronoun *you.*

The history of pronoun development shows a tendency to emphasize the nominative case, particularly in relation to the pronoun *I.* Forms like *methinks* and *meseems,* common some centuries ago, have both been discarded in favor of *I think.* Where first-person cases are used erroneously, it is probably more usual to find *I* substituted for *me (between you and I, Give it to John and I)* than vice versa.

There are further ways of making the first person pronoun impressive. One is the royal or editorial *we,* which is fairly common even yet, despite expert disapproval, as the substitute for the singular form *I.* Other substitutes for *I,* that is, *the author, the present writer, the investigator, your committee,* and so forth, are evasions designed to impress. Although frowned upon by various authorities, they still have a fairly wide currency.

With regard to the second person pronoun, impressiveness has perhaps been served by pushing this second person further away

[2] *The Words and Sounds of Telephone Conversations,* by N. R. French, C. W. Carter, Jr., and Walter Koenig, Jr., American Telephone and Telegraph Company, Monograph B-491 of the Bell Telephone System, June 1930.

from the speaker or writer. The intimate singular forms *thou* and *thee* have been dropped altogether in favor of the originally plural *you*, which was the dative, later the accusative, of the second person pronoun. Thus a formerly oblique usage has become standardized in a way very different from the forms used for the first person.

There is an interesting similarity between this use of the plural *you* for the singular in the second person, and the frequent use of *they* for the singular in the third person. Often, when the speaker does not know whether to use the masculine or the feminine, this plural *they* will be used, as in *"You just had a telephone call." "Did they leave any message?"* This dialogue, marked as established English by the Leonard Survey linguists (No. 31), illustrates this frequent use of *they* as common gender.

THE IMPRESSIVE PASSIVE

At the beginning of this chapter it was suggested that dullness is impressive, and later the first person pronoun and its substitutes were considered. One very frequent substitute for the first person pronoun is the passive voice; instead of saying *In this book I have analyzed verbs* the author may say *Verbs have been analyzed in this book*. Since the passive is thus so closely related to our topic, it may be well to consider it briefly from the historical aspect.

Anglo-Saxon, or Old English, had only one independently developed voice, the active. An inflected passive, called the medial passive, which had existed in the older language and was still to some extent preserved in Gothic, bequeathed only a single verb form to Anglo-Saxon, *hātte,* meaning *He was called,* and appearing in archaic Modern English in its participial form *hight* (*A man hight John*). With the exception of this verb, the Old English passive was formed by means of the auxiliary verbs *bēon* (*to be*), *wesan* (past of *to be*), and more rarely *weorþan* (*to be or become*).

This passive voice has been in use continuously since Anglo-Saxon times, except that the auxiliary has been narrowed to the verb *to be*. It is freely used in Middle English, and even more freely in our modern speech.

It is perhaps a question whether the word *voice* is accurately descriptive of the difference between the active and the passive. Jespersen in his *Philosophy of Grammar* [3] suggests that it might better be called the passive *turn,* since it looks at an action from a different aspect, with the subject and object of the verb turned around.

As just mentioned, the passive is frequently employed to avoid the necessity of using the pronoun *I*. It represents a sort of false modesty, which emphasizes the speaker by means of circumlocution. This passive usage is therefore a good example of linguistic arrogance or desire to impress.

In its modern uses the passive fails to present an impression of swift action or vividness. It is the staple of the report, the research monograph, and the catalogue. Many teachers of correct writing advise against the use of the passive, telling students to choose the active voice as being more interesting and lively. Such instruction, however, has not greatly affected the extent to which passives are used; there must be something impressive about the mere dullness of these verb constructions which gives them their wide currency.

ARROGANCE TOWARD THE FOREIGNER

In all languages certain words have tended to acquire unpleasant meanings, just because of the arrogance of the people using them. Our verb *welsh* has a history interesting in this respect. In early Anglo-Saxon it was a noun applied by the invading Teutons to their Celtic victims; it was spelled *wealh*. Because the Germans were not familiar with these Celts, the word acquired the general meaning *stranger;* and because the Celts were enslaved, it took on the meaning *servant*. In the Anglo-Saxon of Alfred's time the word has the meaning *foreigner, stranger, slave, Briton,* and *Welshman*.

But the arrogance of the conquerors was not to stop there. Gradually the generalized meaning dropped out, and the racial

[3] New York, Holt, 1924.

meaning alone survived; but at some later time in the history of the English language, when Welsh revolts and revolutions caused bad feeling between them and the English, the word *welsh* acquired a verbal meaning given as follows in *Webster's Dictionary:* "to cheat by avoiding payment of debts; to avoid dishonorably the fulfillment of any obligation." Thus the English language reflects the superior attitude of the English people toward a neighboring community, an attitude which, it need scarcely be said, is quite unjustified by the Welsh character.

The word *barbarian* itself reflects a similar attitude, not on the part of the English, but of the Greeks. In early Greek the word *barbaros* meant simply *stranger* or *foreigner,* but very soon it took on the unpleasant meanings it has preserved. Another instance is *outlandish,* with its derogatory meaning.

On the other hand, with the inconsistency characteristic of human nature, things foreign often contribute toward a sense of impressiveness. Far from regarding people of other nations as outlandish or stupid, people often look upon travel and the acquaintance with other cultures as a mark of superiority. There is a distinct tendency toward the overuse of foreign words and phrases, such as *entre nous, faux pas, nouveau riche, terra firma, sub rosa,* and so forth, with the aim of impressing the reader or listener. Some rhetoricians advise against the employment of such foreign words and phrases, recommending that the person speaking or writing English stick to the English language.

Closely allied to this inclination to use foreign words and phrases is the habit of using technical words because of their power to impress. Any specialist, even one of very minor ability, can easily familiarize himself with the patter of his speciality; and such familiarity is frequently an excellent stock in trade, if it is not overworked. One good technical term unfamiliar to the reader and listener will convince him that the specialist is indeed an expert. Too many, to be sure, will baffle him; and so it is a good rule to use such technical terms sparingly. However, to avoid them altogether, as some authorities recommend, would be to display undue modesty and to run the risk of having one's ability underestimated.

THE IMPRESSIVE STYLE

But it is not alone the technician who by using superior words can convince people of his standing. In journalism, up to and perhaps including the present time, there has been a distinct dialect which has been named journalese. Fights were, not fights, but *fistic encounters,* and football heroes were *the gladiators of the gridiron* or *warriors of the pigskin.* Language was inflated, sometimes to absurd dimensions, perhaps partly to fill space, but certainly in large measure to impress the average reader of the paper. The style and technique of journalese have altered in recent years, but probably journalese itself is still active. Today the sports writer is likely to invent terms of his own for the details of his stories, synonyms for *defeat, knock out, ball,* and *player;* but these synonyms are not likely to be quite as pompous as the terms of twenty years ago. Journalese, in short, has simplified itself; but almost anyone scanning the public prints will agree that it is still journalese.[4]

In private life "high-flown" language has traditionally been used to achieve the same effect of elegance and impressiveness. Elegant language was at its height in the Victorian period, and Sir William S. Gilbert in his operas frequently pokes fun at it, as does also Mark Twain, particularly in the famous descriptive passage concerning the school commencement exercises. The climax of high-flown language is a poem by a young lady in which the French word *tête* is used in place of the English word *head.*

Such language is less current today than it was eighty years ago; but impressiveness in today's language is still current, as when *superintendent* takes the place of *janitor,* and *beautician, cosmetician,* and *mortician* come to be current usage. The fashion of the day seems to oppose much inflated language, but the opposition has not yet been made effective.

A minor type of inflated writing is the use of archaic words. A certain sort of individual, when asked to go for a walk or to

---

[4] Another example is the alliterative phrase for boxing coined by the late Bill McGeehan of the New York *Herald-Tribune:* "the manly art of modified murder."

the theater, will reply, "Yea, verily." The same sort of individual will use words such as *mayhap, oft, in sooth,* partly as facetious humor, but also partly for the sake of being impressive. It need scarcely be added that the use of archaic terms is frowned upon by the rhetorical authorities.

MISCELLANEOUS EXAMPLES

In the field of English spelling there is one odd little instance of what may be called arrogant usage. When an ordinary noun ending with a consonant plus *y* is pluralized, a regular rule is that the *y* changes to *i* and *es* is added. Examples are *sky, skies; country, countries; berry, berries.* When, however, the word ending in *y* is a proper name, it retains its individuality and adds the *s* directly to the terminal *y*. Thus the plural of *Mary* is *Marys,* of *Lucy, Lucys,* and *Beatty, Beattys.* It is obvious that the reason for the difference in the pluralization of proper nouns and common nouns ending in *y* is that the proper nouns may retain their individuality and superiority to the common nouns.

Impressiveness may appear in mathematical and legal English. Thus *50 percent* sounds better than *a half,* and when used with *hundred* or *thousand one* sounds better than *a. Free and clear* is much more noteworthy than *unmortgaged,* and many legal terms, such as *convey, devise,* and *subpoena,* are calculated to draw favorable attention. In *The Heart of Midlothian* Sir Walter Scott presents a character, Mr. Saddletree, who exploits legal Latin for this purpose.

The past participle *proven,* which is so frequently substituted for the "correct" past participle *proved,* is a minor instance of the same sort. *Proven* sounds somehow more legalistic than *proved,* and its frequent use seems to be based on the fact of its greater impressiveness. The legal background adds to this impressiveness and is a part of the reason for the popular use of *proven.*

In general, careful or even meticulous grammer is calculated to win admiration. This is especially apparent in the various English constructions known technically as "splits." The split infinitive, while the most publicized of these splits, is only one among many. There are in addition the split comparison, the split prepositional phrase, the split verb phrase, and the split subject and predicate. Examples follow.

1. Split infinitive: I wish to clearly understand you.
2. Split comparison: She was as clever in all her school work as her sister.
3. Split prepositional phrase: He went to, though he did not much enjoy, the party.
4. Split verb phrase: That boy will always and on every occasion do his duty.
5. Split subject and predicate: He, instead of helping me, hindered me.

The split infinitive has been the subject of very wide controversy, and today the rules seem to be undergoing a process of liberalization, so that split infinitives are allowed in most publishing offices. In sentences such as *We can expect the mayor to at least protect our interests* a split infinitive is almost inevitable, since putting *at least* in any other position would give a different meaning from the one intended by the sentence as it now stands. The unsplit infinitive, however, is frequently impressive. Sentences such as *He was able partially to repair the brake* sounds erudite and imposing. There can be little doubt that those few speakers and writers who actually avoid the split infinitive get great satisfaction out of the effect of their avoidances of it.

The other splits are less noticed by the grammarians and are perhaps less important. The adverb *not* always splits a verb phrase, and certain other adverbs regularly are placed between parts of a verb. Unless this adverbial element is very long or otherwise awkward, there is no reason why it should not be used; and the same thing is true for the other split constructions.

SUBJUNCTIVE AND GERUND

According to various authorities the subjunctive mood is disappearing from English usage, especially in England. This subjunctive mood is of old standing; it was already English in the Anglo-Saxon period. As an expression of doubt, desire, condition or concession contrary to fact, indirect imperative, and so forth it has been more commonly used than it is today, when the tendency is strongly to get rid of little and unnecessary inflexional elements.

In *if* clauses the subjunctive is probably disappearing in Modern English. One hears people say freely *if it was summer, if they are here, if summer comes* (rather than *come*). After *as if* and *as though*, also, the indicative is likely to be heard: *He speaks as though he was well educated*. About the only place where the subjunctive is still retained is in sentences such as *I insist that he be called* and *Resolved, that he be called* and, occasionally, *If I were you, I would do it*. By and large, the subjunctive is a disappearing mood, and it is possible that before many years it will be entirely eliminated from the English language.

On the other hand, the very scarcity and preciousness of the subjunctive make it appeal to those who want their speech to be different and striking. A few writers are careful to use the subjunctive whenever it is possible to do so, and a smaller number of speakers have the same predilection. In the subjunctive it is as though grammar leant over backward to be dignified and pompous; and some of this dignity is imparted to the users of the construction.

A like prestige attaches to the individual who observes grammatical tastes and distinctions regarding the gerund and the proper case to use with it. According to the authorities the possessive case is the proper one to use in connection with a gerund: *What was the reason for his* (or *Henry's*) *asking that question?* As a matter of fact the possessive of a noun preceding the gerund is extremely rare in actual usage. It is normal to write *He was pleased over his friend George Baker lending him the money*, rather than to put an *'s* on *friend* or *Baker*. With a name or a common noun the possessive construction with the gerund is almost unknown.[5]

For the pronoun there is slightly more of a tendency to use the possessive case. To say *We talked about him leaving school* rather than *We talked about his leaving school* would seem a little awkward. It is easy to choose the possessive rather than the objective form of the pronoun, and this is frequently done, although by no means universally.

[5] The Leonard Survey linguists list as established English (No. 95) the sentence *What was the reason for Bennett making that disturbance?* In studies made by C. C. Fries it was found that the possessive is used in approximately half of the constructions involving pronouns and almost never in constructions involving nouns.

For both the noun and the pronoun impressiveness demands the possessive, and one may find writers and speakers leaning backward to be correct with regard to both these grammatical constructions. One authority liberalizes the rule, permitting the objective case before the gerund where the substantive has no possessive (for example, the pronoun *any*), when the pronoun is separated from the gerund by modifiers or appositives, and when the act is uppermost in mind. Examples are: *I didn't hear of any of them objecting* and *It was they, the celebrants, turning in an alarm which led to their arrest.*

In actual practice such rules are not very much good. The possessive or objective will be chosen, not so much on the basis of rules, as according to whether or not the speaker desires to make his English meticulous and impressive. Much the same thing might be said for all good and bad grammar. Bad grammar has certain striking aspects; good grammar has others just as striking. In general it will be the tendency to choose good grammar for the purpose of impressing the reader or hearer, since bad grammar is likely to recoil upon its user.

English literature is full of characters who use English grammar and the English language for purposes of impressing. The immortal Pecksniff in Dickens's *Martin Chuzzlewit* is a case in point, as is the exquisite thumbnail sketch of Osric in *Hamlet*. Even Sheridan's Mrs. Malaprop no doubt thought she was being impressive with her "nice derangement of epitaphs."

It must not be concluded from the foregoing analysis that impressiveness is always allied to arrogance and unpleasantness. Much of the desire to impress may arise from worthy motives— a laudable ambition to get ahead, the desire for self-confidence, and so forth. While the English language is ready to serve those portentous and dominant minds who aspire to dictatorship, it is also ready to serve a proper self-appreciation which merely wishes to cultivate a little of the formidable in order to protect itself against possible trouble. We have tried to suggest a few of the ways by which the English language permits this to be accomplished.

MODESTY AND POLITENESS

I F THE QUESTION is asked whether modesty or its opposite is more generally practiced in the world today, it will be almost impossible to get an unbiased answer. This is because of the fact that one blatant, pushing person makes more of an impression than four or five modest, restrained individuals. And this fact brings it about that most observers would probably describe the "average person" as containing a large proportion of forwardness and selfishness.

Chapter Fifteen gave numerous examples of English grammatical usage which is calculated to impress the reader or to convey a sense of domination or aggressiveness. Yet it would be wrong to conclude from these examples that the English language justifies the view of the average person just suggested. On the contrary, such indications as we can find point to the conclusion that the average person speaking English is modest and self-effacing, often even to the point of timidity.

There are, however, naturally enough, more specific examples of aggressiveness in English than of its opposite. This is because modesty leads one to follow in the beaten path of language, while impressiveness will draw one out of it. We shall, however, be able to find considerable evidence on the side of modesty. Aggressiveness in language is not so characteristic as the number and variety of its manifestations might imply.

THE MODEST IMPERATIVE

The imperative mood is of long standing in English and all the other Germanic and Indo-European languages. In Old English (as in Modern English) the imperative was found only in the present tense; but there it had two forms, one for the singular and one for the plural. The plural imperative survived down to the Middle English times, when it disappeared; so that it is the singular imperative from which our modern form is derived.

In Old English there is very little substitution or circumlocution in connection with imperative constructions. When a command or a request was to be made, the imperative was used. This condition, however, began to change in Middle English, perhaps under French influence, which leant toward a courtly style. And today it is changed out of all recognition.

The simple imperative might be called rare or unusual usage in present-day English grammar. People do not issue commands, but rather make requests. While of course customs may differ in various classes of society and in different countries and types of government, still it is true that the average person who speaks English is more likely to use a circumlocution than to issue a direct command.

Suppose a person, an "average person" in the United States, wants someone to shut the window. The wording of the request will scarcely be *Shut the window,* unless the speaker is uncommonly disagreeable or overbearing. A much more likely wording will be *Will you please shut the window?* or *Would you mind shutting the window?* [1]

It is really surprising how many ways there are of putting a request so as not to offend or affront the recipient. It might be interesting to list some of the variations on the theme *Close the door.*

1. Please (to) close the door.
2. Do close the door.
3. Would you mind closing the door?
4. Will (would) you please close the door?
5. Could you close the door, please?
6. Would(n't) you like to close the door for me?

---

[1] It is noticeable that the latter wording may be answered by either *yes* or *no* (*No, I would not mind* or *Yes, I'll shut the window*) and still mean that the hearer will perform the task.

7. Won't you close the door? [2]
8. Do you want to close the door?
9. Would you care to close the door?
10. Might I ask you to close the door?
11. Let me beg of you to close the door.
12. May I ask you to close the door?
13. I should (would) be glad if you would close the door.
14. Please do me the favor of closing the door.
15. May I trouble you to close the door?
16. Let me request you to close the door.
17. Close the door, if you please.
18. I would (should) like you to close the door.
19. May I suggest your closing the door?
20. Would it be too much to ask you to close the door?
21. Would you be good (kind) enough to close the door?

These varied expressions are not uncommon. Taken together, they are undoubtedly far more frequent than the simple imperative; and they show clearly the temper of the average person, which is not dictatorial or overbearing, but friendly and democratic.

But there is more of interest to be found in this list of near-imperatives, since here we actually find modesty used to distinguish the "past" and "present" tenses, without any time distinction entering. This distinction is shown in the tenth and twelfth examples, whose only difference in wording is in the use of *may* and *might*. Obviously *may* and *might* are not used here to express a time distinction; the difference between them is simply that *might* gives an impression of greater courtesy and modesty than *may*.

Precisely the same difference separates *will* in requests (*Will you close the door?*) from *would* (*Would you close the door?*). Here we have again a use of the "past tense" of will to express, not past time, but greater restraint and politeness in making a request.[3] And *can* and *could* might be substituted in these examples with a like difference between them.

[2] The use of the negative in such requests is curious and is allied to some of the constructions discussed on p. 158. See also p. 77.

[3] Frequently obligation rather than time separates *shall* and *should*. Compare *You shall go* with *You should go*. The first shows compulsion; the second duty.

In the twenty-one examples of modest request it will be noted that the question form is very frequent. Requests may be expressed in interrogative, declarative, or imperative styles, and it would even be possible to make such requests in the exclamatory form (*How happy I should be if you would close the door!*) (*What a favor it would be if you'd close the door!*)

It is noticeable also that, not one, but several auxiliaries (*may, can, will, do, let*) are used for this construction. The modest imperative is comparable to the future construction (see page 107) in the variety of forms which may be used to express it. A request may be couched in an almost endless variety of ways, and those given here are only samples of the imperative-equivalent.

It is an odd fact, also, that of all our examples of modest requests, the form using *good* or *kind* (*Would you be kind enough to close the door?*) is one of the least pleasant in its effect. It is not entirely clear how this fact should be interpreted, unless it may be that *good* and *kind* are words into whose use hypocrisy may readily enter, and for this reason the impression they leave is less than their face value. Many people would consider it something of an insult to be called "good-hearted," and the imperative-equivalent with *good* or *kind* is an expression of the same order.

Finally, it is worth noticing that this list of twenty-one forms, with their innumerable variations, will be found used most frequently in talk between equals. In dealing with children (*Close the door, dear*) and servants (*Close the door, Evalinda*) the simple imperative is very much more frequent, and it is noticeable that this simple imperative is thus used today under the same social conditions which three centuries ago called forth the use of the singular second-person pronoun *thou*. *Thou* has disappeared from English, and there is a real possibility that the simple imperative may disappear in the same way. It is quite possible that there will be no imperative mood in English three centuries hence.

Time distinctions seldom operate in *may, can, shall,* and *will* as compared to *might, could, should* and *would*. See Chapter Twenty-two on problems of time.

MODESTY OF ADDRESS

And the observation just made, that courtesy and modesty in making requests will be found oftenest among people in a condition of social equality, leads directly into the understanding of our next example of modesty and courtesy in grammar. This next exemplification is drawn from the conventions of polite address. Manifestly, the way people address each other is some measure of their gentility.

In all languages and in all countries the conventions of proper address are numerous. A married lady must be called this, an unmarried lady that, and a gentleman something else. Now the second person singular is to be used, now the plural, and again the third person. Often even the occupation of the person addressed or of her husband will be incorporated: *Will Mrs. Councillor Schmidt have some tea?*

In France revolution once made a difference, and while revolution did not last, still today the universally used *madame* and *monsieur* may be in some measure a heritage from the liberty, equality, and fraternity of 1789. Address in France is not simple or entirely democratic; the distinction between the singular and plural pronouns in the second person is still maintained, and there are other niceties of usage which contravene strict equality. Communist Russia, with its sexless and universal *Comrade,* has gone further, although of course it remains to be seen whether this *Comrade* will persist as a part of Russian speech or be modified as the French *Citoyen* was modified.

Of the other modern nations, probably Sweden is saddled with the most conventional and the most complicated system of rules for polite address. The second person pronoun is seldom used; the third person pronoun is so much more polite. Distinctions of occupation, sex, marital status, and age are embedded in the welter of forms which the Swedes use in addressing other people.

It would not be fair, however, to assert that Swedish is necessarily a more courteous tongue than English. The rules of address in Sweden may simply be the perpetuation of class and other distinctions in such a way as to defer or even to prevent true democracy. Let us see how the situation stands in English and what deductions we can make here.

The loss of the second-person singular pronoun *thou* has already been mentioned (page 54). This singular form was used under circumstances of great intimacy, to children, and particularly to inferiors, or to show scorn and superiority. It was this last use of *thou* which marked it for elimination. As Englishmen increased in self-restraint and courtesy, this truculent form *thou* fell into disuse, while the more courteous *you* survived for both persons and sexes and for all classes and conditions of mankind.

The pronoun *you* is thus purely democratic in its use in Modern English. Nevertheless there are plenty of discrepancies in other aspects of polite address. Thus we have the distinction between *Miss* and *Mrs.* according as a lady is unmarried or married. A married lady must be addressed by her husband's name if he is living, according to a rule which common sense has not yet succeeded in dislodging. Neither a married nor an unmarried lady may be addressed without her title (*Dickinson, Austen*), although the use of the first and last names together (*Emily Dickinson, Jane Austen*) forms an allowable substitute for the use of *Miss*.[4]

Several students of the English language have commented on the fact that English does not take kindly to diminutives as do some other languages, Italian, Spanish, and Russian, for example. Intimate language in English is not very different from language of a formal sort; in general English grammar has been approaching a single standard in its rules for address, and it certainly seems apparent that this is the most courteous and modest plan to follow. The moment distinctions in address are made, someone is disregarded even while someone else is exalted; and this sets up artificial barriers and unnecessary distinctions.

MODESTY IN STYLE

In Chapter Fifteen we described a number of the expedients which might be used to lend impressiveness to literary style.

[4] Some months ago the authors received an anonymous mimeographed letter suggesting that *Ms* (pronounced *Miss*) be used with all feminine names as a title.

Among them are the use of archaic or obsolete expressions; the use of slang, or, *per contra,* excessively good grammar; and the use of dullness, particularly evidenced by the passive construction. The journalistic style, the impressive use of foreign phrases, the retention of the subjunctive mood were given as examples of the attempt to command the reader's attention and admiration.

But by and large such devices are rarely employed. It is uncommon to find an author indulging blatantly in reader-catching tricks. Pick up a magazine or open a book, and ten to one you will find a page of simple, modest English, forming a clear transparency for the ideas to shine through, an English which does not call attention to itself by using devices such as those mentioned.[5]

Indeed, it has often been observed that the very quality desired by the writer, impressiveness, is best attained with great economy of means, so that just a few touches of archaisms, foreignisms and what not are much better than many. A good example of this economy of means is found in *The Rime of the Ancient Mariner,* which gains its old-world, supernatural atmosphere, not by the lavish use of archaic words, but by carefully and casually planting here an *eftsoons* and there a *gramercy,* and filling the intervals with the simplest and most timeless English. Evidently the best formula for impressiveness is modesty in all but a few excursions into the unusual; and this indicates how much modesty bulks in proportion to literary exhibitionism.

To return to the observation at the beginning of this chapter, it is certain that one mistake or divergence from the normal will stand out in far more than its proper proportion; and this explains the fact that much prose seems to be straining for effect, when in reality it is only a few words or phrases which are properly to be so described.

Modesty in literary style is seen also in the frequent use of questions, particularly in expository writing. Every writer of ar-

---

One might suggest that an even better idea would be to make *M* (pronounced *Em*) a general human title, thus dropping the unnecessary distinction of sex. One is not quite sure what this *M* would stand for, as an abbreviation, but it might be *mankind.*

[5] The modern stylist Ernest Hemingway achieves his effects in part by the eschewing of complex and compound sentences; but he does not employ the attention-getting tricks described in the foregoing paragraph.

gumentative or affective prose knows the value of the question. It gives the effect of deference to the reader's opinion, of consulting him rather than telling him what to think; and yet if properly phrased it can lead him far more effectively than can the positive and dogmatic statement. A *Can we doubt that* or an *Is it not clear that* has often reinforced a weak argument and won over the reader's sympathies. Whether employed naturally or artificially as a rhetorical device, the courteous and modest character of the question makes it effective.

Questions used in argumentative writing are often rhetorical in their nature, and one authority [6] suggests that they are often used to replace a negative statement, as in the example *Would you do better if you were in my place?* a question which assumes the response, *No.* This example shows very clearly the deferential character of such questions; and their appeal to the reader is no less apparent.

OTHER EXAMPLES

Conversational English in its interrogative forms frequently includes a curious combination of negative and positive, which is likewise of a deferential quality. There may be a statement, positive or negative, and then an auxiliary tag of the opposite type: *James will be there, won't he? He didn't refuse, did he? We're all ready, aren't we?* There is no sort of logic in such negative-positive combinations. They are idiomatic, which is to say that they are not susceptible to rational explanation. However, as used in conversation they involve a considerate attitude toward the hearer's opinions, and hence they fall under the linguistic types treated in this chapter.

In an earlier section of this study (Chapter Eleven) certain adverbs (*only, not, merely,* and so forth) were studied, and their frequently early placing in the sentence was given as an example of anticipation or short-cutting. These adverbs also illustrate modesty in English grammar, since the anticipating of these words is a mark of consideration for the hearer. If the speaker began *I had,* it might imply that some considerable possession was about

[6] G. O. Curme, *op. cit.,* p. 140.

to be mentioned; whereas *I only had* shows, even before this possession is mentioned specifically, that the possession amounts to very little.

The same desire to be clear, the same consideration for the hearer or reader, marks sentences such as *I don't think I'll go.* As formerly noted, beginning the sentence with *I think* would imply a favorable answer, while *I don't think* makes matters plain from the second syllable. Honesty, courtesy, and consideration for others, as well as anticipation, characterize such expressions as these.

In all the history of the English language, of its sounds, inflexions, words, and syntax, the general tendency has been toward simplification, despite minor counter-developments which may be likened to eddies and backwashes in a great flowing stream. This very simplification of English is evidence of the essentially modest character of the human nature of those who speak it; aggressiveness would have led to contrary developments. And it is pleasant to think that this modesty, this trend toward simplification, is duplicated in every other language on earth.[7]

It is said that in Modern English, nine words in their various forms make up 25 percent of all the words used in conversation and writing; and in a study of telephone conversations it was found that the 155 most frequently used words made up 80 percent of the total occurrences.[8] These words are the small change of the language; they are the construction words—pronouns, common prepositions, and auxiliaries. They are distinguished sharply from "content" words in that their chief value is syntactical rather than semantic.

These words are the epitomes of restraint and modesty in English, and it is worth noting that their number and scope have been increasing steadily during the past few centuries. They are among the evidences which point to the essentially modest nature of the "average man."

[7] To be sure, modesty is not the only element involved. Others, such as indolence, are considered elsewhere. Notice also that these statements are subject to the reservations expressed on pages 18–19, as are all the analyses presented in this volume.

[8] *The Words and Sounds of Telephone Conversations,* already cited on p. 142.

IMPATIENCE AND ABBREVIATION

IT MIGHT BE THOUGHT that the material of this chapter would be much the same as that of Chapter Eleven, which dealt with expedition and anticipation as aspects of English grammar; but there is a difference. Here we shall consider, not the human tendency to leap over time into future events, but that impatience which leads to the actual discarding of sounds, syllables, words, and constructions, until the English language has become perceptibly shortened and simplified.

In the Federal penitentiaries a common description of breaking rocks, a task often set the convicts, used to be "making little ones out of big ones." The phrase applies very well to the English language, which has undergone a continuous process of attrition and diminution ever since the earliest times of which we have linguistic knowledge. At the same time that words have been multiplying in numbers, they have been decreasing in size, until individually they are often but small remnants of their former selves. And as we shall see in the course of this chapter, it is not words alone which tend to diminish from one century to the next, but all the machinery of language and grammar.

What are the causes for the abbreviation of words? In part, no doubt, they are mechanical. The strong first-syllable stress of English must have played its part in causing, or at least in facilitating, the loss of inflexions during the Middle English period. Moreover, the inconvenience of making contiguous sounds clear may have led to the simplified pronunciation of *fith* for *fifth* and *Artic* for *Arctic*. A desire for ease must frequently have reinforced impatience; and yet it seems apparent that impatience on its side must have reinforced ease, to have produced the very drastic effects observable in our speech of today.

Unquestionably Modern English is brief and compact. If one studies a page-for-page translation out of any foreign tongue, it will be noticed that the English pages are uniformly shorter than those of the other language. Counting syllables in various translations of the Lord's Prayer will show that the English version has fewer syllables than any of the others except the original Hebrew. This may be explained partly by the disappearance of inflexions in English, a development which has cut down the length of individual words. But in this aspect, as well as in other aspects, the change is traceable to the operation of the psychological quality of impatience, which has helped to make English the most nearly monosyllabic of Western languages.

Anglo-Saxon was far more given to abbreviating than Gothic, the earliest known representative of the Germanic tongues. Just a glance at the conjugation of the past tense of the verb *to have* shows the difference. The Anglo-Saxon forms are *hæfde, hæfdest, hæfde, and hæfdon;* the Gothic forms are *habaida, habaides, habaidedu, habaideduts, habaidedum, habaididuþ, habaidedun.* Compare these polysyllabic verb forms to our uniform one-syllable *had,* and it will be apparent how English has changed.[1]

Almost any Gothic word will be found in a shortened form in Anglo-Saxon; we have *þad (cloak)* for *þaida, mœgþ (maiden)* for *magaþs; ierre (angry)* for *airzeis.* Altogether such a comparison as this shows clearly how much Anglo-Saxon already had been simplified from its condition in primitive Germanic.

This tendency to abbreviate and wear away unnecessary sounds and syllables has been accelerated rather than retarded in the thousand-year period between Anglo-Saxon and Modern English. The typical word in Gothic is probably trisyllabic, in Anglo-Saxon dissyllabic, and in Modern English monosyllabic. Counting syllables in the 140 consecutive words on a page in *Beowulf,* we find only 54 monosyllables, and these are largely pronouns, prepositions, and the "construction words" of speech generally.

[1] German is still in the two-syllable stage: *hatte, hattest,* and so forth.

There are 60 words of two syllables and 26 words of three or more. In contrast to this page, 140 consecutive words of Vachel Lindsay's *The Congo* (a poem in the modern manner roughly equivalent in literary type to *Beowulf*) show no fewer than 96 monosyllables, with 35 dissyllables, and only 9 words containing as many as three syllables (none with more).

SHORTENING IN WORDS

The evidence of impatience with regard to individual English words may be studied in connection with a classification according to the three types of abbreviation—initial, medial, and terminal—which have appeared with great frequency in the history of English and are still effective to shorten our speech yet further.

In Anglo-Saxon initial abbreviation was largely confined to words not accented on the first syllable, and the commonest form of such words was that with the syllable *ge* prefixed to the stem. Thus our word *mind* comes from Anglo-Saxon *gemynd,* and *bead* from *gebed* (*prayer*). In the same way *kind* comes from *cynd* and *gecynd,* and *like* from *gelīc, moot* from *gemōt* (*meeting*), *reeve* from *gerēfa, sight* from *gesihð,* and *sound* (adj.) from *gesund.* The strong initial accent of Old English prevented abbreviating other words in this way.

In present-day English initial abbreviation is seen in the forms *bus* for *omnibus, most* for *almost, phone* for *telephone,* and *plane* for *aeroplane* or *airplane.* The abbreviation *most* for *almost* has been condemned by certain authorities, and two examples are marked disputable in the Leonard Survey.[2] *Bus* and *plane* are so common in present-day English as to be accepted as standard forms.

Medial abbreviation is also extremely common in the development from Old to Modern English. Thus *head, hawk, fowl,* and *lord* were the Anglo-Saxon dissyllables *hēafod, hafoc, fugol,* and *hlāford.* Our word *either* derives from the Anglo-Saxon *ǣghwæðer* (also *ǣgðer*), and each from *ǣghwilc.*[3]

---

[2] *He most always does what his wife tells him* (No. 163) and *Most anybody can do that* (No. 147).

[3] In early Anglo-Saxon; in late Anglo-Saxon the form was *ǣlc.*

Many place names show medial abbreviation. Thus *Hampshire* is a boiling down of the old form *Hāmtūnscīr,* and *Clapham* (in Surrey) derives from *Cloppahām; York* from *Eoforwīc* and *Oxford* from *Oxnaford* are stock examples. We might mention also *monkhood* from *munuchād, reckless* from *rēccelēas,* and *forty* from *fēowertig.*

In Modern English this type of medial abbreviation is seen in pronunciations such as *intristing* for *interesting, libry* for *library,* and *cimitry* for *cemetery.* While these pronunciations are not standard and have not led to a respelling of the words involved, still they are widely current and not objectionable to liberal authorities. Their currency is even greater in England than in the United States, the British habit being somewhat more hospitable to this form of abbreviation than the American.

Terminal abbreviation is much the commonest of the three types. It is shown in practically every inflected word in English, in that the inflexions have disappeared or worn down, leaving the word shortened from the terminal end. It is seen also in many words not inflected today which were formerly so. The Anglo-Saxon phrase [4] "Mīne gebrōþra þā lēofostan" is an illustration; it contains four words and nine syllables. The modern equivalent, *My dearest brothers,* has three words and five syllables.

Apart from this kind of abbreviation by omitting the inflexional ending, there is not a great deal of terminal abbreviation in Old and Middle English, since the inflexion itself tended to preserve the latter part of the word. But in the modern period there have recurred what we might almost describe as epidemics of abbreviation. Shakespeare represents one of these, with his *oft* for *often, ope* for *open, writ* for *written* as terminal shortenings, and *e'er* and *o'er* for *ever* and *over, 'tis* for *it is,* and numerous others of the initial and medial types. These Shakespearian abbreviations have failed, however, to pass into the ordinary language, but have remained in the limbo of what is called "poetic English."

Another burst of abbreviation, largely terminal, occurred in the early eighteenth century and evoked the thunders of Jonathan Swift, who stood for words pronounced fully, spelled correctly,

[4] From Aelfric's *Homily on St. Gregory the Great.*

and inflected conservatively. *Mob* for *mobile vulgus, rep* for *reputation, plenipo* and *incog* for *plenipotentiary* and *incognito* were to Swift the worst of linguistic vices, and he denounced them more than once in letters and pamphlets.

Today this sort of abbreviation is so common that authorities seldom bother to attack it seriously. Anyone knows who are meant when the *quins* are spoken of. Any American will talk about *ads* for *advertisements,* the *movies* for *moving pictures, the el* for *the elevated,* without any feeling that he is using bad English or affronting the purists.

Side by side with this tendency to shorten words goes the origination of new words, which brings into the language novel coinages and compounds faster than words can be worn down by the processes of abbreviation. Compounding especially, by putting words together, tends to lengthen them. The processes of linguistic change might be compared to a gigantic mixer, which rounds off and diminishes words as fast as possible, but which cannot cope with the vast amount of new material constantly being poured into it.

ABBREVIATION IN SOUNDS

One of the fundamental principles of sound change is that unstressed sounds tend to be obscured or lost in Modern English. This principle has operated to shorten words and to change sounds in words which have not been shortened.

The principle is seen very easily in compounds. The two Modern English words *wise* and *doom* are from Anglo-Saxon, but the combination *wisdom* shows how their sounds have been shortened and obscured through the placing together of the two words. There is no actual loss of sounds here, but the word illustrates the first step on the path to such loss. In *hussy,* on the other hand, we have an actual loss from the two words *house* and *wife,* which were the originals of the modern compound. In British English *housewifery* is still pronounced *huzzifry; midwifery, midwifry;* and *grindstone, grinstun. Maudlin* illustrates loss of sound from *Magdalene,* its original, and it might almost be said that in any two-syllable word deriving from Anglo-Saxon there is likely to be

found some indication of sound loss, due to this principle of unstress.

It is not always unstress which leads to loss of sounds in Modern English. Very often sounds disappear in abbreviating a word
because the neighboring sound or sounds are inharmonious. The
words *next station* are scarcely ever pronounced fully, and indeed
can scarcely be pronounced fully without conscious effort. What
actually happens is that the word *next* becomes *neck,* and the
combination is pronounced *neck station*—a pronunciation which
is perfectly understood in its context.

In the same way a *g* has been lost from *recognize* and an *n*
from *government* in popular speech and in a good deal of cultivated speech as well. The word *clothes* has approximated itself to
close, and *February* has lost its first *r.* In all these abbreviations
certain definite principles are operative. Besides the unstress principle, which we have already mentioned, there is a principle of
harmony, or concord, which decrees that when sounds are out of
adjustment one will change or one will disappear.

And besides these two principles of sound disappearance there
is found in modern speech simply the impatient tendency to
shorten words without any particular phonetic reason for doing
so. As speech becomes more and more rapid, more and more
sounds tend to be eliminated, until finally only enough is left to
convey the idea. The popular *haya* or *hya* for *How are you?* is
an example in point; it is a hasty greeting and has therefore worn
itself down from its original length. Greetings are particularly
susceptible to this form of abbreviation. *Hello* will become *Hlo;*
Howdy is a diminished form of *How do you do;* and *Goodbye*
was once *God be with you.*

The principle of unstress which results in loss of sounds probably operates more fully in British than in American English,
since British intonation is more modulated than ours, so that a
difference between stress and unstress is more marked. The American immigrant is likely to say *munisip'ple* for *municipal,* while
the Britisher will condense the word into three syllables. The
American will say *interesting* where the Britisher telescopes the
word into *intristing.*

On the other hand, the principle of sound disappearance because of inharmony with contiguous sounds will operate equally well in the two dialects, and abbreviation because of impatience is likely to be more marked in American speech, which tends to be more nervous and hurried than British. Of course it is impossible to make generalizations which will be true for every part of the country. The "Yankee drawl" is slow and long drawn out, and there is a Southern drawl of the same sort. Nevertheless it seems to be true that the speech of the American West, the so-called general American dialect, is somewhat faster in tempo than British English.

ABBREVIATION IN SYLLABLES

A consideration of the kind of abbreviation which involves the loss of syllables from words takes us into the whole question of the dropping of English inflexions. This is usually supposed to have occurred between the Old and the Middle English periods, or even within the latter part of the Anglo-Saxon period; but for the purposes of this chapter it should be considered as not taking place before the late Middle or early Modern period. This is because during the time of "leveled" inflexions no actual abbreviation took place. The Middle English plural form *stones,* pronounced with two syllables, is just as long a word as the Old English plural form *stānas.* There has been a weakening of the vowel of the inflexion, but no actual abbreviation of the word. It is not until the form *stones* (pronounced [sto:nz]) that a syllable is actually dropped.

Early Modern English classics such as Shakespeare's plays and the King James Bible represent a semifinal state in the abbreviating of English inflexional syllables. Shakespeare's metrics must have been greatly facilitated by the current uncertainty or flexibility in the use of inflexional endings. The verb ending *ed* might be pronounced or merged with the rest of the verb; thus *burnished* might be pronounced as two or three syllables, according to the requirements of the meter. In the present indicative of the verb, third person, either the *s* or the *eth* ending might be used— the former merging with the verb, the latter forming an extra syllable. Within half a century after Shakespeare usage had become standardized and the extra syllables had been lost. Shakespeare, however, represents the end of a process which began approximately with the poems of Chaucer, the process of dropping terminal inflexional syllables which had already been leveled under the vowel *e*.

In Modern English a syllable which is unstable and therefore subject to frequent loss is *al*. Such forms as *incidently, accidently,* and even *historicly* tend to supplant the traditional forms *incidentally, accidentally,* and *historically*. While this tendency to drop the syllable *al* is vigorously opposed by conservative linguists, still it is widespread in speech and in writing and may conceivably succeed in establishing the abbreviated forms as standard English.

The adverb without *ly* may be regarded as another phase of the same tendency. Many untutored speakers prefer *correct* to *correctly (Speak correct)*; *quick* to *quickly (Walk quick)*; *slow* to *slowly (Drive slow)*; and *good* to *well (He did it good)*. To be sure, there is historical justification for certain of these adverbs without *ly*. *Deep, hot, sharp, wide, thick, loud,* and *slow* were all adverbs without *ly* in Old English times, and they have been used without the *ly* termination through the centuries.[5]

The substitution of *good* for *well,* which is one of the most widespread of these adjective substitutions, does not constitute an abbreviation of speech; it is perhaps to be explained by the fact that the adjective is thought of as a more substantial word, and therefore a more impressive word, than the adverb. In the other cases given in the previous paragraph, the principle of impatience, of abbreviation, comes into play.

In this matter of syllable abbreviation much the same principles as were described in connection with sounds are operative. Unstress of a syllable will tend to eliminate it, and a syllable which in enunciation is out of harmony with the preceding or the succeeding syllable will also tend to disappear. These two tendencies supplement the pure impatience which abbreviates for the sake of abbreviation.

---

[5] *Dig deep, look sharp,* and *open wide* are examples in common use.

ABBREVIATION IN GRAMMAR

It would take a chapter far longer than this to give a detailed list of all the idioms and grammatical patterns which have been abbreviated in the course of English linguistic history, through the operation of this psychological factor of impatience. For example, it often happens that a preposition will drop out of an expression. Instead of saying *opposite to* one comes to say merely *opposite* (*It stood opposite the bank*). Instead of using *for* with the infinitive (*What went ye out for to see?*) the infinitive is used by itself (*What did you go out to see?*). *Into* is frequently simplified to *in, off of* to *off, out of* to *out,* and so forth through a very long list. The word *home* is often a wearing down of the phrase *at home: James was home all last week.*

Indeed, a very good illustration of how English simplifies itself and thereby changes its grammar is the alteration of the word *way* (or perhaps better of the combination *the way*), which has become a subordinating conjunction. This word *way,* in its meaning *fashion* or *manner,* was often found used with the preposition *in* as the object of a prepositional phrase: *He did it in the way that his father had taught him.* The abbreviating tendency, however, led to the elimination of the preposition *in,* and we now have, as established English,[6] sentences such as *He does not do it the way I do.* Grammatically this makes the words *the way* introduce the subordinate clause *the way I do,* and this noun-article combination has thus become functionally a subordinating conjunction. This construction is extremely common in Modern English: *Read the way you were told; Lift your feet the way I showed you; He lived precisely the way his father did.*

The relative pronoun, which is a creation of Middle and Modern English, has been simplified and abbreviated a great deal, even though it offers opportunity for further simplification. In defiance of logic, the single word *whose* has replaced the awkward *of which* in such phrases as *the paper whose editor he approached. Which that, the which,* and *that which* have all yielded to *which* or *what.* The speech of Caesar (*Antony and Cleopatra,* Act II, scene 2, ll. 88–89)

---

[6] No. 31 in the Leonard Survey.

"To lend me Armes, and aide when I requir'd them, the which you both denied"

with its ambiguous *both,* would be altered in Modern English to *both of which you denied.*

Another type of construction which impatience has simplified is illustrated in the sentence *The man was very amused* (Leonard Survey, No. 140; disputable). Nowadays one is *very interested* or *too discouraged* rather than *very much interested* or *too greatly discouraged.* The exit of *much, greatly,* and so forth from such constructions may be delayed but scarcely prevented by grammarian disapproval.

Another construction, now found almost exclusively in popular or colloquial speech, but tending to rise into the literary idiom, is *kind-of* used as a modifier. From the literary *That is a kind of apple I don't like* and *That kind of man will stop at nothing* the combination has become an adjective equivalent (*He carried a kind of banner*) and finally an adverb (*He felt kind of tired*). This construction is so common that it is written often as a single word, *kinda; sorta* is synonymous and identical in background.[7]

Probably enough examples have been given to show how impatience operates to shorten our speech. Looking at language as a whole, we shall find this impatience neutralized by the tremendous accretion of words and constructions which goes on continuously. Isolated, the shortening process becomes clearly perceptible and finds its psychological roots in the very human tendency to hurry and crowd the expression of one's ideas and thoughts.

[7] An interesting study might be made of the transformation of *of* to what amounts to an inflexional ending in such words as *kinda, sorta, coupla.*

EMPHATIC FRANKNESS

W E HAVE ATTEMPTED to show how language is used impressively to call attention to its originator, and how, on the other hand, language may reflect a modest, courteous, and retiring attitude. Both observations referred language to the speaker or writer, showing one of its subjective aspects. But much, perhaps most, language is objective rather than subjective. It does not contemplate any one personality, whether modest or arrogant. It is concerned with the idea to be expressed rather than with the person expressing it.

In objective linguistic expression one essential is force, or emphasis, and another is clarity. The speaker or writer normally wishes to leave no doubt in the mind of the listener concerning the drift of his message, and he wants to phrase it in such a way that it will have the proper impact. Frankness is also of the essence of his aim; without a clear, frank, and emphatic statement he will not be able to achieve the desired effect.

The foregoing paragraph describes the operation of what may be called the direct approach in language. It by no means describes the only sort of linguistic expression. Language can be and is used to conceal thought, to provoke, suggest, confuse, intimidate, or insinuate, as well as to be frank and direct. But frank and direct language is probably the oldest, and it is still the norm or standard; other sorts of expression must approximate this type if they are to be effective.[1]

---

[1] It is seldom that the verbal trickster will commence by saying, "Now I'm going to pull the wool over your eyes," and yet such a linguistic method is not unheard of. To some extent *Mein Kampf* is an example.

Direct action in language works through rhythm, through repetition, through abbreviation, through sentence order, and through various other miscellaneous linguistic devices which tend to increase the effectiveness of a given expression. Such devices are in general the common machinery by which grammar operates, and yet just as it is possible for a motor to run a car and also to saw wood, so these devices may be used for diverse purposes on various occasions.

EMPHASIS THROUGH RHYTHM

It is only recently that students of language have perceived that all prose, as well as poetry, has characteristic rhythmic patterns which make it pleasing or unpleasing to the ear. Cadence is present in all language whether we realize it or not; and modern teachers advise us to study the characteristic cadences of our sentences, so as to improve them. As has been observed, cadence is more marked in British speech than in American, which is comparatively flat and unvaried. Nevertheless in any sentence there is considerable variation in pitch, tone, and stress, and this constitutes its characteristic rhythmic pattern.

In general, emphasis is served by the distribution of heavy beats so as to make them coincide with the ideas which are to be stressed. This stress may fall upon the subject, as in the sentence *HENRY would not do that,* the object—*Henry would not do THAT,* or it may be the verb which gets the stress, as in *Henry would not DO that.* Stress may even be a matter of local dialect; as is the *I think SO* which is characteristic of New Orleans.

It is more difficult to show stress in written English than in spoken; italics to indicate stress are outmoded and seldom used today, and the exclamation mark also is used very sparingly in contemporary literature. The sentence itself must indicate its own stress pattern, if the sentence is written rather than oral.

Among the many uses of the verb *get* there is one which illustrates how a rhythmic pattern can be suggested in writing. Frequently, in popular speech, *get* is used to convey the sense of obligation, as in the sentence *I have absolutely got to go.* This sentence carries its own emphasis; no one would stress any word but *got.* It is a circumlocutionary expression into which the verb *get* has been imported, probably chiefly for the purpose of showing emphasis.[2]

The word *get* is used in another way for emphasis. It may indicate possession when coupled with the verb *have.* The sentence *I have got my own opinion,* like the example in the foregoing paragraph, carries its own emphasis within it and attains its own effectiveness by adding the word *get.*[3]

In both examples the verb *get* provides a good heavy downbeat on which the voice may rest. The preposition *up,* with its variants *of, out,* and so forth, furnishes another example. As already observed (page 119) the preposition *up* and, to a less extent, the other prepositions tend to enter constructions when they are not necessary, in phrases like *wake up* and *climb up.* Such phrases not only constitute examples of "long-cutting" in English, but also provide an emphatic rhythm which increases the phonetic effectiveness of the statement into which they enter.

EMPHASIS THROUGH ORDER

Akin to rhythm in its importance for the effectiveness of written and spoken English is sentence order. The emphatic position in a sentence is the end; the beginning is also an emphatic position, although to a less degree. Sentences such as *On the whole, discipline is necessary in most cases* is extremely ineffective just because of the weak prepositional phrases at the beginning and at the end. A better order would be *On the whole, in most cases there is a necessity for discipline.* This brings the downbeat of the inflexion at the end of the sentence, stresses the chief word *discipline,* and makes the whole sentence more effective than it otherwise would have been.

In the same way a change from the loose to the periodic structure will often make a sentence more emphatic. *The house fell when the fire had gutted it* is a sentence of a loose type, and it is improved

---

[2] The sentence *I have absolutely got to go* is American English (No. 72 in the Leonard Survey; established). In British English the wording would more likely be *I absolutely have to go.* This wording is perhaps somewhat less emphatic.

[3] This expression also is said to be American English. In British dialect it might be *I've my own opinion,* with diffused stress.

by reordering: *When the fire had gutted it, the house fell.* A good literary style will probably mix loose and periodic sentences, but a style composed of nothing but loose constructions is likely to seem weak.

When a sentence contains a series, emphasis is served by placing the series in climactic order; the strongest member of the series must come at the end, the weakest at the beginning. Thus one should not say *He was cheated, ruined, and annoyed.* The last word forms an anticlimax to the other two and should be eliminated or rearranged. Very often the climactic order is disregarded, with a consequent loss of emphasis and effect.

Transitional elements of a sentence, such as *however, on the other hand, nevertheless, on the contrary,* and so forth, when they refer to a previous sentence, are best placed at or very near the beginning of the sentence, since otherwise emphasis is likely to be lost. In *She had a previous engagement; she broke it in order to go, however,* it is apparent that the word *however* makes a very weak effect in the second clause, while the effect would be considerably strengthened by putting the word *however* at the beginning. In the same way, parenthetical elements normally belong toward the beginning of a sentence or clause: *He decided that, if his duties could be discharged, he would return that night.*

EMPHASIS THROUGH ABBREVIATION

Chapter Seventeen by no means exhausted the subject of abbreviation or its significance to grammar. Abbreviation is frequently productive of emphasis. A clear example is the adverb without *ly.* Such sentences as *He was real lonesome, I was sure glad,* and *He moves mighty quick* are not only symptomatic of linguistic impatience, they are also far more effective in their emphatic aspects than the forms with *ly: He was really lonesome; I was surely glad, He moves mightily quickly.*

The effect of the use of *ly* was demonstrated to the authors the other day by a pamphlet on whose title page was the notation, "Copies of this pamphlet will be supplied freely to anyone writing to request it." The word *freely,* with the *ly* termination, was not only misleading, since it implied a meaning different from the one intended, but it spoiled the rhythm of the sentence, which would have been far more crisp and compact with the word *free*.

The very common use of *good* for *well* in sentences such as *The engine was hitting good this morning* (Leonard Survey, 196; illiterate) shows that greater emphasis is felt to characterize the adjective form. Indeed, *good* has found another adverbial use in colloquial sentences such as *It is good and cold; I was good and sorry*. Such constructions attain a certain emphatic quality through the use of the word *good*, whereas the adverb *very* would seem less strong.

The omission of unnecessary words, which is a form of abbreviation, often serves the ends of emphasis. One phrase which it is almost always better to omit is *as to*. *The question as to whether* will gain effectiveness by being reduced to *the question whether*. Except for a few uses such as the prepositional, meaning *concerning* (*As to John I am undecided*), these words *as to* might well be eliminated from English.

There is a subtle difference, not always definable, between the circumlocution which is emphatic and the circumlocution which is weak. *My Uncle John, he told me the story* is definitely redundant, and yet the repetitive pronoun *he* serves to direct more attention to the person it names. On the other hand, *the question as to whether* is weak and ineffective because of the repetitive phrase *as to*. It can easily be demonstrated that repetition will work both ways, to increase emphasis and to decrease it, and the same thing is true of abbreviation.

EMPHASIS THROUGH REPETITION

One of the commonest ways of securing emphasis in the pronoun is by using the so-called reflexive form as an intensive: *I myself, you yourself, he himself,* and so forth. This emphatic use is probably as frequent as the reflexive use, and the reflexives might almost be renamed the "intensive" pronouns, so regularly are they employed to strengthen written expression and spoken expression.

While this use of the reflexive pronouns is acceptable to grammatical authorities, the repetition of any other pronoun following a noun subject is not considered good English. "My brother he is in Elysium" (*Twelfth Night,* Act I, scene 2, l. 4) might be used by Shakespeare, but today it would be frowned upon. It is frequently true in Modern English that emphatic repetition is regarded with disfavor, even though it might have been good standard English at an earlier period in the language.

There can be no objection, however, to simple repetition, and such repeating is often very effective. The cry of David mourning for Absalom, with its reiteration of words, has echoed down the ages as a supreme expression of grief.[4] Such conscious reiteration is not redundance, but emphatic repetition.

Redundance enters when a repetition occurs casually and without consciousness of its effect. Such a clause as *after he had taken a walk after supper* is awkward because of the repetition of the word *after,* which has no literary justification. In the same way we find somewhat clumsy Shakespeare's frequent pronoun repetitions such as "Oh, she that hath . . . how will she leave" in the first scene of *Twelfth Night.* Modern English would prefer the elimination of one of the pronouns *she.*

The cognate object is by way of being a redundant or repetitious expression. Usually this object repeats the idea of the verb (*He dreamed a dream*), but sometimes it does not. The construction goes back to Anglo-Saxon, where there is a frequent use of such expressions as "Micel wæl geslōg," *He slew a great slaughter.*

In Modern English the use of the cognate object is fairly frequent. One hears *He ran a great race; He fought a good fight;* and *He died an unhappy death.* It is obvious that in such expressions as these the object lends weight and effectiveness to the verb, so that *He died an unhappy death* is much more emphatic than *He died unhappily.* Here we have a good example of the difference between repetition for effect and repetition from weakness.

It must be admitted, however, that occasionally words inserted in a sentence to strengthen it have the opposite effect. Examples

[4] *II Sam.* 18: 33. "And the king was much moved, and went up to the chamber over the gate, and wept: and as he went, thus he said, O my son Absalom, my son, my son Absalom! Would God I had died for thee, O Absalom, my son, my son!"

of such "strengthener-weakeners" as *so, such,* and *very* have already been given. These words have legitimate uses, but as intensives they fail to achieve the desired effect.

EMPHATIC NEGATIVES

The double negative is a most interesting linguistic manifestation of repetition for emphasis. In Anglo-Saxon, as is well known, repetition of the negative was common. The standard example is from the story of *Orpheus and Eurydice* in the Alfredian version of Boethius. "Ond nān heort ne onscunede nǣnne lēon, ne nān hara nǣnne hund, ne nān nēat nyste nǣnne andan ne nǣnne ege tō ōðrum, for ðǣre mergðe þǣs sōnes." *And no hart did not shun no lion, nor no hare no dog, nor no cattle did not know no anxiety, nor no fear of any other, for the joy of the sound.* Almost as thoroughgoing an example occurs in the Prologue to Chaucer's *Canterbury Tales,* in the description of the knight.

> He never yet no villeinye ne said
> In all his lyf un-to no maner wight.

Even Shakespeare employs the double negative; but in the centuries since Shakespeare the construction has been driven underground into popular speech, so that *I ain't got none* is regarded as illiterate English. Yet *I ain't got none* is much more emphatic and definite than *I haven't any.* Perhaps this fact explains the reluctance in the popular mind to conform to the prescribed rules for negatives.

One objection to the double negative, that is, that two negatives really make an affirmative, is absurd; for language does not add negatives in that way; and if it did, all that would be necessary would be to add yet another negative and the sum would once more be negative.[5] It is rather to be regretted that the effective and emphatic double negatives have been reduced in English to a single one per statement; and it is questionable whether the English language has really profited by the development.

A curious rule of present-day English is that which directs the speaker or writer to use *nor* with *neither* and to use *or* with other

---

[5] For the canceling negative see p. 184 below.

negative adverbs, such as *not, never,* and so forth. It almost looks as though the correlative negatives *neither . . . nor* still amounted to a double negative. Certainly logic does not enter this rule.

In addition to *neither . . . nor* Modern English holds several more or less colloquial approximations to the double negative, as in the sentences *We haven't but a few left; I haven't hardly any money;* and *I can't help but dread it.* In each of these cases there is a negative implication, which causes such logical difficulty that all these expressions are regarded by certain authorities as not the best English.

MISCELLANEOUS EXAMPLES OF EMPHASIS

Akin to repetition is the use of the summarizing word, a usage which often makes a sentence stronger and more emphatic. *Girls, boys, men, women, everybody in town was there* gains in emphasis from the summarizing word *everybody.* In the sentence *Orders, telephone calls, letters, memoranda, all the work was finished* there is a difficulty in number, since the summarizing word is singular, while its appositive is plural; still this sentence could scarcely be condemned as bad English, and the use of *all* adds to its effectiveness.

In recent manuals of composition a good deal is sometimes made of the literary value of the various parts of speech. The adjective appears today to be under a cloud, while the verb is praised by teachers of composition as offering possibilities for vividness and emphasis. Students are nowadays admonished to choose forceful, concrete, active verbs, to avoid colorless verbs like *have, do, be,* and to avoid also the weak passive construction. Thus *He somersaulted* is recommended as more vivid than *He turned a somersault; He devoured the book, page upon page* would be preferred to *He read the book eagerly.*

It is a question whether this discrimination between the parts of speech has not been somewhat overdone; a good adjective [6] or a good adverb will be found comparable in effectiveness to a good

[6] Mark Twain never avoided using good adjectives, even when warning young writers away from them. In a letter quoted by the New York *Times* he said, "When you catch an adjective, kill it . . . An adjective habit, or a wordy, diffuse, flowery habit, once fastened upon a person, is as hard to get rid of as any other vice."

verb. Nevertheless it is undoubtedly true that passive and auxiliary verbs tend to induce in the reader or the listener a feeling of dullness and flatness, often without conscious knowledge as to the cause.

An odd little attempt at linguistic emphasis is the use of the superlative in comparing two things: *He is the tallest of the two; Of the two hats that is the prettiest.* This use is called colloquial now, although yesterday it was condemned; it harks back to a fairly early stage of the English language. Obviously the superlative is used as the more impressive and emphatic form, even though the comparative would be more logical.

There is one other construction, occurring in various forms, which perhaps should be referred to the desire for emphasis. In popular English, people say *The reason was because she left; Intoxication is when the brain is affected by alcohol;* and *Cambridge is where the university is located.* In each example there is a clause beginning with a subordinating conjunction which is used as a predicate noun, and all are considered substandard English. Why there should be this tendency to use the subordinating conjunction and its clause in place of the predicate noun is not clear, unless it is that *when, where,* and *because* are regarded as somewhat stronger and more explicit than a noun would be (*The reason was her leaving*).

All the examples which have been given illustrate the unconscious or semiconscious desire on the part of the speaker or the writer to be frank, clear, and emphatic—a desire which is present in most minds, though not in all. The English language has clearly been shaped so as to facilitate this frankness and emphasis. Its grammatical and linguistic patterns embody this desire and its fulfillment.

CONFUSION AND PROFUNDITY

IT IS no simple matter for the human mind to express itself with clarity, directness, and candor. People are prone to fall into confusion innocently, through ignorance of the effective way of saying a thing; and as Chapter Eighteen suggested they may confuse their language deliberately, for a purpose. Mental fatigue may cause an ambiguity, and a too-great preoccupation with one's words may temporarily blur self-criticism. From whatever motive or lack of motive, much of the English we hear and read today is less than well-ordered for the accurate transmission of its central message.

Three types of English appear to be fertile breeding places of linguistic confusion. These are the emotionalized, the illiterate, and, oddly enough, the erudite. We do not say that all expression under any type will be confused, but just that these three types seem most liable to the failing. Our concern in this chapter will be chiefly with the last-named of the three.

CONFUSIONS OF AFFECTIVE ENGLISH

Emotional English is to a large degree a development belonging to the Era of Dictators, within the present century, although certain prototypes are found earlier, such as Antony's famous speech in *Julius Caesar*. Emotional English, which may also be named affective, doped, or demagog English, is utilized by dictators, propagandists, and others wishing to induce a state of impassioned acquiescence in their hearers. Among its literary exponents are Gertrude Stein and James Joyce. Religiously it is best exemplified by the colored evangelist who calls himself Father Divine. Politically, examples are scarcely needed, since anyone can supply the names.

Emotional English operates through words used so as to turn the hearer or reader from thinking to feeling. It holds itself superior to grammar and frequently departs from traditional form and sequences, as in the following example from Father Divine's paper, *The New Day,* dated November 4, 1937: "These candidates which will be mentioned namely, or by name again tonight before we leave here,—we request the honor of your presence as an endorsement of them by voting for them definitely,—these Councilmen selected,—that they might also be elected on Tuesday, Election Day."

Emotional English involves the suppression and distortion of thought, rather than clarity and frankness, although its general drift, as in the above example, is obvious. It induces the actions desired through its very peculiarity of expression. Its aim is not enlightenment, but a certain sort of activity on the part of the recipient, although it may use facts and truths, the more obvious the better, for the purpose of initiating the acquiescence it aims at.

Fascinating and profitable as it would be to analyze fully this emotional English and its multiplying manifestations in modern life, the task would take us too far afield; a separate volume is needed for this purpose, and the need is urgent. The public should be protected against the wielders of the linguistic weapon which has already helped to create so much enslavement in a supposedly free world.

CONFUSIONS OF IGNORANCE

One scarcely needs to give particulars concerning the errors and confusions arising from lack of education, since these are set forth in great detail in any of innumerable handbooks of correct writing and speaking. It has been made easy for anyone to count his grammatical sins by means of the lists arranged in books of reference. For this reason all we need to do here is to distinguish the confusions arising from illiteracy from the incorrectnesses which entail no confusion.

Grammars and rhetorics frequently try to prove too much, condemning words and constructions which are historically permissible and logically acceptable. Most of these condemned constructions are of a sort which may be called substitution; a "wrong" word or phrase is substituted for one which the books designate as "right." Thus the uncultivated speaker may say *yourn* for *yours; done* for *did; ain't* for *isn't, am not,* or *hasn't; git* for *get;* and so forth. Such substitutions are merely violations of grammatical convention; they do not indicate any lack of clarity. In its proper local or class setting *He ain't got none* is as clear as *He hasn't any.* Hence substitutions such as this do not enter into the material of this chapter.

Closer to our subject, because more liable to confusion, are the various illiteracies of sentence structure. The uneducated speaker will tell a story in the form of a single sentence consisting of independent clauses connected by simple conjunctions such as *and* and *but: I went along and I met John and he says howdy but I didn't let on I'd heard.* From the stylistic aspect this conglomerate construction is far from admirable. The speaker is too likely to get tangled up in his connectives, losing the thread of the narrative in the process.

At the opposite extreme the illiterate writer or speaker will occasionally use too many short sentences, especially if he has been warned against his natural method of speaking. Some of these will be complete sentences, and others may be nonsentences, that is, phrases or clauses written as sentences. Such a sequence of short units is unpleasing to the ears of the discriminating or cultivated critic and is open to the danger of confusion.

It must not be concluded that nonsentence usage is bad in itself; the nonsentence is frequently used to great advantage for literary effect, but the nonsentence which is used by mistake through a confusion of thought about what constitutes a sentence is poor English. And such blundering nonsentences appear frequently in uneducated usage.

Within the sentence the illiterate speaker is altogether too likely to say what he does not mean, or at least fail to say what he does mean. A frequent comment of the composition teacher, even in college classes, must be "What you mean is plain, but you have not said it." The illiterate or semiliterate speaker is too likely to get confused by his own thoughts, tangled up in his own words, and to emerge finally from his statement on a grammatical basis different from the one he started with.

Here is an example, from a student paper: "If one could read to get a clear idea, judge what is good in literature, and a good knowledge of events, and tendencies of thought, and although he is interested in one or two particular things he would be well enough informed to ask intelligent questions on the subject being discussed." Another example, from a customer's letter, follows: "Sorry I couldn't come down personally, as my business hours are very late and couldn't possible do it, am sending the coat with my sister which I have stated in the letter that I really couldn't pay for it and that was no use of my keeping it, wishing you can give me a refund as at the present time my father isn't working and it is very hard for me to purchase another coat."

Thus ambiguity, lack of coördination, disunity, and clumsiness dog the heels of the ignorant or inexperienced user of English. As the ignorant one teaches himself or is taught, he learns to say what he means, neither more nor less, with clarity and directness.

MISTAKES OF PROFUNDITY

Unfortunately the student of English does not always stop at the point of handling language in this desirable fashion. He explores the inviting reaches of scholarly fields, and he learns to write the English of erudition. In making this endeavor new temptations to confusion will be found lurking. If he comes to distrust plain and direct expression and to feel that academic English is something above and beyond plain English, then he is almost certain to manifest the errors and confusions of profundity.

One elementary sort of error into which he may fall is the overuse of phrases and other word combinations which have very little meaning and yet sound profound. Here is a list of a few of these. No one of them is in itself a sign of linguistic error. It is the overuse of such meaningless phrases as these which characterizes writing in which simplicity has been violated.

to the end that

in the case of

along the lines of

on the condition that

in the nature of

in this field

explore every avenue

such is by no means the case

in this connection

some difference of opinion

brings us to the conclusion that

for the purposes of this discussion

it is necessary to recognize

on this basis

of this character

in the degree that

in an extreme degree

similar if not indistinguishable from

according as to whether

relative to

if any

Abstract phrases such as these are reinforced in erudite English by abstract words, often holding no very clear meaning—words like *progression, rationality, relative,* and so forth. A recent author who gives a vigorous argument against such abstractions is Stuart Chase, whose *The Tyranny of Words* scarcely sets forth a new linguistic science as he seems to surmise, but does reinforce the dicta of Quiller-Couch, Woolley, and many others concerning the advantage of keeping language concrete.

CONFUSIONS IN SCHOLARLY NEGATIVES

In erudite English, abstractions are often accompanied by a curious negative usage which may be called canceling negation. It is to be distinguished from the double negative, used for emphasis, which was discussed in Chapter Eighteen. The use of two or more negatives does not make a stronger negative; rather the negative elements cancel each other, and the result is negative or affirmative according to whether the number of negative words is even or odd. *He was not unaware* gives a positive meaning, but if we add *that it had not been completed* the whole becomes negative.

Novelists such as George Meredith and John Galsworthy, who are interested in the minutiae of idea and character dissection, are likely to be attracted to the canceling negative. Here is an example from a well-regarded author: "It was not unlikely that he would not at any future time be inacceptable to his wife's family." The four negatives here build up to a positive, so that the whole means "Probably his wife's family would accept him from now on." But this meaning must be searched for; it is by no means on the surface of the cryptic original sentence.

Canceling negation is very often encountered in scholarly works, not excepting scholarly works on the English language. One grammarian even says, "Ambiguity is perhaps not to be regarded too unfavorably in English"—a dubious sentiment, expressed in somewhat dubious English. Ambiguity is the crowning sin against speech, because it is the negation of speech itself. The end of speech is communication, and ambiguity mystifies rather than communicates.

Like the positive constructions already listed, the canceling negative often operates through stock phrases, a few of which are given below.

It must not be that . . . not	Never has the world seen less
Why this should not be . . . is unknown	by no means inconsiderable
	no such unlikelihood
not less important than	It cannot be denied that
One cannot but think that . . . not	It is not unlikely (impossible, improbable) that

Just what constitutes the attraction of the canceling negative to the scholarly writer? It is an interesting question. We can only surmise that it may be another instance of the unconscious desire to impress, analyzed in Chapter Fifteen. The canceling negative not only tests the reader's mental agility, but also displays well the mental powers of the writer; and if his writing occasionally topples over into confusion through an incorrect use of such negatives, that is considered a small penalty.

OTHER ERUDITE CONFUSIONS

Frequently it is merely long sentences which trip up the writer of erudite English. Academic sentences are markedly longer than other sentences, and the liability of a sentence to error (ambiguity, circumlocution, inconsequence, and so forth) seems to increase in geometrical proportion to its length. Even when it is sufficiently clear, the longer sentence is too likely to lack coherence, moving from one idea to another until the end bears small relation to the beginning. In the following example the reader is likely to become bewildered by the rapid shift of ideas and references. The meaning is there, but the turns and twists of thought, the parentheses, and the commas keep it from yielding an easy and smooth significance.

To the present writer, the small differences in the meanings or uses of words that he encounters in reading an English book are (if they are not an Englishman's reproduction of an "American" conversation) pleasant and interesting rather than irritating; certainly, unless an unusual measure of slang is present, they can never be, to any moderately literate American, the cause of serious unintelligibility.[1]

The great number of phrases and clauses inserted along the way impede the thought and make it necessary for the reader to stop and wonder about the meaning. This is not the kind of sentence that would never demand a second reading.

It is not alone the longer sentence which is subject to confusion. Here is a short one which falls into the same difficulty: "James Payn, editor of *Chamber's Journal* in the middle of the nineteenth century and later on of the *Cornhill,* being a Victorian, wrote grammatically." To be sure, on a careful reading one can see that the third *of* phrase does not depend upon the word *middle* and that the subject and verb are at the beginning and end of the sentence, respectively. But it is doubtful whether James Payn himself would have passed the sentence for the *Cornhill.*

It sometimes happens, indeed, that scholarly enthusiasm carries away a writer (even a writer who is also a grammarian) and leads him to violate the most rudimentary rules of agreement and modification. On a careful reading of a scholarly work, it is by no means difficult to collect numerous violations of the rules stressed in the textbooks, rules of concord, of punctuation, of antecedents, of parallel structure, of climax, of repetition, and of ineffectiveness. Such writers have succumbed to erudite English instead of mastering it. The very length and complexity of their sentences render them liable to confusion; the very weight of thought is calculated to strain grammar to the breaking point. And such slips as have

---

[1] For obvious reasons no name and book references are given with the sentences on this page; but it must be remembered that the authors quoted here will find themselves in very good company in their defections from English of the highest standard.

been pointed out are by no means isolated phenomena. They characterize overeducated writing only less than illiterate. At their base lies confusion of thought, which results in confusion of expression.

Among other errors to which the overeducated are especially liable is the clumsy nominative absolute, of which a few examples are given below.

> all possibilities now having been covered
> other circumstances being equal
> the English language having sloughed off unnecessary forms
> account being taken of the contrary fact
> due consideration having been given to
> this stage in the process now being reached
> This possible objection forestalled

For examples of poor English no one needs to look further than manuals purporting to teach how to write. Hackneyed expressions, dull passives, and even poor grammar are rampant—with a few notable exceptions. The old joke rule "Never use a preposition to end a sentence with" estimates the proportion between preaching and practice in most instruction books.

Perhaps the least attractive sort of erudite English is that which leans backward to be correct, preferring *whom* to *who* whether or not the preference is according to rule, employing the subjunctive whether or not usage requires it, and meticulously obeying the rules (more honored in breach than observance) for the possessive of *somebody else,* for *an* before *h,* and for *he* or *she* as the singular pronoun of common gender, rather than *they.* Happily such meticulousness seems to be growing less frequent rather than more, and even scholars are learning to write as they speak.

The final judge must be the reader himself. Take the five most recent publications on a technical subject with which you are familiar and read a chapter in each with careful attention to the English used. How many examples of erudite English can you find? How many confusions? How many violations of the grammarian's rules? One such book, published a few years since, a monument of careful scholarship in the linguistic field, yielded to one reader three single-spaced typed pages of errors and defects of a linguistic sort.

Of course it is human to get tangled up in one's thoughts, no matter how well one knows a language, when those thoughts are abstruse and intricate. We are not censuring the writers of erudite English. We are merely pointing out the human side of this linguistic accomplishment. And we might add that erudite English is on the whole becoming rarer in the modern world. An increasing proportion of scholars, even in addressing their intellectual peers, use clear, frank, direct English, as nontechnical as may be. Erudite English, with the confusion it so often entails, is going out of scholarly fashion.

SLOTH AND SLOVENLINESS

THERE IS a curious affinity between laziness and efficiency, which was well brought out in a recent short story about a bank clerk who was so lazy that he invented for his bank numerous laborsaving devices, thereby winning promotion and the Girl. We have named our chapter opprobriously, but it might as well be called "Ease and Efficiency" so far as its subject matter would indicate.

One advantage of using the title actually chosen is that we are so familiar with its second term. Every student of grammar has heard of "slovenly speech" or "slovenly English." To be sure, the word *slovenly* in this phrase is not meant to characterize the system of English grammar as a whole; it has no psychological-linguistic implications. It is simply a convenient phrase to use in condemning a way of talking or writing which is unpleasing to the condemner, and its onus falls not on the English language but on the individual who dares to pronounce or to grammaticize in the condemned fashion.

Our use of the term *slovenly* in this chapter is out of the ordinary, since we are applying it not to individuals but to the English language itself as a joint product of countless men and women who have followed the normal human tendency to avoid unnecessary work. It is English itself which we shall try to exhibit as lazy, slovenly, or, if you please, laborsaving.

SLOTH AND CONTEXT

One of the greatest facilitators of slovenliness in language is context. This word *context* is basic in the study of language, since no word has meaning in itself, but only attains meaning in connection with other words. Only the sentence has meaning. Words like *dog* or *hide* may seem easily definable, but in fact the definer must have a context before he can so much as tell whether they are nouns or verbs. It is context which determines meaning, and the significance of individual words is conditioned by context.

This dominance of context is seen clearly in the example *He was formally a lawyer, but is now on relief.* While the sentence can be made to "make sense" as it stands, anyone reading it would know that *formally* is used by mistake for *formerly* and would interpret the whole accordingly. Another example is *His intemperance mitigated against his success,* where the reader finds no difficulty in interpreting *mitigate* as *militate.*

Sloth is obvious in these examples. The writer or speaker is either too ignorant or too lazy to use the exact word, relying on context to convey his meaning; and context is equal to the task. Once in a while such aberrations even become part of the language. This is especially evident in what are called "popular etymologies," forms like *belfry* for *berfrei, penthouse* for *appentis, ravenous* for *rapinous, hiccough* for *hickup, rarebit* for *rabbit,* and so forth, where a word has been changed because of a mistaken concept of its derivation.

Context is the key to understanding the "portmanteau words," which were named though not originated by Lewis Carroll in his classic *Alice* books. *Chortle* has entered English, its meaning self-evident as a merger of *snort* and *chuckle.* More recent examples are *slanguage* and *insinuendo,* both of which are included in the latest editions of *Webster's Dictionary* as good humorous English words.[1]

By making semimeanings clear context thus acts as a sort of vent for linguistic laziness. Errors arise from individual laziness, but individual errors always tend to be transferred to the language itself, actually changing the form of words or constructions. The English language contains many instances of the results of such individual sloth.

---

[1] Related to these examples, but illustrating originality rather than sloth, are Walter Winchell's word-coinages—for pregnancy, *infanticipation;* for to marry, *to middle-aisle;* for divorced, *renovated.* In each case one or more existing words form the basis of the new creations.

To consider for a moment the workings of context in English grammar, we may glance at the rule, said to be one of the most fundamental of all rules, directing the speaker or writer not to use a pronoun with no antecedent or a vague antecedent. Thus such a sentence as *Tom told his father he would soon get a letter* is called defective, because it is not clear whether *he* refers to father or to son. Alternative corrections would be *Tom would get a letter soon, he told his father* or *Tom told his father to expect a letter soon.*

Violation of this rule is called slovenly grammar, and yet this rule is one of the most frequently violated on all levels of education and cultivation. Usually it is violated with impunity, because the context, perhaps in another sentence or paragraph, makes the meaning clear. And when it does not, it ordinarily does not matter whether or not the meaning is exact. In the example in the previous paragraph the reader knows that a letter is coming, and if not informed by the context in another sentence, he may not care greatly whether the letter will be addressed to Tom or to his father.

Devotees of the pronoun with no antecedent or a vague one should should be encouraged by the fact that this construction occurs nowhere more often than in the King James version of the Hebrew Scriptures, that translation which is regarded, and rightly so, as the noblest literary expression of the English language. In fact it might almost be called a rule that the Bible relies on context to identify pronouns.

A random example is I Sam. 18:3: "Then Jonathan and David made a covenant, because he loved him as his own soul." Here one may say that it does not matter to which of the two the pronoun *he* refers. Another example is I John 3:3: "And every man that hath this hope in him purifieth himself, even as he is pure." An examination of the Greek text proves that both *he* and *him* refer to God; but there is no such indication in the English translation.[2]

SLOTH IN BREATH AND VOICE

English sounds may be divided into breath sounds, that is, those which are made without any vibration of the vocal chords, and

[2] Other instances are Gen. 24: 31–33; Mark 9: 20; I John 5: 16.

voiced sounds, those in which the column of air passes the vibrating vocal chords. The distinction applies only to consonants, since the vowels are all voiced. Within the consonant group we have a number of pairs of sounds of which one is breath and the other voiced; examples are *p,b; f,v; t,d; s, z;* and *k,g.*

Now it may appear that the breath sound would be the easier of the two types, since it requires a certain amount of energy to cause the vocal chords to vibrate; but the fact is just the contrary, since the breath sound requires a much greater expenditure of force in breathing than does the voiced sound. Anyone may verify this for himself, pronouncing, for example, the consonant *p* without a vowel, and then the consonant *b.* It is apparent that *b* is a much "easier" sound than *p.*

Sloth in English phonology has led to the disappearance of three breath consonants, *hl, hr,* and *hn,* which were current in Old English. A fourth, *hw,* has survived in reversed spelling, *wh,* in America at least, where school children are warned against pronouncing *when* like *wen, whale* like *wail,* and *which* like *witch.* In standard British English, on the other hand, the breath sound has entirely disappeared and we have only the voiced sound *w* to take care of all of the words which formerly had the breath sound.

This actual change in the sound system is by no means the only instance of a leaning toward voice on the part of the English language. It was a general rule in Anglo-Saxon that when a breath consonant came between two vowels it became a voiced sound; and this tendency has given Modern English approximately a dozen plurals such as *knives, wives, thieves, loaves, wolves,* and so forth. The breath consonant *f* of the singular has been changed by contiguous vowels into the voiced sound of the plural.

Certain instances of the substitution of *z* for *s* can also be given. In words such as *his, is,* and *was,* Chaucer undoubtedly pronounced the final consonant with its breath value; but sloth has led to the pronunciation with *z,* which is current in present-day English. It is a fair prediction that as the English language continues to develop, breath sounds will tend progressively to be replaced by voiced sounds, until finally English may contain no breath consonants at all.

This is apparent also in several alternative pronunciations of words. The nouns *truth, path, oath, house* all end with breath sounds; but in the plural the breath sound becomes voiced, either commonly or always. This voicing is simply a characteristic manifestation of the tendency toward ease in language.

OTHER PHONETIC SLOTH

It might be asserted that all or almost all phonetic change in the history of English has been in the direction of ease, laziness, or slovenliness. Much of such change, for example the alteration of *k* near a front vowel to *ch* (Anglo-Saxon *cinn,* Modern English *chin*), is a matter of the accommodation of one sound to another for greater ease of utterance.

Even the insertion of sounds, such as the intrusive *d* in the word *thunder,* can be explained on the basis of ease of utterance. The tongue has been held against the gums in making the sound *n,* and the addition of the sound *d* completes the motion of the tongue and introduces the following vowel. This is a different development from the *d* added to words like *sound,* where the consonant *d* is introduced through the influence of the past termination *ed.* The latter instance is not concerned with linguistic laziness.

Of the sound changes from Old to Modern English, the greater part have been matters of the accommodation of one sound to another. Even the rising of the long vowels, which has puzzled phoneticians, may be explained on the basis of accommodation. Since some 85 percent of the consonant sounds of English are made with the active point or blade of the tongue held high in the mouth, it would be natural for the vowels to rise so as to accommodate themselves to these high consonants.[3] Such a combination is of course a matter of vocal ease, and hence it falls under our chapter heading.

Sound accommodation or accord is frequently named "assimilation," and assimilation really means an approximation of sounds to one another in the interest of ease. Such a word as *gossip,* formed

---

[3] The theory thus summarized is set forth in full in *Why English Sounds Change,* by Janet Rankin Aiken, New York, The Ronald Press, 1929.

from *godsibb,* where the *d* has been changed into *s,* is a very obvious example. A somewhat less obvious instance is *impassable,* where the point nasal consonant *n* has been changed to the lip nasal *m* to agree with the following lip consonant *p.* Such assimilations are extremely common in English, and, indeed, in all modern languages, since the same principle of sloth and slovenliness will tend to operate in one language about as readily as in another.

A final group of examples of ease, accommodation, or assimilation in sounds is based on the frequent discrepancy between spellings and pronunciations in English. Typically the spelling preserves an earlier pronunciation which has yielded to a new one. Such common words as *short, folk, know, gnaw,* and *brought* are worth studying in any analysis of linguistic indolence.

In its earliest English form the word *sceort* was no doubt spelled phonetically, with a sibilant *s* preceding the *k.* It is not certain just when this combination of a sibilant and a back consonant altered, but at some time before Danish influence had become fully operative the two sounds merged, becoming a single sibilant, a little farther back in the mouth than the original *s.* Later the double vowel simplified also, so that *short* shows two sounds fewer than its ancestor. Here we have another undoubted instance of accommodation for the purpose of ease.

The word *folk* shows another possibility. In Anglo-Saxon this word, spelled *folc,* was phonetically written, the four letters all being sounded. However, we have a point consonant *l* between a back vowel *o* and a back consonant *k.* This unbalanced phonetic situation resulted in the disappearance of the *l* and the present pronunciation with two component consonants instead of three.

In *know* and *gnaw* still another possibility is illustrated. We have in Anglo-Saxon a full pronunciation (*cnāwan, gnagan*); again, however, we have an unbalanced phonetic sequence, with the back consonants *k* and *g* preceding the point nasal *n.* This time the point nasal remained, and the preceding, difficult-to-pronounce sounds were lost.

Our final example is the past tense *brought,* which in Old English was *brōhte.* Here a guttural consonant, spelled *h,* was interposed between a back vowel and a point consonant *t*. This guttural consonant, which in some dialects of German survives (in words like *ich*), disappeared from English phonology and in doing so lowered the vowel slightly, so that in Modern English instead of having the sound *o* we have the sound *aw*. It is obvious that not only this lowering of the vowel but also the disappearance of the guttural are matters of vocal ease.

EASE IN THE ALPHABET

A great and universal defect in the present-day teaching of phonetics is the regarding of vowels and consonants as two separate systems not related to each other. As a matter of fact, the consonants overlie the vowels in mouth position, extending farther forward to the lips, and farther back to the soft palate, the vowels forming a compact mass below and within the consonant areas.

Many of our phonetic terms need revision to bring out this interrelation between vowels and consonants. For example, the term *front* as applied to vowels really indicates those vowels which are made with the center of the tongue, and this region is actually behind the part of the tongue active in forming most consonants, that is, the mobile tip or point. What are called high vowels are uniformly lower than their neighboring consonants, and the back vowels are not so far back as the back consonants, where actual contact between tongue and hard palate is maintained.

In an accurate and complete analysis of the sound system of English it would be simple to chart the innumerable accommodations which have been made and are being made within English words. With consonants and vowels artificially separated, such correlation is difficult or impossible.[4] It is no exaggeration to say that if English words should be analyzed on the basis of their mouth positions, consonants and vowels being included in a single system, every word, perhaps even every syllable, within the English language would show some effect of the principle of ease or indolence. This will be made clear if the student simply consults any good dictionary and compares the Modern English word with its earlier

---

[4] For an attempt at a joint consonant-vowel analysis see Chap. 8 of *English Present and Past*, by Janet Rankin Aiken, New York, The Ronald Press, 1930.

equivalents, noticing what phonetic alteration has taken place. While occasionally there may be a change which seems out of the line of ease, such sporadic instances can be explained by other factors.[5]

OTHER EXAMPLES OF LAZY SPEECH

Turning from the subject of English sounds, let us look at the ordinary grammatical dicta concerning "slovenly English." A popular authority is John B. Opdycke, whose *Get It Right!* [6] is called "a cyclopedia of correct English usage."

Mr. Opdycke admits (page 582) that language tends to become more and more "euphonious" with the passage of time. This euphony is what we have just described under the name "accommodation," where the examples *impassable* and *gossip* were given. However, according to Mr. Opdycke euphony evidently ends with past years, because he considers it not euphonious but slovenly to try to make contemporary speech euphonious. Such an amalgamation and simplification as the ordinary *didja* for *did you* is called simply vulgar, quite irrespective of the fact that the latter is almost never heard. The dropping of the *t* from *let's (less go)*, which is obviously a matter of ease in speech, is included among vulgar pronunciations.

Is colloquial English slovenly English? This question seems to be answered in the affirmative by Opdycke and other authorities, who too often include the two in a general condemnation. Sentences such as *He was without an excuse, She is against that politician,* where a preposition does the work of a verb, are good colloquial English and easier to frame than such alternatives as *He lacked an excuse, She opposes that politician,* where less common words must be found and used as verbs. Yet such sentences are condemned by Opdycke and other authorities.

The examples given in this chapter are only meager hints for a full study of ease or indolence in language. Just as, according to Wright, ablaut may be discerned in every word of the English

---

[5] Thus the obtrusive *f* in *laughter, draught, cough,* and other words has been explained by Krapp as "an infantile substitution."

[6] New York, Funk and Wagnalls, 1935.

vocabulary, so it would be difficult, if not impossible, to find an English word into which the principle of ease has not entered in some fashion. Our examples have been concerned with native words, but it would be no task at all to point out manifestations of the same principle in foreign importations, where modifications of spelling, pronunciation, use, and meaning regularly take place in the adaptation of the word to English use.

Ease may be called the all-pervading linguistic principle, ever ready to operate, negated now and then by stronger impulses in contrary directions, but corresponding in general to that fundamental axiom of economics, "Man seeks to satisfy his desires with the least possible effort." Man's desire is to communicate. So long as comprehension is secured, he does not very greatly care about elegance. In most situations he will communicate in the easiest, laziest manner possible; and the English language, like the bank referred to in the first paragraph of this chapter, receives the benefit of this human indolence. For no one comparing Anglo-Saxon to Modern English can doubt that slovenliness, at any rate in the past, has worked to the benefit of our language. Perhaps it may be the same way with much of what is at present called "slovenly English."

INDECISIVENESS

ONE OF the most conspicuous traits of the human mind, and perhaps more particularly the educated human mind, is indecision. The more one knows, the harder the task to "make up his mind," as the quaint idiom puts it. Many people struggle with indecision throughout life; many end, as Queen Elizabeth is said to have done, by adopting indecision as a settled policy; only a few naturally possess or are able to develop the capacity for coming to quick and positive conclusions.

All this is not to say that indecision is necessarily an evil. One might assert, on the contrary, that snap judgments are at least as likely to be wrong as right and that modern civilization has been kind to man by removing from him the necessity of excessive alertness and permitting him to substitute for it the joys of ratiocination. One needs but to turn to the illustration given in the previous paragraph: Queen Elizabeth's reign was at once the least decisive and the most glorious of English history. Perhaps society might do well to demote its leaders of force and emphasis in favor of the Elizabethan type—if it can be found.

Be that as it may, it is evident that the English language reflects in full measure the indecisiveness of its individual users. It spends generations, often even centuries, making up its collective mind concerning this or that sound, spelling, or construction. Occasionally it is arbitrary, eschewing a given locution for no very good reason; at other times it is prone to boggle at the oddest and easiest decisions, making a speech pattern which is full of alternatives— sometimes two and sometimes as many as a dozen or more.

METATHESIS IN WORDS AND SOUNDS

A good illustration of linguistic indecisiveness is the phonetic phenomenon called metathesis, which involves shifting the order of sounds within a given word. Take such a simple monosyllable as Modern English *run*. If we go back to Gothic, as representing the earliest known stage of the Germanic tongues, we find the verb *rinnan,* which can easily be connected with the modern form and which, except for the inflexional ending, is identical with the Scottish verb *rin.*

It looks like a very normal and easy development, but it is not so in fact. In Anglo-Saxon the letters of *rinnan* became transposed, so that the standard forms were *iernan, arn, urnon, (ge)urnen.* Later a second metathesis restored the Gothic order, resulting in the word we have today. The indecision over the form of this word thus has extended over a millennium and a half.

The word *horse* in Anglo-Saxon was *hors,* but there existed also a metathesized form *ros* or *hros* in Germanic; and this metathesized form is present in our word *walrus,* which is literally the *whale-horse,* the first part being derived from *hwæl, whale.*[1] Indecision here has been resolved by the recognition of both forms—one separate and one compounded.

Anglo-Saxon included two forms, *rōt* and *wyrt,* which showed past metathesis and have given us *root* and *wort* in such words as *bloodroot* and *liverwort.*[2] A decision has been made, however, by recognizing both the original and the metathesized forms, as though an individual should decide between two pairs of gloves by wearing both.

The foregoing examples bear out the fact that *r* is the most metathesized consonant in English. Our modern word *grass* was *gærs* in Anglo-Saxon, *cress* was *cærse,* and *bird* was *brid(d), burn* [3]

---

[1] Modern *walrus* comes from old Norse *hvalross,* the Anglo-Saxon form being *horschwael,* again an example of indecisiveness, this time in compounding.

[2] A list of more than 150 words combined with *wort* is given in *Webster's International Dictionary,* while *root* is a part of fewer than 90 combinations.

[3] Variously spelled *beornan,* and *biernan,* with principal parts *bearn, burnon, (ge)burnen.*

was *beornan* (Gothic *brinnan*), *wren* was *werna,* and *fresh* and *thresh* were *fersc* and *þerscan,* respectively.

Other consonants liable to metathesis are *l* and *s.* In the word *ask* this metathesis is still active, *ax* [aks] being a form in common use, especially among negroes of the South. Chaucer speaks of the abbot as *lipsing,* where we would say *lisping,* and A. A. Milne has perpetuated in a child's poem the frequently metathesized *wops* for *wasp.* The English language has not yet come to a sharp conclusion about some of these forms, and where decisions have been made they have required a long period of time.

But metathesis is not to be found only in sounds. Metathesis in words is just as prevalent, and one example which practically defies the ministrations of the grammarians is *He asked him a question* as compared to *He asked a question of him.* In the first example it is possible arbitrarily to call *him* an indirect object, but it looks more like a direct object, particularly since it directly follows *asked* and may be used alone: *He asked him.* One scarcely likes to admit the possibility of a verb taking two direct objects, and yet the metathesis in these sentences is very difficult to resolve on any other basis. This is by no means an isolated example, as several authors have pointed out.

In a number of phrases, such as "sow a field with corn" for "sow corn in a field"; "blame the war on Germany" for "blame Germany for the war" . . . "beg a favor of one" for "beg one for a favor"; "threaten death to him" for "threaten him with death"; "clean the spot from the floor" for "clean the floor of the spot"; one has to do with a word-metathesis.[4]

Not only are such examples common in English, but also they seem to be growing more common with every generation. In *The Philosophy of Grammar* Jespersen pointed out that frequently the object of a verb expresses, not what undergoes the action of the verb, but what the result of that action is, as in the example *to dig a hole,* where the hole obviously does not undergo digging, but is the result of the digging process. English construction seems

[4] George H. McKnight, *English Words and Their Background,* New York, Appleton-Century, 1923, p. 199. Quoted by permission.

to be less and less decided about the difference between a subject and an object. Metathesis of all kinds is common, and context is invoked to make the meaning clear.

INDECISION IN VERB AND SUBJECT

One of the matters about which the English language has never succeeded in making up its mind is the construction after the conjunction *either* followed by a pair of personal pronouns. When the personal pronouns are both in the third person, as in the sentence *Either he or she is wrong,* the decision is easy. The verb agrees with both subjects, showing the alternative by being singular instead of plural. But when the two pronouns are of different persons, there is no clean-cut or standard decision. One may say *Either he or you is wrong or Either he or you are wrong;* and either sounds about as bad as the other. When it comes to *Either he or I,* the verb *am* is as awkward as the verb *is,* while *Either he or they* repeats the difficulty of *Either he or you.*

The ordinary ruling in cases such as this is that the verb will agree with the nearest subject, but in actual practice generally the sentence is expanded so as to read, for example, *Either he is wrong or I am;* the difficulty here is circumvented rather than met. Theoretically English should have a solution for constructions such as these, but practically it has never come to a decision about them.

Oddly enough our next example of indecision involves precisely those expressions in which a preference or a decision is being expressed. English has at least seven alternative fashions of expressing preference idiomatically.

would rather	would better
had better	had sooner
had rather	had liefer
	had just as lief

It is impossible to choose among these alternatives, except perhaps to say that the last two are somewhat archaic. The sentences *I'd like to make a correction* and *I had rather go at once* are listed in the Leonard Survey as established English (Nos. 40 and 30). A few decades ago grammars used to oppose the abbreviation of *would* into the single letter *d,* prescribing *had rather* as the expansion of *I'd rather. Would* is undoubtedly the more logical form historically, while *had* is more idiomatic. No decision concerning these alternatives has been arrived at, or is likely to be.

On the other hand, the decision concerning the vexed question of *will* and *shall*, which has already been discussed, seems to be clarifying, since the grammarians are succumbing to the popular tendency to choose *will* in all cases of future time. The omission of the form *shall* from at least one modern minimum English vocabulary is a sign of the trend, and it might be said that *shall* is obsolete in expressions such as *My colleague and I shall be glad to help you,* which, although the Leonard Survey lists it as established English (No. 8), would scarcely be heard in actual use.

Where, as in the case of *shall* and *will*, linguistic indecision involves the opposition of the grammarian to popular practice, it frequently happens that of two possible wordings, both sound wrong. This is notably true in the case of *It is me,* of which H. E. Palmer says, "It therefore follows that the unfortunate student, whichever form he uses, will be corrected and warned against that particular form." [5] Other examples in which the speaker must choose between sounding stilted and incurring condemnation by authorities are *He don't, everybody else's, I felt bad* (or *badly*) *about it,* and *Do it like I do. To get the worse of it* is a construction prescribed by grammarians, but it would certainly be avoided by any speaker who wanted to sound normal and natural. The indecision between this form and *to get the worst of it* is perhaps not so much because of indecisiveness of speakers as of the aberrations of grammarians.

One of the most awkward indecisions in English grammar is that involving *ain't I, aren't I,* and *am I not.* The first is condemned as vulgar, the second has been called "kittenish," and the third is obviously clumsy. It would be a happy day for the speakers of English and might at least end the present disagreement between dictionary and grammar if the language could make up its mind definitely to use some one easy standard form for the negative question with *I* and copula; but there seems only a faint hope of such an occurrence.

[5] *A Grammar of Spoken English,* New York, Appleton, 1924, p. 44.

INDECISIVE INFLEXIONS

The letter *s* is one of the worst generators of indecision in the English language. Since it looks like a plural, it naturally suggests the plural verb *are,* and many English words are commonly used with both *is* or *are.* One may say *alms is* or *alms are, tidings (news) is* or *tidings are, amends is* or *amends are,* and so forth through a long list.

Indeed, in the history of English this tendency to regard a final *s* as a sign of the plural has been effective in changing the form of a number of words, such as *girdle, riddle, bridle, burial, pea,* and *cherry,* all of which from the historical aspect should be written with the final *s* which at one time or another they possessed. In the singular this final *s* led to indecision and finally to the introduction of a logically incorrect form which would be easier to recognize as a singular. In Modern English the same process is now operative in the mistaken forms *serie* and *specie,* which are very often found instead of *series* and *species,* words which look as though they might be plurals.[6]

In addition there are, of course, numerous indecisive plurals in which the form in *s* is alternated by some other plural termination, usually foreign or classical in origin. Words like *appendix, index, vortex, curriculum, formula, cherub, seraph, bandit, radius* have two or even more possible plurals, and it cannot be said of any one that it is the only right form. In *Webster's Dictionary* there are listed 316 words having more than one correct plural, a list which constitutes a monument to the inability of the English language to make a decision and stick to it.

These are not the only indecisive inflexions in English. There are likewise plurals which have no termination or the *s* termination, as, for example, the word *fish;* there are alternative comparative forms such as *less* and *lesser;* and there is a considerable number of alternative past participle forms, such as *melted* and *molten.* English inflexions cannot be looked at as positive and definite, since in every department of the language there are irregularities

[6] This *specie* is of course different from the dictionary word meaning *money.*

and alternative forms which reflect the inability of the language to designate one form and only one as correct and standard.

ALTERNATIVES IN SENTENCE CONSTRUCTION

Probably in no other language are there so many alternative ways of saying any given thing as in the English language. In the first place, English has a vast number of synonyms or near-synonyms which may be substituted, the one for the other, in an almost endless variety. It is true that the language seems to dislike exact synonyms, preserving some shade of difference even between words so nearly alike as *begin* and *commence, great* and *large, sanguine* and *hopeful*. Frequently the distinction will be based on the difference between a learned and a popular word—a distinction made the subject of a chapter in *Words and Their Ways in English Speech*.[7] When a writer notices a repetition which he wants to remove, there is seldom any difficulty in finding another word which will fit as well as the first selection. The English language, in short, is full of indecision about the exact name for any one of the ideas it includes.

And in the same way there is indecision about ways of expressing ideas in sentences. In telling a story, while the past tense is usually employed, the present tense may be used for vividness or emphasis. In many instances this leads to an alternation between present and past, which are jumbled together in the same story or synopsis. If the English language could first fix upon a single method of story-telling, this difficulty would be eliminated.

Another stumbling block to inexperienced writers, stemming directly from the indecisiveness of the English language itself, is the alternation of pronouns. In giving directions for making something, very often the reader will first be addressed as *you,* then the passive will be used, then perhaps the third person pronoun *one* or *he,* and possibly the first person plural *we.* Again we have indecision in speaking, which is rooted in the indecisiveness of English.

Closely allied to this difficulty is the difficulty with the imper-

[7] Greenough and Kittredge, New York, Macmillan, 1901, pp. 29–41.

sonal construction. There are some half dozen ways of saying that a certain report is current.

one hears it said that	we have heard that
they say that	I hear it reported that
you may hear it said that	It is said that

Thus all the pronouns, in both genders, are usable for this impersonal construction. What wonder that the inexperienced writer does not know which one to use or, perhaps, uses them all in rotation?

OTHER EXAMPLES OF INDECISION

It is impossible to keep psychological phenomena in isolated compartments so that an illustration is susceptible of one and only one explanation. In previous chapters there have been numerous examples which show alternatives and which therefore illustrate indecisiveness as well as courtesy, short-cutting, or what not. For instance, all varieties of the modest request instanced on page 151 prove not only that the English language lends itself to the expression of courtesy but also that it cannot reach a precise decision on the form proper for this purpose.

The variety of tenses in English, which has been mentioned so far as the future tense is concerned and which will be discussed further in Chapter Twenty-two, amounts to the same thing. A language which has several kinds of present tense (present, present perfect, present progressive, and present passive), as many pasts, at least six futures, and any number of other odds and ends of tenses, cannot be said to be clean-cut or decisive, as is, for example, classic Latin, which had one tense, and only one, for the expression of a given time relationship.

It is true that English tends to manufacture a distinction where none has existed. Synonyms are differentiated, and curious differences have arisen, such as that between present and past in *He discovered that there was (is) a God*. The use of the past refers the discovery to its discoverer, without committing the speaker concerning the validity of the discovery, while the second recognizes the existence of a deity as a timeless truth. While indecision has not been completely eliminated, since many speakers use present and past indiscriminately in such constructions, still the two usages have been differentiated to some degree.

It was intimated at the beginning of the present chapter that indecision in general might not be a bad thing. Certainly the broad range of choices offered by English in grammatical constructions is distinctly to the advantage of the individual. Frequently English even permits the avoidance of a linguistic difficulty by the simple expedient of omission. For example, the person who does not know whether to use *who* or *whom* in sentences like *That's the person (who* or *whom) he thought her to be* has simply to omit both pronouns in order to avoid the whole difficulty.

The mere fact that in English there are innumerable ways of saying the same thing insures that no one will be forced to use a way of speaking which raises problems of grammar, of meaning, or of form. If one has a request to make one can modulate it nicely to the exact degree of courtesy desired or can adapt it to one's own peculiarities of grammatical usage. In asking a question, expressing a preference, or planning for the future, one finds abundant linguistic alternatives.

For generations the English language has been seeking to make decisions on points of greater or less importance in the linguistic field. A few such attempts have succeeded; more have proved abortive. Perhaps some day the attempt itself will be given up and English will be abandoned to an effective and complete indecisiveness. English, like England, may find its Elizabeth to make it glorious.

PROBLEMS OF TIME

ALL STUDENTS of the human mind will agree that the average individual has a very imperfect sense of time. Alarm clock precision in consciousness is rare or nonexistent. In actual human experience the hours may drag or they may fly; there is even a belief that time is longer in youth than in age. One may live in the past, the future, or, less probably, the present. The last is not only uncommon but also almost impossible, since the present is after all a mere point between past and future, with as little thickness as a point in geometry. Unless the present is able to extend itself into past or future, it is negligible from the aspect of bulk; and it is noticeable that when people talk of the present they usually mean a slice of time including some of both future and past.

Now the English language, like all other languages, has to cope with these human attitudes and reactions concerning time. There are two main devices for doing this: semantically, by words of time content (*Monday, then, later,* and so forth) and grammatically, by means of the verb. English has evolved a system of six primary and six secondary tenses in various voices and moods, an indefinite number of alternates, substitutes, and other odds and ends to cover special cases. Our task in this chapter will be to examine these verb forms and see how well and logically they operate for the purpose of showing time.

LINGUISTIC SCHEME OF TIME

Time is ordinarily divided into past, present, and future; but this threefold division is less than adequate for grammatical purposes.

A grammatical expansion has been suggested by Jespersen, who adds a before-past, an after-past, a before-future, and an after-future, making seven time divisions in all.[1]

This suggested plan brings us nearer, though not quite to, the naturally evolved divisions of English grammar. While a "before-present" may not be defensible logically, since all before the present is the past, still such a heading does exactly correspond to the present perfect tense of English and therefore should be included in spite of logic. We therefore propose a minimum, simplified time-grammar plan of nine divisions, as follows:

Time	*Tense*	*Example*
Past		
1. Before-past	Past perfect	He *had eaten* by ten o'clock
2. Past	Past	She *called*.
3. After-past	. . .	In 1703 she met the man whom she *was to marry*.
Present		
4. Before-present	Present perfect	He *has read* the book.
5. Present	Present	I *hear* music.
6. After-present	. . .	He *is to sail Monday*. He *is about to say* goodbye.
Future		
7. Before-future	Future perfect	He *will have finished* before six.
8. Future	Future	He *will call*.
9. After-future	. . .	Tomorrow at this time he *will be about to start*.

The foregoing outline raises numerous interesting points. As is well known, the English verb has had but two inflexional time divisions, past and present; therefore our future tense is not a single word like *hear* or *called*, but a periphrastic verb, *will call*. The same tendency to look behind or around rather then ahead is seen in the fact that the six standard English tenses represent simple time or before-time, while after-time is not so much as named. And in the case of the after-future, or the future-in-future, its linguistic expression is both rare and awkward.

It is noticeable also that in several of the examples the precise

[1] In *The Philosophy of Grammar*, New York, Holt, 1924, p. 257.

time-bearing of the verb is determined by a separate word or phrase: *Monday, in 1703, by ten oclock, tomorrow at this time.* The verb gives only a rough approximation to time; *has read,* for example, might indicate *yesterday* or *fifty years ago.* But oddly enough, if either of these additions is introduced to import exactness into the sentence, the present perfect tense at once becomes inappropriate, changing to the past (not *Yesterday he has read the book,* but *Yesterday he read the book*). Vagueness is not only tolerated by, but inherent in, these English tense forms, including even a present verb such as *hear,* which normally indicates not a present, but a very recent past (*I hear they eloped*).

Moreover, the more closely we study this ninefold schedule of the time forms of English verbs, the more apparent it becomes that such a plan fails to represent accurately English verb usage as a whole. If, for example, we scrutinize the form *hear,* we shall find that while it can be used in the present tense to indicate approximately present time, it has also numerous other uses. In *I am never lonely when I hear good music* the verb *hear* is timeless; in *I hear they eloped* it is past. In *Tomorrow I hear the president's speech* it is future.

In fact, what is called the simple present tense in English is probably more commonly used to indicate simple present time than to indicate habitual action. And what is true of *hear* is true to a greater or less extent of all the other verbs in the examples given in the time plan. There is no single one (unless it is the after-future) which is found invariably as used there. All are shifting in their indication of time, and the context must decide their meaning.

To illustrate these facts, it may be profitable to list a few of the other time indications which may be shown by verbs in the same past and present forms as those just cited.

Tense	Example	Time Meaning
Past perfect	He *had left* by six.	Before-past
	If he *had left* then, he would be here now.	Past
	Would I *had known!*	Wish or desire; vaguely in past

Tense	Example	Time Meaning
Past	He *called*.	Past
	Henry came before I *left*.	After-past
	He *danced* then but now he plays the violin.	Habitual past
	It is time he *called*.	Present
	If we *named* him Percy, would he thank us when he *grew* up?	Future supposition
After-past	He *was to be* here by two.	Past
	If they *were to appear*, it would not surprise me.	Timeless
Before-present	I *have called* three times.	Before-present
	I *have lived* here six years.	
	Before I *have finished* I shall probably regret having started.	Before-future
	Always men *have tended* to take the short view.	Timeless
Present	He *walks* up and *talks* to me.	Past
	Time and tide *wait* for no man.	Timeless
	This *tastes* sweet.	Present or near-past
	While I *sew*, you may read to me.	Future
	We *leave* tomorrow.	Future
After-present	Harry *is to call* at nine.	After-present
	Iago is the character who *is to cause* all the trouble.	After-past
	We *are to start* tomorrow.	Future
	You *are to understand* that there was no unpleasantness.	Present

From an analysis of this array of different times it is apparent that within certain limits English verbs are completely shifty and indecisive in indicating time. One might almost say that time in English verbs is as you desire it; it is to be understood by the reader or hearer from indications usually thrown out by the surrounding words. In itself the English verb can scarcely be said to indicate time at all.

Thus far we have been dealing with the nine verb forms which are most often said to indicate concrete time relationships. But this is only a part of the story. English verbs have somewhat more than 130 different forms,[2] if we include all the periphrastic verbs

[2] 134, according to Aiken, *A New Plan of English Grammar*.

and verbs with auxiliaries. Of these many verb forms, only a few are framed to express time. The majority show other relationships.

An easy example, drawn from modern usage, is here given. Suppose one wants to say that generosity is characteristic of a certain individual. The following constructions might be used:

You always *were* generous.   How generous you *are!*
You *would do* the generous thing.   You always *will be* generous.

Here past, present, and future, as well as the so-called "past" of the auxiliary *will,* are used to indicate a single idea. And this is typical of the time confusion of English verbs.

Another example which may be adduced is the use of the auxiliary *must.* There are eight possible verb forms combined with this auxiliary; of these two are so rare as to be negligible, and several others are of infrequent use. The following list indicates what part time plays in these words.

Tense Form	*Example*	*Indication*
Present	You *must stay.*	Compulsion or urging, present or future
	I *must go.*	Duty, present or future
	He *must think* so.	Strong probability, past, present, or future
	He said he *must accept,* and he did so.	Duty or obligation in the past
Present perfect	He *must have called* before we came.	Strong probability in the before-past
Present progressive	She *must be leaving* at this very moment.	Strong probability, present tense
	I *must be going* within an hour.	Duty in the future
Present perfect progressive	He *must have been working* very hard.	Strong probability in the past or before-present
Present passive	John *must be called* at six o'clock sharp.	Duty or compulsion in the future
	I *must be mistaken* about the name.	Strong probability in the present
Present perfect	He *must have been warned,* for he has escaped.	Strong probability, before-past

Tense Form	Example	Indication
Present progressive passive	At this moment he *must be being fed.*	Strong probability in the present
Present perfect progressive passive	He *must have been being fed* before this.	Strong probability in the past
	He *must have been being fed* at a later hour than six o'clock.	Strong probability, after-past

From this list it is apparent that the verb forms with *must* are used mainly to express two ideas: duty, compulsion, obligation, on the one hand, and probability on the other. Certain forms may express either of these two ideas; others only one. And in no case is there any form which expresses one time and only one. Time is secondary, indecisive or absent in all the verb forms with the auxiliary *must*.

No attempt has been made at completeness in the examples just listed. The reader can probably suggest others and may be able to add to the list of meanings expressed by the auxiliary *must*. Our aim has been simply to show to what extent time is dissociated from English verb forms.

SEQUENCE OF TENSES

If the time relations of verbs are difficult and shifting, what is called the sequence of tenses in English is more so. The rules on this subject, as given in grammars, are in the highest degree uncertain and mixed. The upshot of actual usage seems to be that almost any sequence of tenses may be followed, provided context is taken into consideration.

One rule formerly given for the sequence of tenses is that when the governing proposition has a past-tense form, a past tense should be used in the following clause or clauses. For example, the sentence *He promised that he would buy the book* would certainly read awkwardly if the future verb were substituted for the past: *He promised that he will buy the book.*

This example is obvious, and yet there are so many exceptions to this rule that it can scarcely be said to hold. For example, one might say *He said he is planning to buy the book, He said that he will buy the book tomorrow,* or *He promised that the book will please you,* thus following a past tense with a present or future tense.

An often-heard construction is illustrated by the sentence *Henry said that he telephoned Bill but since that time he did not hear from him.* This is certainly awkward and would be improved by substituting *has not heard* for *did not hear.* However, no general rule could be formulated from this example, since precisely the same sequence of tenses is possible in *Henry said that Bill invited him, but he did not go.* While they are common in modern speech, such sentences as *After dressing he ate his breakfast* would be more conservative grammatically if the first two words were changed to *after having dressed.* This is even more evident in *Leaving for Chicago, he arrived the next day;* here the combination of the present participle and the past tense is certainly clumsy. All these constructions are common in popular modern speech.

Sequence of tenses is regularly disregarded in the case of the past infinitive. We are told to say, not *He wanted to have gone,* but *He wanted to go.* Here the rule, and a very sensible rule, is that the past infinitive is used only when past time is not indicated elsewhere in the sentence. Such a rule accords with a major tendency in the development of the English language, the tendency not to repeat unnecessarily inflexions or their equivalents.

Perhaps as good a way as any other to define the best present practice concerning sequence of tenses is to state the rule that the tense of the verb in a subordinate clause should fit with related words in a main clause. However, this is a very elastic rule, since, as has been shown, most tense forms in English are so flexible that a misfit will be very unlikely. The present tense, for example, is used so regularly to express not present but past, future, or timeless action, that it will fit with a verb in almost any other form.

The very phrase "sequence of tenses" is misleading, since this rule applies as well to a combination of verb and adverb as to a combination of verb and verb. In the sentence *I am here since six years,* the discrepancy appears in the relationship between the present tense of the verb and the time-phrase *since six years*. This foreignism is contrary to English idiom, but is not a matter of sequence of tenses.

A construction frequently heard is *The bell didn't ring yet,* in which the past is substituted for the conventional before-present. Another example may be found in the sentence *I have asked her yesterday.* Such sentences violate the feeling of the English speaker for the verb, but the violation appears only in the words *yet* and *yesterday,* which are not felt to be compatible with the tenses of the verbs. If a dash instead of a comma were placed before the last word of the second example in this paragraph, it would be understood as a disjointed construction and would thus be defensible grammatically.

ASPECT IN THE ENGLISH VERB

The term *aspect* is today found useful to express certain modern uses of the English verb. Curme, Jesperson, and others have been forced to adopt this word in order to express what is not covered by terms such as *tense, mood, voice,* and *person.* All these latter terms envisage a state of the language in which distinctions are sharp and clear-cut; aspect is distinctly a psychological term, and it leads to interpretations which are often of the most subtle and even indefinable character.[3]

A good example will be found in the four words *he would do it.* As a verb, *would do* is ordinarily classified as the past corresponding to *will do,* which is called a future. On the other hand, the time interpretation as well as the meaning interpretation of *would do* depends entirely on the context.

If we add four words to the base clause, *would do* in *He would do it, but he was prevented* indicates desire in the past. This use is now felt to be rather archaic. We find it frequently in Shakespeare, but in Modern English the verb *like* is generally added: *He would like to do it.* However, the old use lingers on in more than one construction.

If we form the sentence *He would do it; he is that sort of man,* we find *would do* in the aspect already mentioned, used to show

[3] The term *aspect* is used in a broader sense in chap. iii, p. 22.

a characteristic trait or propensity leading to action of a given sort. In *If he would do it, he would be happier,*[4] we have the familiar conditional aspect, with no indication either of desire or of propensity. In *He would do it that way as a boy, but now he prefers a different plan,* we have an aspect of habitual action, which differs from all the other instances. Is it not evident that aspect in the English verb is psychological rather than logical, a matter of human intent rather than a fixed system?

The foregoing remarks merely touch upon a few of the grammatical bearings of the English verb in its relation to time. It would be valuable to have a complete analysis of a typical verb such as *call,* in all its 134 forms, to show their varying, overlapping, and shifting meanings and indications. Perhaps enough has been said, however, to prove the general point that the English verb in its time indications is by no means to be regarded as a logical element, operating according to logical rules. Perhaps no part of speech is so completely governed by what is loosely called "human nature" as is the verb.

[4] The usual English idiom would, of course, be *If he did it.*

THE FUTURE OF ENGLISH

THE FOREGOING CHAPTER concerning linguistic problems of time suggests just one of the innumerable allied and fascinating by-paths which might well be pursued in the course of an investigation such as the present one. Another allied problem which we shall not attempt to study fully is the matter of sex and maturity in English, or, in other words, the psychological effect of the special talk of childhood and femininity or masculinity upon the language we speak.

No doubt children have what amounts to a little language of their own. This is particularly true in homes where "baby-talk" is current, though such homes are increasingly rare. It is easy to identify certain words, such as *naughty, bye-bye, pattycake,* as distinctively juvenile. In a cartoon which appeared some years ago in *Punch* the word *lookit* was put into the mouth of an elderly woman as American dialect, whereas any American would know that *lookit* is not an adult word.

This little language of childhood has been considerably studied within recent years, although the studies have been mainly either phonetic or numerical—that is, concerned with the sounds children use or the number of words they know. The psychology of juvenile speech is a fruitful field for the investigator and one as yet largely unexplored. The reason for omitting the language of children from the present study, however, is that this language is not homogeneous, but shows such great diversification of type and pattern as to minimize its influence upon the adult idiom. While some influence might be traced, it would probably be found that it is not very extensive.

In speech and in writing women as well as children have followed a linguistic pattern detectably different from that of men. This was especially true in periods when the education and the customs of women were very different from those of men, making a social barrier between the two sexes. Yet the earliest Bible document which scholars think to be contemporary with the events it portrays, the fifth chapter of the book of *Judges,* is traditionally by a woman, and the song of Deborah does not indicate any special feminine linguistic traits. Amid the raucous derision of late nineteenth-century scholars Samuel Butler, himself a male of rather feminine perceptions and intuitions, maintained that the *Odyssey* is the work of a woman. Butler's conclusion was based more on the subject matter of the Greek epic than on its language, which does not seem distinctively feminine.

Today it may be said that certain pieces of writing can be identified readily as feminine or masculine in their origin, but that these are on the whole the exception rather than the rule; the conclusion would rest as much on the subjects and literary treatment as upon grammar or vocabulary. It would be a bold analyst, indeed, who would undertake to specify in what respects the English of Dorothy Thompson differs from that of Walter Lippmann or that of Virginia Woolf from that of Walter Pater and who would then generalize to a conclusion that sex differences in English are recognizable. And since these differences, if they do exist, are so random and indefinable, they can scarcely be studied with profit in such a broad investigation as the present one.

PRINCIPLES OF ENGLISH DEVELOPMENT

In the foregoing chapters we have attempted to show that English has in general developed along lines determined by the human characteristics of the eager, lazy, undecided, arbitrary, partial, modest, and arrogant persons who have spoken and written the language during the many centuries which have gone into its making. These innumerable individuals may be said to have built themselves into the language after the fashion of polyps, and English is the coral reef in which the mentality of

every one of them infinitesimally appears. The reef itself is in-
finitely varied and heterogeneous; it is only on biased or casual
inspection that it looks mechanical or symmetrical.

Despite the heterogeneity and contradictoriness of English
linguistic history, it is possible to formulate a few general tendencies or principles which have directed or defined its growth
from the earliest times to the present. The growth is continuous
and has not slackened in recent times; on the contrary, it may
in some respects be said to be proceeding even faster today than
formerly. The conservatism of grammarians has succeeded in ar-
resting only a small proportion of changes.

The first great principle of English linguistic change is formal
simplification. Such simplification is exemplified in English sounds,
inflexions, and syntax, and to a less extent in words and idioms.
It operates so widely and generally that it is often emphasized
to the neglect of its converse principle, which we shall consider
later. Perhaps its most obvious examples fall in the field of
phonetics, where it is known by such names as assimilation and
accord.

Psychologically, simplifications in English may arise from any
of several causes; but the chief human traits leading to this end
are probably indolence, ease, and short-cutting or impatience.
These traits operate irrespective of rules and formulas, and they
are today active in evolving an English which will be easier for
both native and foreign speakers. Unquestionably they produce
a better language, however much conservative speakers may cling
to the old ways.

This principle has been the means of bringing about an actual
narrowing of the speech area for the formation of English sounds.
Theoretically, the sounds on the fringe of the speech area should
require greater effort to pronounce and hence should tend to disappear. This is just what happened in English; the gutturals
spelled in Anglo-Saxon g (dæg) and h (liht) have long since been
dropped from standard English speech, and they are tending to
disappear also from the Scottish dialect and from many dialects
of German, where they persisted much later. Contraction of the
speech area is thus by no means a phenomenon peculiar to stand-

ard English, though clearly exemplified in the development of our language.

Other types of simplification are to be seen in the tendency to eliminate breath sounds, a tendency which is not confined to the four sounds *hl, hr, hn,* and *hw,* which have actually disappeared from British speech. The breath sound is invariably more difficult than the voiced, and in any word it will tend to be replaced by the latter unless strong stress prevents the replacement. The pure breath sound *h* has so tended to disappear from modern speech that it is seldom or never heard in unstressed position.

Simplification, or the tendency to ease, accounts for the fact that any unstressed vowel will either disappear or become obscured to [ə] or [ɪ]. Often the speech experts will call for a clearly identifiable vowel sound in an unstressed syllable, for example the *e* sound in the termination *ment;* but such a sound is practically never heard, even on the lips of careful speakers.

The simplifying tendency is no less clear in the field of accidence, and many examples of such simplification have already been given. Even inflexions which are presumably stable, such as the *s* termination for the plural, are slipping, as may be seen by the tendency to syncopate such phrases as *two loaves of bread* and *three bottles of milk* into *two bread* and *three milk.* The singular is replacing the plural also in certain alternating usages, such as the following from a letter: "After the death of her father and mother we regret we have been unable to identify the policies on the life of Mary Doe and Susan Roe;" here the words *death* and *life* are what might be called distributive singulars, and this singular usage appears to be increasing in English.

It has long been recognized that the possessive inflexion is disappearing; today it is confined largely to pronouns and words indicating living beings. It has been replaced by the inflexionless noun with an adjective function, as an earlier chapter indicated. There is no inflexion in English which is universal or regular.

In syntax also simplification is widespread. Sentence order has become more standardized with the passage of time, until as pointed out in an earlier chapter, it can be formulated very definitely under a score or so of heads. In its broad outlines sentence order is probably simpler in Modern English than in Elizabethan.

One might compare sentence construction in Modern English to the Arabic notation in mathematics as contrasted with the Roman plan typified by former stages of the language. Order is so important in English that it leads to some curious ambiguities, as in the sentence *The boy who boasts seldom is worth while.* Here order can work two ways, and without order to guide us, the meaning is also double. Normally a certain order admits of one meaning and only one.

It has been remarked that except in textbooks of English for foreigners sentence order is almost entirely neglected in studies of the English language. Sentence order has a grammar and a psychology, and both are worthy of fuller study and exploration.

PRINCIPLE OF DIVERSIFICATION

It has been asserted that simplification is an important, but not the only, principle of the growth of the English language. While it is human to be lazy and to short-cut, it is just as human to be expansive and to decorate or to ornament one's speech. It is significant, however, that the second principle we are about to formulate has no name, this fact showing the comparative neglect which it has suffered at the hands of linguists. While many specific applications have been recognized, the principle itself has been less than adequately defined.

Perhaps the best single word for it is "diversification." [1] It corresponds to the centrifugal force in physics, simplification being the centripetal. Side by side with a decrease in what may be termed the essential parts of the linguistic machine goes a very greatly increased production. Our language, less and less complex in its mechanics, grows daily richer in other aspects, until the resultant effect might easily seem to be that of increasing complexity.

The outstanding example of this greater richness of linguistic pattern is of course the vocabulary. One of the standard diction-

---

[1] In relation to phonetics this principle is called "grading" in Aiken, *Why English Sounds Change* and *English Present and Past.*

aries of Anglo-Saxon [2] includes approximately 70,000 entries, though by no means all these items are separate words, many of them indicating merely alternate spellings. But even assuming that Anglo-Saxon, including the words unknown to dictionaries, had a vocabulary of 70,000 words, it is a far cry from that to the number in our modern dictionaries, estimated variously at from 200,000 to 2,000,000 or more.[3]

At the risk of some degree of repetition it must be emphasized that this enormous increase of vocabulary has involved no increase in speech sounds, but rather the reverse. English phonetics has decreased in complexity with the centuries. The approximately forty speech sounds of Modern English are ample to cover all the entries in modern dictionaries. To be sure, homonyms abound: *bear, bare; borne, born; our, hour; sun, son; whale, wail* (in British English). Context is crucial for the interpretation of such words in the oral language. And in the literary idiom there is an abundance of words which are spelled alike, but pronounced differently: *read* (present) and *read* (past); *row* (a series) and *row* (a quarrel). Still the language, both oral and written, is able to carry on with a minimum of misunderstanding. Most of the vagueness or ambiguity of English is semantic rather than grammatical.

SUBORDINATION EXTENDED

The richness of detail and ornamentation which characterize Modern English are shown nowhere more clearly than in the increase of grammatical subordination in our present idiom. Like a tree putting out twigs and branches the English sentence has put out clauses which more or less copy the order and construction of the main trunk, or independent clause. Questions have made themselves into relative clauses, verbs have taken on clause modifiers, and the result is a diversity in unity which has transformed the English sentence into something surprisingly different from its forerunner in Anglo-Saxon.

This enormous increase in subordination has necessitated the

[2] John R. Clark Hall, *A Concise Anglo-Saxon Dictionary for the Use of Students,* 3d ed., rev. and enl., Cambridge, The University Press, 1931.

[3] Robert L. Ramsay, "Taking the Census of English Words," *American Speech,* February, 1933, pp. 36–42.

creation of many more connectives than the few which joined the parts of sentences a thousand years ago. Progressively English has been augmenting its stock of connectives by pressing into that service words of every other function—nouns, adjectives, verbs, adverbs, and even interjections. And the process has not ended. Today a whole group of verbs in *ing,* which used to be called danglers, are passing into the preposition class.

Sentences like *Considering everything, his trip was wise* used to be condemned on the grounds that the opening word was a verb in participial (that is, adjectival) form without a proper governing word, since a trip does not consider anything. But gradually it came to be perceived that really such words are neither verbs nor adjectives, but connectives (prepositions). On this basis, there is no dangling construction; and thus words like *examining, speaking (generally speaking), viewing, regarding* are reinstated in grammatical respectability.

PRINCIPLE OF ABSTRACTNESS

A third principle of English linguistic development, and the last which we shall consider, is the growth of abstractness. As is obvious, primitive language is concrete in its terms, and often primitive tongues are difficult for the translator, just because of their lack of generalized and abstract words. Probably the first step toward abstractness which most languages take, and a step which is still apparent in English, is adding abstract meanings to concrete words, as *blossom* (verb) may mean concretely *bloom,* or more abstractly *come into being.* This addition of meanings was almost a principle of the Hebrew language, where, for example, the word *ru'ach* means both *wind* and *spirit;* and precisely the same duality of meaning is seen in the Greek *pneuma.* As language develops, the concrete meanings of such words sometimes drop away, and a wholly abstract group of words is built up.

Adjectives, which isolate qualities from concrete things, should probably be classed with abstractions, and so should most or all of those construction words, or morphemes,[4] little indefinables

---

[4] For a definition and description of the morpheme, see Aiken, *A New Plan of English Grammar,* pp. 10, 186–191.

like *of, as,* and *not,* which are among the most commonly used words of the language. Worn down to almost nothing by the grinding of centuries, these words carry the burden of communication, though they are ordinarily balanced in the sentence by one or two concretes.

It is a curious phenomenon, and one probably belonging distinctively to modern life, that we distrust the abstract word. Theoretically the ability to move in the realm of thought might seem evidence of increasing civilization; nevertheless it is the foible of a group of modern linguistic philosophers to regard the abstract word as somehow unreal and therefore to be avoided. While an over-reliance on abstractions, as occasionally manifested in the erudite style (Chapter Nineteen) is questionable, still the genius of the English language seemingly refuses to take seriously the opposition to abstraction so dogmatically stated by Ogden, Richards, Chase, Korzybski, and others. The language itself seems inclined to side with those other philosophers who have suggested that the abstract may be nearer reality than the concrete; certainly language seems to be headed toward that sort of reality.

We are recurringly told that human nature does not change; and if this is true, then we may expect the English language to go on under the influence of the same impulses which have shaped it into its present character. Bradley has been quoted as saying that the simplification of English cannot continue, because just about every simplification which could take place has already occurred. A like assertion about the vocabulary has not been heard; we are not told that English has so many words that the language cannot hold any more. Nor has it been prophesied that the abstract character of English will increase.

Yet by all indications these three principles will continue and, along with the motives which have been suggested in the various chapters of this study, will evolve the English of a thousand years hence. What this English will be like we do not know; that it will be different from the English of today we can scarcely doubt. Perhaps within the next millennium men will discover how to control the kind and direction of linguistic change so that English can be approximated to a laboratory ideal. Perhaps mathematical and scientific notation, a phonetic alphabet, or some other mechanical device may govern communication in the future. Or possibly English itself may decline with deterioration in the national fortunes of the English-speaking civilization, suffer conquest, and undergo modification comparable to that which it experienced after the conquest of 1066. Conceivably, in a thousand years there may even be no English language.

But these speculations are probably somewhat visionary. A language is greater than the vicissitudes of its speakers, more leisurely than the necessities of the passing day, and more persistent often than the race itself. It has a logic above the choplogic of its apologists, the logic of the interactions and aspirations of humankind.

INDEX